PLAYING FOR SCOTLAND

THE HISTORY OF
THE ROYAL SCOTTISH NATIONAL ORCHESTRA

PLAYING FOR SCOTLAND

THE HISTORY OF
THE ROYAL SCOTTISH NATIONAL ORCHESTRA

CONRAD WILSON

HarperCollins*Publishers*

HarperCollins*Publishers*
P.O. Box, Glasgow G4 ONB

First published 1993

Reprint 9 8 7 6 5 4 3 2 1 0

© 1993 Conrad Wilson

ISBN 0 00 434595 9

A catalogue record for this book is
available from the British Library

Printed in Great Britain by
HarperCollins Manufacturing, Glasgow

To the memory of Walter Susskind, and to all the conductors and members of what is now the Royal Scottish National Orchestra, in gratitude

Contents

Introduction

The idea of a book about what was formerly the SNO was first suggested to me by Alexander Gibson in the early nineteen-seventies, when the orchestra was enjoying a period of prolonged success: it had made its first major tour of Europe, its first significant appearances at the Edinburgh Festival, its first really good recordings and, with Scottish Opera, had completed its first (and, sadly, what turned out to be its only) *Ring* cycle. But having just written my history of Scottish Opera's first ten years, I did not want to start immediately on another chronological trail.

So I said no, not at the moment, and the suggestion lay dormant until, in the autumn of 1991, when the centenary of what was by then the Royal Scottish Orchestra had been reached, it was put to me again, this time by Christopher Bishop, the orchestra's chief executive. Would I be interested? This time I said yes. A history of the orchestra, based, as far as possible, on personal experience, was what I proposed; and having just quit *The Scotsman* after almost thirty years as music critic, I now had time to write it.

Apart from the Reid Orchestra (Tovey's old ensemble) in Edinburgh, the Scottish Orchestra, as it was simply called in my boyhood, was the first orchestra I ever heard in a concert hall. I learnt the symphonic repertoire through its performances at the Usher Hall, and in particular through the imaginative programmes devised by Walter Susskind, who was my boyhood conductor. Since it was he, more than anyone, who first awakened my musical instincts, and who set me my first musical challenges – even Brahms at that time seemed a challenge – I would like to dedicate this book at least partly to his memory. I owe him grateful thanks.

But I would also like to thank those who, still alive, have told me something about the pre-Susskind years – Hugh Marshall especially, who was the Glasgow Choral Union's and later the

SNO Chorus's pianist from the age of seventeen until his retirement six years ago at the age of eighty-one. He was also, for a while, the orchestra's vice-chairman. In both capacities, he got to know many of the conductors, from the nineteen-twenties onwards, and his memories, as well as his thoughts on the orchestra as it is now, have been of great help.

Helpful, too, have been all the orchestra's surviving administrators, from Robert Ponsonby onwards. Sir Alexander Gibson, about whom I am writing a separate book, has spoken to me for hours – in his house, in his garden, over lunch, over supper and over the phone – about his twenty-five years with the orchestra. Various players and ex-players have aired their views, privately and publicly, on the state of the orchestra at different periods in its history. Members of Christopher Bishop's office staff, particularly Fiona Ferguson, have fed me facts I needed, and have given me access to files and press cuttings. Lynne Walker, former publicity manager and editor of the orchestra's magazine SNOScene, supplied much information. But inevitably, in the pages that follow, many names will remain unmentioned, and many tributes unpaid.

For a hundred years the orchestra has been a national institution, much loved, much criticised. All concert-goers in Scotland have their fund of anecdotes about it, and if mine do not always coincide with yours, or if I have omitted things you hold dear, then that simply proves how prodigious the orchestra's history is, and how much it has achieved.

At present, however, it is at a cross-roads, with a new name, a new conductor, an experienced but controversial administrator, who, as this book goes to press, has announced that he will leave the orchestra in the autumn of 1993, a new hall and a new century of performances to look forward to. In its first hundred years it worked with some famed conductors and soloists: Koussevitsky, Weingartner, Barbirolli, Szell and Boult seem not a bad roll-call for the years between the two world wars. It survived some major crises, as well as what look, in retrospect, like periods of slave labour. Its leaders have included Horace Fellowes, David McCallum, Jean Rennie and Sam Bor, to mention just four distinguished names from the past. And its tally of premieres and Scottish premieres, listed at the back of the book, is impressive.

To have given the premieres of Iain Hamilton's Sinfonia for Two Orchestras, Thea Musgrave's Horn Concerto, Peter

Maxwell Davies's *Stone Litany*, Luciano Berio's *Bewegung* and *Still*, Harrison Birtwistle's *Melencolia I* and Lyell Cresswell's Cello Concerto, to mention seven of my favourites, is something to be thankful for; and to have introduced Stockhausen's *Gruppen*, Ligeti's Double Concerto for Flute and Oboe and several works by Hans Werner Henze to British audiences shows an orchestra alert to some of the most important music of the day.

There has also been a continuity of which, in writing this book, I have become increasingly aware: George Szell, as teacher and influence, is a recurring theme; Barbirolli, who raised the orchestra to international status in the nineteen-thirties, helped to secure Alexander Gibson's appointment as musical director in the nineteen-fifties; Neeme Järvi, who briefly appeared as an unknown quantity in the nineteen-sixties under the name of Naeme Yarvi, reappeared as musical director in 1984. Beecham and Boult, Horenstein and Kletzki left their mark over a long period. Artur (who preferred to call himself Arthur) Rubinstein gave his debut performance of Tchaikovsky's First Piano Concerto in Scotland in 1915, and returned as an octogenarian to present two marathon concerto programmes with Gibson in the nineteen-seventies.

Rather than resort to quoting old reviews, I have relied wherever possible on my own memories of performances, amplified where necessary by interviews and research. Whether now as the Royal Scottish National Orchestra or long ago as the orchestra of the Glasgow Choral Union, the players – even on their most *ad hoc* basis – have always been more than a provincial band. The achievement of their first century is something to celebrate.

Their second – well, who knows? But their 1993 programmes, announced in a bright new brochure, promise performances of Mahler's Ninth Symphony and Messiaen's *Turangalîla*, Shostakovich's Fifteenth Symphony and Berg's Violin Concerto. As I was proof-reading this book, Witold Lutoslawski was in Glasgow rehearsing a complete concert of his works. And Walter Weller, whose repertoire is not of the largest, has agreed since becoming musical director to learn his first Scottish work, Iain Hamilton's *Aurora*. This must be good news.

Finally, some points of style. Conductors knighted in the course of the orchestra's history receive their title at the appropriate point in this chronicle. Thus I write of Alexander Gibson until 1977, Sir Alexander Gibson thereafter. The orchestra, too, will be differently known at different times. Transliterations of Russian names

xii   PLAYING FOR SCOTLAND

are, with one exception, those employed in the *Collins Encyclopedia of Music* and its various offshoots in which I was involved as editor. In my preface to the 1976 edition of the encyclopedia, I wrote that I preferred the modern spellings – *Petrushka* rather than *Petrouchka*, Rakhmaninov rather than Rachmaninov, Chaikovsky rather than Tchaikovsky – that are used by the *Financial Times* on its arts page and wherever editors believe in progress. My preference still stands, but I have accepted, in the circumstances, a plea from the RSNO management to spell one famous name in the traditional way the orchestra still favours.

Conrad Wilson,
Edinburgh, Scotland, and Introbio, Italy, 1992

1

Henschel and After

What's in a name? Quite a lot, if Scotland's national symphony orchestra is anything to go by. True, during what might be termed its pre-history, it had no name at all. At that time it was simply an *ad hoc* outfit recruited to accompany choral music in Glasgow, and to give orchestral concerts on the side. Then it became known as the Orchestra (or perhaps simply the orchestra) of the Glasgow Choral Union. Not until 1891 did it gain its own identity as the Scottish Orchestra, and not until 1893 did it actually play under that name. But once it did so, the name stuck for fifty-seven years until, after much soul-searching, it became the Scottish National Orchestra in 1950, in honour of its brave new status as a full-time orchestra.

As the SNO – its long familiar acronym – it enjoyed its widest renown and, with Alexander Gibson as conductor, its longest period of stability. From these years dated its momentous performance of Mahler's Eighth Symphony at the 1965 Edinburgh Festival, its first LP recordings, its first substantial foreign tours (though there had been a brave foray to Holland with the Dutch conductor, Willem Kes, in 1898) and its productive association with Scottish Opera, when it performed not only *The Ring* but Berlioz's *The Trojans*, Henze's *Elegy for Young Lovers*, Stravinsky's *The Rake's Progress*, and much else, to international acclaim.

Then suddenly, in quick succession, came two more changes. With Glasgow as European City of Culture in 1990, and with a grand new concert hall built to commemorate the occasion, Royal status was conferred on the orchestra as well as on the auditorium in which, it was assumed, the players would be the principal occupants. In haste, the SNO was renamed the Royal Scottish National Orchestra, but the monicker seemed clumsy. After a few months, a further name was devised, the shorter, trimmer Royal Scottish Orchestra.

Yet people vocally and in writing regretted the passing of the word 'national'. Was this, they asked, a necessary change? But as Lord Goold, the latest in the orchestra's long line of chairmen, was to explain, the SNO had burst out of its national enclosure into the wider world. Even if, in some quarters, the new name was thought retrogressive, and even if, by a twist of the tongue, the new acronym could be made to sound less than seemly – indeed rather rude – it was considered good for international business. As the Royal Scottish Orchestra, the players would be loved by the Japanese, as well as by sponsors to whom such matters mattered; but by December 1992 it was again – although who could say finally? – the RSNO.

In 1893 and earlier, sponsorship took different forms but was equally essential to the orchestra's survival. Annual guarantees from private individuals helped to keep music flowing. Shortage of cash meant fewer concerts; a surplus extended the season. It was a capital sum of £20,000 from James A. Allan, a rich West of Scotland shipowner, which made a proper Scottish Orchestra feasible. With the money a limited company was formed 'for the purpose of organising and maintaining an efficient orchestra which would be suitable for concerts throughout Scotland over a much longer period than has hitherto been possible'.

Much longer, yes, but still not long enough. The shortness of the Scottish Orchestra's season, devised to last from November until February each year, and divided between a 'serious' and a 'popular' concert series, as well as, geographically, between Glasgow, Edinburgh and other places, was regarded as scandalous by the time John Barbirolli had been appointed conductor in the nineteen-thirties. And although the season, or what the Committee of Management – ancestors of today's board of directors – liked to call 'The Scheme', was later extended, it was done so with less than whole-heartedness. Indeed the pusillanimity of the committee, and its desire to cram as much as possible into the shortest space of time, was still provoking outrage as recently as 1949 – for the very good reason that the orchestra continued to be run on a part-time basis and was disbanded each summer, leaving the players to eke out an existence in seaside resorts where piers and pavilions required a holiday band.

But even in the days when it lacked a name, the orchestra did not lack personality. It was one of the first professional orchestras in Britain. It attracted – as it still does – players from far beyond

Scotland. It had plenty to do. Music flourished during Queen Victoria's reign, even if much of it consisted of now forgotten oratorios performed by choral societies throughout the land. These events were the soap operas of their time, and orchestras – with the challenge of an occasional *Dream of Gerontius* as proof of the validity of the genre – depended on them for their survival.

A riffle through any bundle of nineteenth-century Scottish concert programmes shows what went on. Glasgow had its Musical Association for the Performance of Oratorios and its Harmonic Society which merged with each other in 1855 to form the Glasgow Choral Union, fountainhead of what is today the RSNO Chorus. But for every *Elijah* which such societies sang, there were dozens of *Redemptions*, *Prodigal Sons*, *Last Judgments* and the like. Yet not until 1844 did Glasgow hear a complete performance of *Messiah* and, instead of apologising for the oversight, bragged that it was the first of its kind in Scotland (Edinburgh, more modest, could have made a similar claim seventy years earlier).

Glasgow was not always so slow to seize its opportunities. True, the Choral Union astoundingly turned down a chance to have Berlioz conduct two concerts in 1853, opting for its own chorus-master, Julius Seligmann, instead. But in other respects it was on the ball. In 1800 the city had combined with Edinburgh to invite Johann Salomon, the London impresario, to direct performances of some of the Haydn symphonies he had recently commissioned. Hans von Bülow, the world's first virtuoso conductor, flitted in and out between 1874, when he was soloist in Beethoven's *Emperor* concerto, and 1877, when he fulfilled a promise to his friend Johannes Brahms that he would conduct the composer's First Symphony in Glasgow a year after its Karlsrühe premiere.

Arthur Sullivan showed his prowess as a choral conductor before turning his attention to composing operettas. Julius Tausch, who succeeded the hapless Schumann as conductor of the Düsseldorf Music Society, wintered in Glasgow in 1878. August Manns, famed for conducting with white kid gloves, regularly took time off from his Crystal Palace engagements to bring his professionalism as a trainer and programme planner to Glasgow's and the rest of Scotland's musical life (he specialised in cycles of symphonies performed in chronological order).

There were times when orchestras had to be imported from elsewhere. London, Liverpool and Manchester were among the regular suppliers, and in 1870 a band of German players sailed from Hamburg (and got ice-bound on the Elbe on the way home) to accompany a Sullivan oratorio. But this only made the need for reliable local forces all the more evident. Scratch orchestras, hustled together from here and there, could not suffice for ever. The expertise of August Manns, who insisted on longer seasons and bigger and better orchestras to take part in them, did much to make the eventual founding of the Scottish Orchestra a reality.

By the early eighteen-nineties, as many as ninety players were being assembled each season to take part in the Choral Union 'scheme', with its interweaving of vocal and orchestral events. All that was now needed was the initiative to transform them into the Scottish Orchestra, and James Allan's £20,000 provided the incentive. No doubt one of the local chorusmasters could have been invited to become conductor, but Glasgow was thinking bigger than that. It asked Georg Henschel to do the job. As a solo baritone, he had sung with the orchestra in 1888, and was already famed for his ability to perform Schubert's *Winterreise* and other Lieder while accompanying himself on the piano (there are recordings of his efforts). Though born in Breslau, he was to become (like Solti and Menuhin) a British citizen, to change (like Handel and Szell) his name to George, and to be knighted for his contribution to British music.

Scotland astutely grabbed Henschel when he had begun to divide his career between singing and conducting. Having risen to the role of Hans Sachs in a concert performance of *Die Meistersinger* before its Munich premiere, and having taken part in the *St Matthew Passion* under Brahms's conductorship in Cologne, he had agreed in 1881 to become conductor of the Boston Symphony Orchestra, newly founded by a banker and Civil War veteran, Major Henry Lee Higginson. This, and a salary of $10,000 at a time when a British conductor was lucky to earn £10 a concert, might have made him seem too big a fish for Glasgow to catch, but in fact Henschel had lasted only three years in Boston. By 1886 he was teaching singing in London, and running a concert series with a taste for the new and unusual.

So tempting him to develop a new Scottish orchestra was probably not difficult, and Glasgow's soft spot for German musicians found its perfect embodiment in a man who could claim to be one of Brahms's best friends. Music dictionaries are prone to say that Henschel became conductor of the Scottish Orchestra in 1891, which is why many people expected the orchestra to celebrate its centenary in 1991. But because of the traditional tendency of Scots to bicker among themselves, the launching of the orchestra was delayed and the first concert did not in fact take place until 1893.

In the circumstances it was lucky that the newly christened orchestra got going at all. The immediate problem lay in whether or how the Scottish Orchestra should combine with the already existent Glasgow Choral Union – a matter which, incredibly, had not been previously sorted out. But it also lay, as it was to do until 1950, in the length of the winter season, even although the value of an extended season had been 'admitted' by the Scottish Orchestra Co Ltd to be that it 'would provide orchestral facilities for concerts at reasonable intervals, and so afford the orchestra sufficient time for the rehearsal and study necessary to secure first-rate performances'.

Even with James Allan's £20,000 subsidy to create a mood of optimism, it was feared that the initial season might prove 'too short, perfunctory and uninspired'. On the other hand, a longer season might result in an enormous loss. While these matters continued to be thrashed out, with no likelihood of an immediate outcome, August Manns craftily recruited his usual Choral Union Orchestra, complete with ninety players, for a ten-week stint including performances of Berlioz's *The Damnation of Faust* and a new cantata by Hamish MacCunn entitled *Queen Hynde of Caledon*. By the man in the white kid gloves, the Scottish Orchestra Co Ltd had been gloriously outwitted.

By the time, two years later, it had got its act together, the rivalry between the two organisations had become lethal. In retaliation to Manns, the Scottish Orchestra filched the Choral Union's manager, John Wallace, and the leader of its orchestra, Maurice Sons, to work with Henschel. And in order to make the Choral Union's ten-week season seem puny, a season lasting twenty-six weeks was announced. The Choral Union lost £3,000, and the Scottish Orchestra presumably a lot more (the precise sum was never divulged). Manns, crestfallen, retired at the end of the season, his fourteen years of faithful service to Scotland having ended in disaster. But it left the field free in 1894 for the joint venture that should have been agreed upon in the first place. Henschel celebrated his triumph with a performance of Beethoven's Ninth Symphony, a work he had conducted the previous year in London, prompting Bernard Shaw to remark that it was a masterpiece that mattered more to him than all the other eight symphonies put together.

But triumphant though he was, Henschel at the age of forty-four was also prudent. The twenty-six weeks of the 1893 season, incorporating thirteen 'classical' concerts and fourteen 'popular' ones in St Andrew's Hall, were reduced in 1894 to twenty weeks – and still made a loss. This time the amount was disclosed (£5,743) but at least the artistic rewards were considerable. Dvořák's *New World* symphony received its first Scottish perform-ance less than a year after its world premiere in America (where Seidl, not Henschel, had conducted it). Later came a concert per-formance of *The Flying Dutchman*, and Henschel conducted one of his own works, setting a precedent that Weingartner, Szell, Susskind and Rankl would later eagerly follow.

Henschel remained conductor until 1895, and departed on what appears to have been friendly terms. As guest conductor he was welcomed back, and grew so fond of Scotland that he settled there, writing his memoirs of Brahms in 1907 and becoming the Laird of Alltnacriche in Inverness-shire, where he died in 1934 (a year that had already claimed Elgar, Delius and Holst). At Avie-more, where he and his wife are buried, he is commemorated by a plaque 'erected by residents and friends in grateful remembrance', though his own memory of Brahms striding across the Baltic island of Rügen was undoubtedly more vividly worded: 'For a long time I looked after him out of the carriage window, in spite of the wind and the still pouring rain. It was a picture never to be forgotten. As far as the eye could reach, nothing but moor and clouds and – Brahms.' It could have been Scotland he was writing about. Henschel must have enjoyed bad weather.

From the first conductor of the Boston Symphony Orchestra, the management committee turned to the first conductor of the Concertgebouw Orchestra, Amsterdam. Willem Kes, a violinist pupil of Joachim and Wieniawski, was forty when he was appointed as Henschel's successor. A Dutch disciplinarian, he was known for the thoroughness of his rehearsals and for his intoler-ance of ill-behaved audiences – people were discouraged from coming and going during performances (not until Paavo Berglund famously stopped a performance for the same reason in the nineteen-eighties was the orchestra to work with so irritable a con-ductor) and the hint of a whisper was heard and frowned upon.

During Kes's reign, the orchestra became fully established under its new name but its links with the Choral Union were tactfully retained under a co-operative arrangement. By 1898, The Scheme, as it continued to be known, was consolidated under the title of 'The Choral and Orchestral Union of Glasgow'. Until the formation of the Scottish National Orchestra in 1950, this was the name which, in large type, adorned the top of the orchestra's Glasgow concert programmes, with the component parts – the Glasgow Choral Union and the Scottish Orchestra – squeezed beneath, to left and right, in considerably smaller letters.

In career terms, Kes's three years as conductor of the Scottish Orchestra were an interlude between his Concertgebouw period, for which he will be principally remembered, and his appointment to the Moscow Philharmonic Society and Music School in 1898. As a conductor, it is clear, he had already fulfilled himself before coming to Scotland. Nothing he did later had the pioneering spirit of his work in Amsterdam, and by 1905 in Koblenz his disciplinary powers were confined to the world of academe.

Still, he brought Joachim to Glasgow, as well as Sarasate, and he never regarded the orchestra as beneath his dignity. He was the first and – until Alexander Gibson seventy years later – the only conductor to take the orchestra abroad. True, it was no farther than his homeland; but at a time when foreign touring was by no means commonplace, the orchestra's fortnight in Holland in 1896 was a major event. The Dutch Government laid on a special train, Kes was decorated by the Queen of the Netherlands after a concert in The Hague, and his successor at the Concertgebouw, the great Willem Mengelberg, gave a special concert with the Dutch orchestra for the Scottish visitors in which the main work was Tchaikovsky's *Pathétique* symphony, a masterpiece not yet known in Scotland.

For its own part, the Scottish Orchestra worked hard in Holland, with a schedule – two concerts per day – that would cause rebellion now. The repertoire contained works by the then still living Dvořák, Rimsky-Korsakov and Gustave Charpentier, a composer more famed for his opera, *Louise*, than for his symphonic suites, but whose music lay close to Kes's heart. A report in *The Scotsman* said that in most of the towns it 'rained wreaths', and that the 'utmost enthusiasm' prevailed. The orchestra's own summing up of the trip agreed that 'the honour and reputation gained were great', though 'the losses for the limited company continued.'

In 1897, indeed, the season was ominously reduced to nine weeks, and it was this, more than anything, that prompted a really binding merger between the Scottish Orchestra and the Choral and Orchestral Union the following year, with a proper, durable constitution. By then Kes had been succeeded by a German nonentity, Wilhelm Bruch, nicknamed Sleepy Billy, who lasted two seasons before being replaced by the Jamaica-born Frederic Hymen Cowen, son of the private secretary to the Earl of Dudley. Though he could play Mendelssohn's D minor Piano Concerto at the age of twelve, Cowen, too, was deemed dull. His worst enemies, said Bernard Shaw, could not accuse him of vivacity, and Elgar ambiguously called him someone who 'never imposed his own personality on the music.'

So safe was Cowen that he lasted ten years in Scotland, while simultaneously working with the Liverpool Philharmonic and directing the Handel festivals at the Crystal Palace in London. But since his idea of an adventurous season was to conduct all the Beethoven symphonies, it was inevitable that he would be accused in the end of lack of enterprise. As a trainer he was efficient. Nobody complained of slipshod playing under his baton. It was just that others conducted better than he did, especially Richard Strauss, whose visit in 1902 at the age of thirty-eight was a milestone in the orchestra's early history.

For his programme, Strauss chose only his own music: two of his established symphonic poems, *Don Juan* and *Death and Transfiguration*, the neo-Mozartian Serenade for Thirteen Wind Instruments and the Brahmsian choral cantata, *The Wanderer's Storm Song*, a work so choked with counterpoint that its effect – to quote Norman Del Mar's study of the composer – is of unrelieved heaviness. The audience, predictably, preferred the symphonic poems to the other items, and Cowen, cashing in on their success, himself repeated them a few weeks later. But in 1903, Strauss was back in person with two more symphonic poems, *Till Eulenspiegel* and the unwieldy but picturesque *Aus Italien*.

Though undoubtedly the orchestra's most lustrous catch, he was not the only one. Edouard Colonne, founder of the Colonne Concerts in Paris, was another (his orchestra, thirty-seven years after his death, had the honour of opening the very first Edinburgh Festival in 1947). So, too, Fritz Steinbach, disciple and 'strenuous' conductor of Brahms, who presented a three-day festival of his master's music, and Henry Wood, founder of the London Proms, whose progressive rehearsal techniques were welcomed. Peter Raabe, on the other hand, was a more dubious visitor. Curator of the Liszt Museum at Weimar, he was to become by 1935 a notorious Nazi and head of Hitler's racialist Reichsmusikkammer.

Yet in spite of the variety of visitors, one cannot help suspecting that during the first decade of the century the Scottish Orchestra marked time. It was there; it had gained a degree of security; but apart from the occasional local premiere – Cowen introduced Sibelius's and Elgar's first symphonies to Scotland – not very much was actually happening. Yet something significant had been established, which Cowen referred to in a farewell tribute in 1910. The orchestra, he pointed out, consisted mostly of able young players, 'and indeed it has been the nursery for all other orchestral institutions'.

Now that was a fact that needed stating. At the turn of the century, an adolescent Gustav Holst had toured for several seasons as the Scottish Orchestra's second trombone (his daughter, Imogen, in her biography of him, said he was 'not an outstandingly brilliant trombonist', but he was competent and proud to have been praised by Hans Richter). In later years, Leon Goossens, Evelyn Rothwell, Barry Tuckwell and Stuart Knussen were among the many gifted players who passed through the orchestra's ranks.

No doubt there was a degree of self-interest in Cowen's valedictory comment about how the orchestra's responsiveness stemmed from 'constant performances under a single conductor', but clearly there was some sort of artistic policy at the time, and it was paying off. Later, especially during and immediately after two world wars, the average age of the players would rise and the character of the orchestra would change.

James Robertson, today's orchestral manager and a former bassist, can remember a time when most of the players, of an obviously older generation, spent all their free moments playing cards, and rehearsals took place in a fog of tobacco smoke. But in recent years the average age has dropped again and the personality of the orchestra has once more changed. Like those in London, Birmingham and elsewhere, Scotland's is now a young orchestra, alert, serious, dedicated and intensely critical, with a steadily rising number of women members, through whom many an old-fashioned attitude – not least on the part of conductors – has required to be adjusted.

In Cowen's day, most of the Scottish Orchestra's conductors were already into their forties before they were appointed. Henschel had been forty-three, Kes a slightly more youthful thirty-nine, Cowen himself a mature forty-eight. His successor, Emil Mlynarski, was forty. Not until the arrival of Barbirolli would there be a really young conductor, a Simon Rattle of his time, and the difference was immediately apparent, just as it was again later when Alexander Gibson, at the age of thirty-three, succeeded a pair of ageing Austrians.

Mlynarski, an impressively qualified Pole, certainly did not set the Clyde on fire, though at least he was a more colourful personality than the pallid Cowen. A pupil of Anton Rubinstein, as well as of Leopold Auer, he was to become Artur Rubinstein's father-in-law. Before they became so closely related, however, he enticed the young virtuoso to play Tchaikovsky's B flat minor Piano Concerto for the first time in his career at St Andrew's Hall, Glasgow, and the Usher Hall, Edinburgh, in 1915.

Rubinstein, in his autobiography, admitted that at the morning rehearsal, his short acquaintance with the difficult concerto showed 'many imperfections', but Mlynarski, instead of getting impatient, was kindness itself. Inviting Rubinstein to have lunch with him in his room at the Central Hotel, he went through the score and, in the pianist's words, 'proved how wrong it was to play too quickly the valse sequence in the second movement. I never play this work without being conscious of his words. And, thanks to him, I had a real success in Glasgow and Edinburgh.'

To prepare himself for the performance, Rubinstein had spent two months at Forres, near Inverness, as the guest of Sir William Gordon Cummings, a 'charming gentleman' who put a piano and billiard table at his disposal, and fed him on grouse which he ate 'to the music of bagpipes played by men in kilts who marched around the table'. In return for the hospitality he played the piano late into the night, while Sir William and friends listened to him in their dressing gowns.

In Glasgow, St Andrew's Hall was the orchestra's prime acoustical asset, a traditional Leipzig-style Gewandhaus, where quality of sound was judged more important than richness of decor or soft upholstery. The seats, indeed, were seriously uncomfortable, but then worse could be said of Bayreuth. Good acoustics and human comfort are rarely compatible. Yet a glance at the pictures in Leo Beranek's *Music, Acoustics and Architecture* shows a hall

similar in its shoe-box shape and proportions to Vienna's Musikverein, Amsterdam's Concertgebouw and Boston's Symphony
Hall. The European conductors who came to Glasgow in the old
days must have felt thoroughly at home there, and no doubt it
was a major element of the Scottish Orchestra's attraction for
them. To get an impression today of what it must have been like,
and how it sounded, you have only to visit the smaller-scale City
Hall and you will see and hear.

The fate of St Andrew's Hall is a subject to which I shall return.
Barbirolli, Beecham and Boult adored it, and Alexander Gibson,
when his time came, did so also. Edinburgh, on the other hand,
lagged behind Glasgow in acquiring an auditorium of international
quality. The cramped, classical elegance of the Music Hall in
George Street, where the orchestra first appeared, was never a
long-term possibility. The mightily resonant McEwan Hall, from
1907, was just another temporary solution, though Berlioz's
choral music must have sounded thrilling there – it still would
today.

But the answer, after characteristically endless Edinburgh pro-
crastination, was provided by the opening of the Usher Hall in
1914. George Henschel was invited back to conduct Beethoven's
concert overture, *The Consecration of the House*, and the official
inauguration, a few weeks after the assassination of Archduke
Franz Ferdinand at Sarajevo, was attended by King George V.
The £100,000 that had been provided by Andrew Usher in 1896
for 'a centre of attractions to musical artists and performers and
to the citizens of Edinburgh and others who might desire to hear
good music' had risen in value to £136,000 by the time Stockdale
Harrison's designs reached realisation up the hill from the Caledonian Hotel. Not even that amount of cash, however, could
provide the backstage facilities the hall still desperately needs (the
conductor's room, which has to be shared with any soloists and
contains only one lavatory, resembles a shanty-town if Mahler's
Eighth Symphony is being performed).

Yet, while lacking the acoustical perfection of the Glasgow auditorium, the Usher immediately established itself as a 'good' hall.
It had presence, and a handsome design, circular rather than
rectangular. What it could not provide was the combined lumin-
osity and warmth of tone that defines a truly great concert hall.
Barbirolli thought it acoustically patchy, Beecham said he could
never achieve a real fortissimo there (though he undoubtedly did

so) and Gibson insisted that a large body of strings was required
to make the result worthwhile.

Today, like many another famous hall, the Usher seems to have
acquired a sort of acoustical patina through usage – or perhaps
one's ears have just grown accustomed to it. Yet the procession
of great orchestras (as well as some bummers) that have passed
through it since the foundation of the Edinburgh Festival in 1947
have tended to prove Furtwängler's dictum that there are no bad
halls, only bad orchestras. And there have been times – though
they are less and less frequent – when Scotland's national orchestra
has sounded bad there.

Though Glasgow remains its home, the Scottish was ever a
national orchestra. From the beginning it toured the country,
visiting halls large and small, in a way that its continental counter-
parts do not. Critics, from time to time, are dismissive about this.
Great orchestras, they claim, should not need to go on the road.
Country cousins should come and hear them in their home base,
rather than the other way around. What is the point of playing
Brahms symphonies in buildings too small for them?

Yet what, it could equally be asked, is the point of playing
Brahms symphonies in buildings too large for them? Not until
halls, for the sake of box-office returns, began to expand beyond
a capacity of two thousand seats did serious acoustical difficulties
arise. Audiences who are able to sit inside the sound of an orchestra
hear what the composer intended more satisfactorily than those
who sit outside it. The effect of the *Eroica* symphony in a small
or smallish hall is quite different from its effect in a large one. Ears
accustomed to the glossy, bottom-heavy textures of music played
by big orchestras in big modern halls can be startled by the impact
of somewhat smaller orchestras in smaller-scale surroundings.

So playing, and listening, in halls of different characteristics is
not necessarily a bad thing. Edinburgh, Aberdeen and Dundee
were quickly established as the Scottish Orchestra's principal
venues outside Glasgow. Ambitiously, in 1923, the Tayside centre
of Britain's jute industry built itself a grandiose Gewandhaus
above the docks with the help of a gift of £100,000 from Sir James
Caird. King George V had laid the foundation stone nine years
earlier (around the time he did the same for the Usher Hall).
And the new Caird Hall, for all its vastness, proved an acoustical
success, even though Sir Thomas Beecham said that conducting a
concert there was like performing music down Regent Street.

Not to be outdone, Aberdeen's city fathers acquired the already existent Music Hall in Union Street in 1928 for £34,000, rescuing the century-old building from possible decline and providing the Scottish Orchestra with the permanent use of yet another rectangular, flat-floored Gewandhaus. Though smaller than Dundee's, it possessed good if rather boomy acoustics, and was more than adequate for symphony concerts (a major refurbishment in 1986 improved its facilities without doing acoustical damage).

So now the orchestra had four imposing buildings to perform in, but any other town with enough money and adequate premises was also on its itinerary. Greenock, Perth, Forfar, Ayr, Inverness, Paisley, Dunfermline, Stirling and a dozen or more other places could hear the Scottish Orchestra perform. Today, with the BBC Scottish Symphony Orchestra and Scottish Chamber Orchestra also touring the country, concerts have been rationalised, and the SCO has taken over some of the symphony orchestra's previous dates; but as part of its centenary celebrations it went out on the road again in 1991, visiting many places – including Orkney, Shetland and Lewis – in which it had not played for years. I heard it in the institutional surroundings of Stirling's Victorian Albert Hall, and thought that Dvořák's *New World* came to life there in a way it would never have done in the antiseptic modern MacRobert Centre across the river.

In 1916, Mlynarski's six years in Scotland ended abruptly when wartime attrition caused symphony concerts to be replaced by chamber ones. The signing of the Armistice in 1918 was commemorated with – of all things – Elgar's *The Spirit of England*, sung by the Glasgow Choral Union under David Stephen. Today, when even the first *Pomp and Circumstance* march is apt to be greeted with hostility in Scotland, the choice would be considered thoughtless. On that occasion the performance was hailed as magnificent, as it also was, many years later, when Sir Alexander Gibson recorded the work as part of a substantial Elgar survey.

To Landon Ronald, in 1919, went the task of rebuilding the orchestra, though Mlynarski remained popular enough to be invited back regularly as guest conductor. The pre-war tally of about sixty concerts per season – twenty-seven of them in Glasgow on Tuesdays and Saturdays, and a dozen on Mondays in Edinburgh – was restored, and by 1920 a total of seventy-five players had been recruited.

The reliable Ronald, dedicatee of Elgar's *Falstaff*, was clearly the right man for what was required of him, and in 1922 he was knighted for his efforts. But, like Cowen, he was not the most thrilling or adventurous of conductors. When Barbirolli, a later, greater exponent of *Falstaff*, exclaimed to him how wonderful Elgar's symphonic study was, Ronald replied that he could not make head or tail of it.

To offset the conservatism of his programme planning, Julius Harrison was brought in as associate conductor. Though more at home in the opera house than the concert hall, he made a sensation by presenting Skryabin's *Poem of Ecstasy* (today, no doubt, it would be Messiaen's *Turangalîla* symphony) several times in a single season. Other works to which he treated his Scottish audiences were less colourful. They included the cantata, *The Great god Pan*, by his teacher, Granville Bantock, Holst's *Hymn of Jesus* and Elgar's *The Music Makers*, but a galvanic new force was soon to arrive and sweep away this world of cosy English music-making.

2

i

Koussevitsky

After its four-year marriage to Sir Landon Ronald ended in 1923, the orchestra entered a more fickle phase in its life. Or perhaps it simply had difficulty attracting another full-time partner. At any rate, no fewer than five conductors were announced for the following season, the most seductively exciting of whom was Serge Koussevitsky. Russia's one-time virtuoso of the double bass had already appeared – as Joseph Barnes, the prolix but durable manager of the management committee, worded it in the annual brochure – with 'sensational success' in Edinburgh, and his Glasgow concerts would therefore be of 'epochal importance.'

Koussevitsky, he promised, was 'undoubtedly an outstanding personality among present-day conductors and a worthy successor to the late Artur Nikisch.' But just in case anyone feared that the absence of a permanent conductor might lead to bad habits, Barnes prudently added 'It is a condition of each conductor's engagement that he shall rehearse the orchestra for all concerts to be conducted by him, so that the disadvantages usually attaching to a plural conductorship are obviated.'

The use of deputies, whether by conductors or players, was one of Britain's musical diseases, today no longer virulent. Koussevitsky, rising to Glasgow's challenge, compiled an opening programme which undoubtedly demanded his presence in person, and which was audacious enough to show why he was regarded as a genius by some, a charlatan by others. In Britain, only Sir Thomas Beecham had Koussevitsky's sort of cheek, though some would prefer to call it arrogance, and others insecurity.

Like Sir Thomas, he mostly got away with it, thanks to his ability to thrill an audience simply by walking on to the platform. Not many of today's conductors have that ability, though in Scotland the Estonian Neeme Järvi and the Russian Yuri Temirkanov have been able to do the trick. But if trick is the word, and if the quality is an essential ingredient of a certain sort of conductor's make-up, then Koussevitsky had it in abundance. Who else could have, or would have, launched a concert season with a programme consisting of a Handel suite, a C. P. E. Bach concerto ('orchestrated by M. Steinberg'), the prelude to Musorgsky's *Khovanshchina*, the Wedding March from Rimsky-Korsakov's *Golden Cockerel*, Rakhmaninov's *Vocalise*, Lyadov's *Baba Yaga*, and Brahms's Fourth Symphony? Koussevitsky had arrived in town, and wanted everybody to know it.

In fact, it was a concert brilliantly devised to suit his special talents. Like Beecham he was no purist, but he knew how to make corrupt editions of classical music acceptable through the force of his personality. His treatment of the dawn music from *Khovanshchina* was famously slow – the slowest in history – but planted alongside the glitter of the *Golden Cockerel*, the fizz of *Baba Yaga* and the romance of Rakhmaninov's wordless *scena*, it must have spun an irresistible web of Russian magic. Then, as a final belly punch, he proceeded to give the same treatment to Brahms.

Though there were musicians who said they could 'see through' Koussevitsky, nobody could explain the electricity and neurotic frenzy he was able to bring to Tchaikovsky's *Pathétique* symphony, which turned up later in the season (there is an old Boston Symphony Orchestra recording of this work that confirms the intensity of Koussevitsky's interpretation). People claimed that he could not read a score, basing their slander on his unconventional habit of getting a pianist to run through every new piece with him before he rehearsed it. Stravinsky, more pointedly, said that nobody messed up his Symphonies of Wind Instruments the way Koussevitsky spectacularly messed it up.

Yet with the help of his rich wife, he enriched the orchestral repertoire. The quantity of Koussevitsky commissions was prodigious, and few of them were duds. The masterpieces included Bartók's Concerto for Orchestra, Ravel's orchestration of Musorgsky's *Pictures at an Exhibition* and Stravinsky's *Psalm Symphony*, 'composed for the glory of God and dedicated to the Boston Symphony Orchestra on the occasion of the fiftieth anniversary of its existence'. Sir George Henschel had been the Boston Symphony's first conductor. Koussevitsky, a year after his Scottish season, was to become the most famous of all Boston's baton wielders, and many of the works he commissioned were to take their place in the international repertoire.

If none of them turned up in Scotland in 1923 (quite a number of them had yet to be written) Koussevitsky's Scottish programmes were nevertheless packed, sometimes eccentrically, with surprises. As prelude to Tchaikovsky's *Pathétique* symphony, for instance, he conducted Mozart's *Eine kleine Nachtmusik*, the Bacchanale from *Tannhäuser* and Strauss's *Till Eulenspiegel* (he was a phenomenal Straussian).

A programme with Skryabin's *Poem of Ecstasy* as its radiant climax reached that point via Haydn's Thirteenth Symphony, Weber's *Oberon* overture, the Prelude and Liebestod from *Tristan and Isolde*, Siegfried's Funeral March from *Götterdämmerung*, and Debussy's *Rêve* and the *Prélude à l'après-midi d'un faune* – in that order. Something described as Vaughan Williams's Concerto for Orchestra with Organ – he wrote no such work but perhaps it was a Koussevitsky arrangement of *The Lark Ascending* – formed the start of another Koussevitsky adventure that progressed to Tchaikovsky's *Francesca da Rimini*, Lyadov's *Five Russian Folksongs*, the Glasgow premiere of Rimsky-Korsakov's *Flight of the Bumblebee* and Beethoven's Fifth Symphony.

How well did the orchestra respond to a conductor notorious for his towering rages? At his first rehearsal, it is said, Koussevitsky put down his baton after five minutes and remarked to the leader, Horace Fellowes, in German 'I am surprised at the inferior quality of the playing, I cannot understand it, because this is a *recognised* orchestra.' The players, on being told what he had said, rose to the challenge and produced what was reported to be 'a fantastically good performance'.

Sir Adrian Boult – or Adrian C. Boult as he was known at the time – was Koussevitsky's sober British rival for the hand of the Scottish Orchestra in 1923, but could offer nothing as blazing as this. What Boult, for his part, could provide were things Koussevitsky was incapable of – Parry's *Symphonic Variations*, for instance, and the Glasgow premiere of Delius's *On Hearing the First Cuckoo in Spring*.

Debussy's *Petite Suite* and Gordon Jacob's transcription of a set of virginal pieces by William Byrd could have been anyone's territory, but it was Boult who conducted them. His repertoire was always wider than people gave him credit for. This pillar of the English establishment conducted, after all, the first British performance of Berg's *Wozzeck*, and his truthfulness to whatever he touched won him the long and warm-hearted support of

Scottish audiences, right up to his last years, half a century later, when he conducted Schubert's Great C major Symphony with perfectly sustained momentum and generated the long central crescendo in the finale of Sibelius's Second Symphony with an equilibrium few others could match.

Behind the appurtenances of a military moustache, a stately bearing and a baton like a fishing rod, Boult could bring to works such as these a sense of excitement that grew from within the music instead of being superimposed on it. I remember, in a single season, hearing Beethoven's *Eroica* symphony conducted first by the Birmingham-born Boult, then by George Weldon, another conductor with Birmingham associations. Boult, waggling his stick but otherwise standing stock still, set each movement in motion in such a way that – to quote his own perceptive little book on conducting – one got the impression that the whole symphony was laid out in front of him on two vast pages of music. Nothing, in short, impeded the progress of the performance. Weldon, on the other hand, lashed himself into a lather with the wild array of gestures he brought to anything from Dvořák's *Carnival* overture to Ravel's *Bolero*, but for all his visual allure he made singularly little impact on the drama of the *Eroica*. The audience, responding to sight rather than sound, nevertheless cheered Weldon more loudly than Boult.

The other conductors that season were two old friends, Landon Ronald and Emil Mlynarski, and one newcomer, Maurice Besly, who arrived from The Queen's College, Oxford, and slid into a legal career after a fleeting appearance in the 1954 edition of *Grove*. Boult, who could have been a prime candidate for the orchestra's conductorship, went to the City of Birmingham Orchestra instead, and from there to the newly-formed BBC Symphony Orchestra in London. Koussevitsky, like Szell a decade later, went instantly to America, where he would be the acclaimed conductor of the Boston Symphony Orchestra for the next quarter century. Mlynarski returned the following season, but his relationship with Scotland was by then on the wane, and thereafter he was to be found more often in Paris, Philadelphia and Warsaw, where he conducted the premiere of Szymanowski's *King Roger* in 1926.

Weingartner

However cautious they may have been in some respects, Joseph Barnes and his committee knew a big name when they saw one, and knew how to go about netting it. Scottish parsimony seems never to have been an obstacle when a top conductor was there to be grabbed – and if he came from Austria or Germany, so much the better. Sir George Henschel's main credential had been his friendship with Brahms, but Felix Weingartner's trump cards thirty years later were his links with Liszt and Wagner and, on an impersonal but metaphysical level, his communion with Beethoven. That the centenary of Beethoven's death was approaching when he reached Glasgow in 1924 made his two seasons with the Scottish Orchestra all the more timely and, no doubt, all the more mystic.

But Weingartner had other assets also. One of them was his imposing track record with the Vienna Philharmonic and Vienna Opera, where he had been Mahler's successor; another was his proven expertise as a composer, arranger and author. But everything, even Weingartner's own symphonies, circled round Beethoven. When he married for the sixth time – so the story goes – his new wife was nicknamed the Pastoral. Like many a good anecdote, however, this one was not quite accurate. Weingartner had only five wives, so the last was the C minor.

Predictably, Beethoven was the subject of Weingartner's opening concert in Scotland, on 18 November 1924. In one of his self-congratulatory printed statements, Barnes had exclaimed about the 'desirability of engaging conductors of the highest eminence'. Felix Weingartner, he declared, 'stands without compare in the sanity of his readings and in the truly classical interpretation of the compositions of the great masters'. As if that were not enough, the eulogy went on to say 'His book, *Die Symphonie nach Beethoven*, is the standard work on the rendering of the symphonies of Beethoven, and is recognised as authoritative'. The last four words were rammed home in bold type.

Faced with such a build-up, the audience must have waited with

bated breath to encounter the authority of his opening programme. In choice of music, it looked by no means unimaginative, consisting as it did of two movements from *Prometheus*
(rather than simply the usual five-minute overture to that still
neglected ballet), an 'Andante for String Orchestra', the *Egmont*
overture and the *Eroica* symphony, in that order.

The prospectus, sadly, did not identify the andante for strings,
but it must have been a Weingartner arrangement of a movement
from one of the string quartets – an unfortunate but not
uncommon trait of the time, and one that was revived by Leonard
Bernstein in America as recently as the nineteen-seventies. The
audience, however, was destined not to find out, because Weingartner on arrival changed the programme to a more conventional
combination of the *Coriolanus* overture, the First Symphony, the
Egmont overture and the *Eroica*.

But disappointment, if there was any, must surely have been
swept aside by the *Eroica*, one of Weingartner's most deservedly
acclaimed interpretations, as his recording of it with the Vienna
Philharmonic has long testified. If a complete Beethoven cycle had
been hoped for by the orchestra's supporters, however, it was
soon denied them. Apart from a performance of the Ninth Symphony a month after his arrival – with Weingartner's own arrangement of Gluck's *Alceste* overture and a bleeding chunk of *Die
Walküre* to precede it – Beethoven for the remainder of the season
was displaced by Weingartner's other enthusiasms.

So the 'Symphony No 5 in C minor' which he presented in
Edinburgh in December turned out not to be Beethoven's but
Weingartner's own. Whatever the quality of the music, it received
a big build-up. 'Written specially for the British public', bragged
Barnes, 'and finished only this year, the orchestral parts were
copied in Vienna, in Berlin and in London as Mr Weingartner
journeyed towards us. The ink of some of the parts is scarcely
dry.'

The work itself, to judge by the programme note, was equally
portentous. Listeners were assured that it was 'orthodox in design,
following the classical German models and having as last movement a great fugue on two themes'. The music, they were
informed, possessed no definite programme, but 'each hearer has
Mr Weingartner's permission to imagine for himself or herself the
picture or the romance or the vision which it suggests to him or
her'. Everybody was expected to perceive the integrity of the final

Poco maestoso, bringing 'the whole impressive work to a fitting and dignified close'. Weingartner's own more modest comment was that it was 'simply a symphony, a genuine symphony'.

But Weingartner was no Mahler. His symphonies, recognised as the price that had to be paid for his excellence as a conductor, fell on stony ground wherever he performed them – as did those of his fellow Viennese, Karl Rankl, in Scotland thirty years later. And even his excellence as a conductor was at times disputed. Some British critics, including Neville Cardus, praised the quietness of his platform manner – 'his laundry bill probably disappoints those who attend to the weekly linen of most other conductors' – and extolled his constant respect for the composer's own notes and instructions. Others, however, thought him aloof, neurotic and vain – qualities possessed by many other conductors, it's true, but combined in Weingartner's case with what was reckoned to be a disappointing lack of personality and, even worse, of fire. As for his much vaunted statement that 'My aim in conducting has been and is to reproduce the work soulfully and with the greatest simplicity and fidelity', who could accept it from a man who so ruthlessly truncated Wagner's operas and touched up Beethoven's orchestration to suit himself? In other words, Weingartner in Vienna or in Scotland was a conductor like any other, and less defensible than most.

Yet the best of his recordings suggest otherwise. That of Beethoven's Seventh Symphony tempers Toscanini-like tempi with Viennese grace. Scotland did not fail to note these qualities, even though he was by then in his middle sixties and soon to become director of the Basle Conservatoire in Switzerland – a fact that prompted some people to deduce that his powers were on the wane. But perhaps it had more to do with political canniness, for he died in Winterthur, near Lake Zürich, at the age of seventy-nine in the middle of the Second World War,

Certainly, as late as 1939, he was earning plaudits at Covent Garden for his Wagner conducting, and it is tantalising to know that he wanted to conduct Berlioz's *Benvenuto Cellini* and his own version of Weber's *Oberon* in Britain the following season. Beethoven was not his only hero. He championed Weber and Berlioz long before others saw fit to do so, and was a committed Wagnerian to the extent that he included the overture to *Das Liebesverbot* -a real rarity – in his first Scottish season, along with Elgar's *Enigma Variations*, Mendelssohn's *Scotch* Symphony, the

Glasgow premiere of Respighi's *The Fountains of Rome*, Delius's *First Cuckoo* and his own arrangement, rivalling Berlioz's, of Weber's *Invitation to the Dance*.

But his fickle, restless and irascible nature prevented him from ever becoming dedicated to the Scottish Orchestra even to the limited degree that Szell was to be later. He came and he left, just as he also did in Vienna, Berlin, Hamburg, Boston and wherever else he briefly settled; and though, during his two Scottish seasons, he conducted most of the concerts himself, he seemed perfectly content to share the Scottish Orchestra with Václav Talich, Landon Ronald and Hermann Abendroth, without showing the slightest interest in what was happening when he was not there in person.

By 1926, any hopes of a pre-centenary tribute to Beethoven in Scotland were dashed. Instead, for his second and last Scottish season, Weingartner chose to concentrate on Brahms and Liszt (opting for what is now a rarity, the symphonic poem *Tasso*), on Berlioz (the *Symphonie Fantastique*) and odds and ends such as the air from Bach's Suite in D, the pizzicato scherzo from Tchaikovsky's Fourth Symphony, two movements from Holst's *Planets* suite, and Felix Mottl's long-discredited arrangement of Schubert's keyboard Fantasy in F minor. He did not, however, forget to leave space for more of his own music – this time his *Tempest* suite, with which, in December 1925, he bade farewell to Scotland.

But if self-interest seemed to characterise Weingartner's Scottish programme planning, it was perhaps only to be expected. Václav Talich's programmes during the same period were, on the other hand, a model of Czech integrity. Though his name, in international terms, was less renowned than Weingartner's, he was a no less impressive scoop on the part of the management committee, a conductor who was as great as, if not greater than, Rafael Kubelik among more recent Czechs.

Championed by Dvořák and befriended by Nikisch, Talich had been leader of the Berlin Philharmonic while still in his twenties and conductor of the Czech Philharmonic by the time he was thirty-six. Burly in build, with a shock of dark hair, he must have looked very different from the elegant, ascetic Weingartner. He was every inch a Czech, and the pioneering champion of Janáček's operas. He was also a great teacher, whose pupils included today's most zealous Janáček conductor, Sir Charles Mackerras.

What attracted him to Scotland two seasons running remains

obscure. Perhaps he just had an occasional longing for the north
– the only other non-Czech city to which he was regularly lured
was Stockholm. Or perhaps Glasgow was musically more appeal-
ing at that time than people now realise. One of the eternal mys-
teries, after all, was the meeting between Brahms and Hans von
Bülow in Baden when the latter – his mind still reeling after the
premiere of Brahms's First Symphony in Karlsrühe – offered to
conduct it the following year in Glasgow, where he was appearing
regularly with the Scottish Orchestra in its pre-natal state.

Talich was no Hans von Bülow, but he was a conductor of
immense talent and insight who compiled his Scottish programmes with the single-mindedness he brought to all aspects of
music. Before his first Glasgow appearance at the age of forty-one,
the orchestra committee hailed him as 'one of the most promising
of the younger school of continental conductors'. If calling him
'young' and 'promising' now seems a touch patronising, we
should remember that those were days before a Welser-Möst or a
Simon Rattle could be offered a key appointment while still in his
twenties.

Glasgow did not give him Weingartner's sort of priority. He
was simply slipped into the 1924–25 season in January 1925, after
Weingartner had been able to make his initial impact and Landon
Ronald had conducted the Glasgow premiere of Delius's *Brigg
Fair*. But he immediately scored a hit with a programme containing a selection of Dvořák's *Slavonic Dances* as a rousing Czech
visiting card and Skryabin's Piano Concerto (with the Scottish
soloist, Lilian Mackinnon) as evidence of his range of interest. A
week later he conducted Albert Roussel's *Pour une Fête du Prin-
temps*, a piece of French post-impressionism that nobody in Scotland yet knew – it was revived, still a rarity, by Jane Glover as
guest conductor in 1992, during the orchestra's centenary celebrations.

The following year, when Weingartner was winding down his
relationship with Scotland via Bach's Air on the G string, Talich
consolidated his position as one of the orchestra's most desirable
guest conductors by giving the Glasgow premiere of Mahler's
Fourth Symphony, Richard Strauss's suite of Couperin arrangements, and three of the movements from Holst's *Planets* suite
which Weingartner, a few weeks earlier, had failed to show interest in. Best of all, however, he compiled a series of five programmes each devoted to a single country or group of countries,

an imaginative idea to come from a guest conductor who could all too easily have arrived in Scotland with a flamboyant portfolio of party pieces.

Czechoslovakia was naturally given pride of place, with rarities by Dvořák and Fibich, but the Russian, Austrian and Scandinavian programmes were no less thoughtfully devised, and the Italian one was notable for the presence of music by Sinigaglia, Geminiani, Martucci and Sgambati, a protégé of Liszt. Today such concerts would be virtually inconceivable. Guest conductors no longer think that way, nor have they the time to do so. But Talich's relationship with the orchestra was too good to last: his Czech responsibilities were increasing and after one more season, when he had the orchestra entirely to himself, he was gone, leaving the players to a new triumvirate consisting of Vladimir Golschmann, Hermann Abendroth and Albert Coates.

Golschmann, founder in 1919 of the 'Golschmann Concerts' in Paris, was famed as a progressive, with a flair for the music of the Gallic group of composers known as Les Six. Today, perhaps, he would have found a niche in Musica Nova, but towards the end of the nineteen-twenties in Glasgow the orchestra was in too impecunious a state to use his talents to that sort of advantage. The Frankfurt-born Abendroth, an established Wagnerian in Germany, reached Scotland via guest dates with the LSO in London, but left no lasting impression. The 46-year-old Coates, a specialist in Russian music, was a more valuable visitor, but at a time when the orchestra was going through one of its musically patchier phases, this in every way imposing conductor – born of English parents in St Petersburg, initially a scientist but soon to be a protégé of Nikisch – failed to make the impact he might otherwise have done.

By now, with a tally of anything up to six conductors per season, each of them equally favoured, the players were struggling to maintain a standard and a continuity, and perhaps – though it seems unlikely – a house style. But suddenly in 1930 a new name, planted among nonentities such as Robert Heger and Albert van Raalte on the one hand, and more interesting figures such as Landon Ronald and Nikolay Malko on the other, appeared and proved immediately prophetic. 'That upstart Barbirolli', as his rival Sir Thomas Beecham called him, was a 31-year-old Italian Cockney and former cellist who had been showing his strength in London and elsewhere as an opera conductor. The Scottish

Orchestra was to bring out his qualities in the concert hall and thereby help to steer him towards a different musical career which, as it developed, would earn him affection around the world and, with it, the nickname of 'Glorious John', bestowed upon him by Vaughan Williams.

3

The Barbirolli Years

During the nineteen-twenties, unless there was a Russian around, the Scottish Orchestra's programmes had tended to be Teutonic. When British music was performed, it was generally of a sort that attracted the German and Dutch conductors upon whose services the orchestra relied. The same would happen in the nineteen-fifties, when two Austrians in succession reigned over the programmes. But in 1930 came a tiny breath of fresh air, an awareness that not everything revolved round Beethoven and Brahms. John Barbirolli provided it. He arrived from London with no preconceived notions about what the orchestral repertoire should or should not contain. At the age of thirty-one, he had never been in full-time charge of a symphony orchestra, but he knew what he wanted to conduct, and he knew how he wanted to do it.

Today's orchestral players are prone to say that young conductors 'use' them in order to learn the repertoire. Simon Rattle was not quickly forgiven by members of the BBC Scottish Symphony Orchestra for employing them (as they saw it) as patient guinea pigs for the perfected performance of Peter Maxwell Davies's exceedingly complex First Symphony he would later conduct so tellingly with the Philharmonia Orchestra in London. But Barbirolli, for all his inexperience, came to Scotland formidably well prepared.

No doubt his Franco-Italian ancestry – he had an Italian father, a French mother and had been christened Giovanni Battista Barbirolli – contributed to his breadth of musical taste. At first it had seemed likely that he would be a cellist, in which capacity he was a member of two string quartets, gave a recital at the Aeolian Hall and appeared as soloist with the Bournemouth Municipal Orchestra. But then, when he founded his own string orchestra, he discovered that he wanted to conduct it. Yet he was always a cellist at heart. His left hand, with its large thumb, played on the orchestra as if it were a cello. And when, at the 1948 Edinburgh Festival, he conducted an ecstatic performance of Dvořák's Cello Concerto with Piatigorsky as soloist, he grabbed the Russian cellist's instrument from him at the end and played a few notes himself. Like Toscanini, also a cellist, he was capable of being rude about a former bassist called Koussevitsky.

Again as with Toscanini, the Italian side of his personality was inevitably attracted to opera – he was an incomparable, if infrequent, conductor of *Aïda*, *Otello* and *Madama Butterfly*, two of which he recorded – and he might well have concentrated on an operatic career had not, from 1930 onwards, a series of symphony orchestras wooed him.

Since the Scottish Orchestra was the first of these, we must speculate on whether Scotland is to be praised or blamed for tempting him away from the opera house. But if, thereby, an outstanding interpreter of Verdi and Puccini (and, on the evidence of the memorable *Tristan and Isolde* he once conducted at the Empire Theatre, Edinburgh, a possibly great Wagnerian) was largely lost, an equally outstanding conductor of Elgar, Mahler, Bruckner and Sibelius was undoubtedly gained. If his first two guest appearances with the Scottish Orchestra played relatively safe in choice of music, they were nevertheless compiled with the flair for which he would become famous – one of them consisted of Rossini's *Siege of Corinth* overture, Delius's *In a Summer Garden*, Mozart's *Jupiter* symphony and Debussy's *La Mer* – and the quality of the conducting was unmistakable.

A new force had arrived. True, Barnes's 1930 concert syllabus went no farther than to say that Barbirolli was 'regarded as one of the most promising of British orchestral conductors' – a surprisingly low-keyed statement to come from the orchestra's ponderous but usually by no means unappreciative head of the management committee. But then, nobody in Glasgow at that time probably knew just how good Barbirolli actually was and how lucky they were to get him. Nor, presumably, did they want to offend the four other conductors alongside whom Barbirolli would be appearing.

But of the four, Nikolay Malko was the only one who by then cut much ice. A pupil of Rimsky-Korsakov, Lyadov and Glazunov, he was perhaps less colourful than some of the orchestra's other Russians, but he did not lack vivacity and he did not inflict on the players anything as terrifying as Koussevitsky's temper. Robert Heger, on the other hand, was to be summed up by the Anglo-Austrian writer, Mosco Carner, as 'a great routinier, no more and no less'. Born in Alsace, he was one of those useful people who, like Heinrich Hollreiser later, have a way of turning up everywhere and producing a decent performance of almost anything, no matter how difficult.

In 1953 at Covent Garden he conducted the British premiere of Richard Strauss's last opera, *Capriccio*. A typical Heger concert in Scotland consisted, in 1931, of the Love Scene from Strauss's *Feuersnot*, Nikolay Metner's Piano Concerto (with the Russian composer himself as pianist) and what the programme brochure listed as the Glasgow premiere of what was misprinted as Verdi's *Sforza del Destino* overture, perhaps in the belief that the family whose destiny it dealt with was none other than the Sforzas of Milan. Heger – who also championed Bruckner's symphonies at a time when it was brave to do so in Scotland – made his final appearance with the orchestra in 1933, but survived another forty-five years before dying, at the age of ninety-two, in Munich.

With four orchestral interludes from the opera, *Intermezzo*, Albert van Raalte also showed himself to be a Straussian with a taste for the unusual. But in no other respect could this pupil of Nikisch be said to have left his mark on the orchestra, even though he appeared five seasons running. Holland was where his heart lay. Not only did he found the Radio Hilversum Orchestra but he contrived, during the Second World War, to run what *Grove* described as 'an exclusively Jewish orchestra for exclusively Jewish audiences', after which he was sent to – and survived – a concentration camp for artists and intellectuals.

With Sir Landon Ronald past his peak – by 1930 he was sliding into academic life and a repertoire increasingly dependent on Elgar – Barbirolli clearly had the opportunity to assert himself as Britain's brightest young conductor, and to reveal his own devotion to Elgar, in an exciting and positive way. Yet the orchestra's programme brochure still refrained from eulogising him, and in 1931 he continued to take his place as part of a line-up that now included Basil Cameron, Constant Lambert and Issay Dobrowen in addition to Albert van Raalte and Sir Landon Ronald. Indeed, not until Barbirolli had introduced Sibelius's Second Symphony, Vaughan Williams's *Job* and Bax's Fourth Symphony during the

1932–33 season did Joseph Barnes begin to realise what sort of conductor he had acquired.

But then, in those grim years of poverty and depression he must have had much else on his mind. His introduction to the 1933–34 programme brochure spelt some of it out. After thanking the subscribers and guarantors who had enabled the management committee to overcome the 'severest crisis' in the orchestra's history, he said that to have abandoned the season would have been a 'veritable catastrophe'. The orchestra was 'something that we cannot willingly let die'. The music-lovers of Glasgow and the West of Scotland were praised for 'deeming it not only a duty but a privilege' to stand together and provide the funds necessary to carry on.

'Owing to the severe depression from which the whole world has been suffering', he added, 'this has involved serious personal sacrifices.' But the result, Barnes disclosed, was that the guarantee fund had actually increased and now exceeded £6,000. Even better news was the fact that Barbirolli had been engaged as conductor for the whole season. 'Mr Barbirolli', said the brochure, abandoning its previous reticence about him, 'last season won the cordial admiration and esteem of his audiences and his appointment will give universal satisfaction'.

With an increased number of concerts, Barbirolli was able to incorporate more of the music he cared about. Indulging his taste for Mozartian opera seria, he conducted Busoni's arrangement of a suite from *Idomeneo*, a work at that time neglected everywhere – its British premiere, by the Glasgow Grand Opera Society conducted by Erik Chisholm, took place that very year. The Sibelius experience was continued with a performance of the Fifth Symphony, a work Barbirolli would conduct again with the orchestra at the 1969 Edinburgh Festival, a year before his death, drawing such intensity from the double basses at the climax of the finale that the instruments audibly creaked with the strain.

Adolf Busch played Elgar's Violin Concerto. The Second Viennese School made one of its first Scottish intrusions via Schoenberg's *Verklärte Nacht*. Stravinsky's *Petrushka* received its first complete performance in Scotland, and the exploration of the music of Arnold Bax continued with a performance of the Third Symphony. There was even, at the end of the season, a performance of Strauss's *Ein Heldenleben*, a work requiring so many extra players – Barbirolli made do with a total of eighty – that it might, in 1934, have been thought beyond the orchestra's financial resources.

Announcing the 1934–35 season, Joseph Barnes was even more effusive than the year before. 'John Barbirolli', he said, 'has been reappointed conductor for the whole period and the unqualified success which attended his engagement last season makes this a matter of supreme congratulation.' Though there were times when Barnes's congratulations carried more than a whiff of self-esteem, he had plenty at that time to be proud of.

For his opening programme this time, Barbirolli chose Bax's tone poem, *The Tale the Pine-trees Knew*, which the composer had dedicated to him three years earlier. Thereafter the deaths earlier in 1934 of England's three leading composers – Elgar, Delius and Holst – inevitably loomed over the rest of the season. A memorial evening to all three of them was conducted by Barbirolli on 20 November, his choice of music consisting of Elgar's Funeral March from *Grania and Diarmid*, the first Scottish performance of Delius's *Eventyr* (which Beecham was to revive on one of his Scottish visits after the Second World War), movements from Holst's *Planets* suite and the Elgar Violin Concerto with the orchestra's leader, David McCallum, as soloist.

But commemorations spread into other concerts also. From Barbirolli there were performances of Elgar's Second Symphony and *Engma Variations*, and of Delius's *North Country Sketches*. The Glasgow Choral Union sang *The Dream of Gerontius* under its chorusmaster Wilfred Senior. Extracts from *Parsifal* (Barbirolli again) added to the season's valedictory air, but not everything took place beneath a mantle of melancholy.

In one classic Barbirolli coupling, Artur Rubinstein was soloist in Falla's *Nights in the Gardens of Spain*, and two of the orchestra's section leaders, Charles Meert and David Nichols, played the cello and viola parts in Strauss's *Don Quixote*. It was characteristic of the conductor to insist that his own principal cellist, rather than some international star, should perform the title-role in that work. Strauss himself, who never regarded it as a star vehicle, would have been pleased. The Scottish premiere of a little-known Sibelius symphonic poem, *Pohjola's Daughter*, completed the programme.

Barbirolli knew how to coax the best out of individual players. To Eileen Grainger, his youthful sub-principal viola, went the honour of performing Walton's Viola Concerto during the same season. Barbirolli had spotted her talents when she played in the

Covent Garden Orchestra, had put her on trial in the Scottish
Orchestra and had asked her to stay on for £8 a week – which was
one pound above the going rate. A member of the management
committee, it is said, objected to this lavish sum, and asked, to
murmurs of agreement from his colleagues, 'Why should we pay
that money to a girl?' Barbirolli's unanswerable reply was 'I'm
not bringing you a girl, I'm bringing you a viola player'.

By then, indeed, he had recruited as many as ten women players
– no great achievement by today's orchestral standards, but
impressive enough in the year 1934. One of his most far-sighted
appointments was the oboist Evelyn Rothwell, who replaced a
recalcitrant Belgian who had walked out on him; she later became
a distinguished soloist as well as his wife. When he revitalised the
Hallé Orchestra a decade later, his forces included a woman hornist, a woman trombonist and, most famously, a woman timpanist,
Joyce Aldous. Few conductors have won more devotion from
his players. Nevertheless Barbirolli could be testy, and at times
maddeningly insistent. Melvyn Bragg's television profile of him
showed him rehearsing the start of the scherzo of Bruckner's
Seventh Symphony over and over again, stopping the players
constantly in a way they traditionally detest.

In the deceptively simple opening bars of Sibelius's Second
Symphony – one of his favourite works – he was reputedly even
worse, expending limitless time and patience over the pulse, the
accents and the quiet crescendo of these first eleven subdued notes
and their subsequent repetition. And there were times when the
attention of the players wandered, which resulted in an imperious
rap of the baton and a throaty-voiced rebuke. 'Most of you seem
incretinated this morning' was a familiar piece of Barbirolli abuse.
Yet though his methods could infuriate them, the end product
won their respect. Not for nothing, at the end of the season, did
the Scottish Orchestra rise and sing to him 'Will ye no' come back
again'.

Return he did, for one season more. Everybody had guessed by
then that they could not hang on to him much longer, and the
annual brochure now regularly included a clause along the lines
of 'owing to a prior engagement, Mr Barbirolli will be absent
from two of the Saturday concerts'. Yet by today's standards he
was stupendously present. During his five years in Scotland, either
as guest or as principal conductor, his time with the orchestra
amounted to a total of sixty weeks. In some weeks he conducted as

many as seven concerts. Considering the shortness of the Scottish season, there is no doubt that the management committee got its money's worth.

But Barbirolli gave value in other ways, too. His rehearsals brought a cohesion and rich beauty to the playing that it had only intermittently possessed before. What the strings lacked in numbers, they made up in expressiveness and with a new precision of bowing. Charles Reid, in his biography of the conductor, has told how Barbirolli and his leader, David McCallum, would spend their train journeys between Edinburgh and Glasgow seated in their first-class compartment with orchestral scores and string parts spread out on the seats opposite them. McCallum would play a passage on his violin, while Barbirolli listened 'with microphonic ears and the eyes of a hawk'. Passage after passage would be subjected to alternative bowings and phrasings before the conductor pencilled in definitive ones. The point, the heel and the middle of the bow would all be tried out before it was decided that the point was best after all. Once, in publicly declaring the Scottish Orchestra to be the only permanent orchestra of its size in Scotland, Barbirolli said that his definition of the word permanent meant an orchestra that rehearsed as an entity every day of the week.

Yet he was no obsessive workaholic. He knew how to enjoy himself. Like George Szell, who succeeded him, he was a keen cook. Unlike Szell, he liked to treat his players to late-night supper parties at his Glasgow flat in Charing Cross, where his own perfected recipe for spaghetti bolognese was served straight from the pan. Needing little sleep, he coped easily with post-concert parties thrown by patrons and subscribers, and was known to arrive at the following morning's rehearsal still wearing white tie and tails, ready to dismantle the opening bars of Beethoven's Seventh Symphony, another of those works to which, every time he conducted it, he devoted the most meticulous attention.

What he could never comprehend was a management committee that was unable to see beyond a thirteen-week season, lasting from November until February, and that allowed its players to drift away for the rest of the year. To Barbirolli, this seemed utterly absurd. Not only did it fail to attract players of a desirable quality, but it undid all the days and weeks of work he himself put into transforming the orchestra each year into an integer. In speeches and printed statements, he returned to the subject again and again, pointing out that putting on an excessive number of concerts in the winter, and none at all in the spring, summer and autumn, was no way to run an orchestra.

Grudgingly, the management committee decided that 'as an experiment' it would lengthen the 1935–36 season by two weeks. Announcing this in the annual brochure, it added that Barbirolli's re-engagement would give 'universal satisfaction'. But the conductor himself was not so satisfied. In his opinion the two-week extension – which meant that the orchestra would now be giving no fewer than eighty-six concerts in fifteen weeks – did not alter his basic complaint, which was that a maximum amount of work was being crammed into the shortest possible amount of time.

Nevertheless his programmes ranged as widely and attractively as ever. In memory of Sir Alexander Mackenzie, who had died earlier in the year, he conducted the touching little instrumental *Benedictus* which was revived (after a long period of neglect) during the 1992 proms. No doubt Barbirolli found an Elgarian streak in this *morceau* by a Scottish composer born ten years before Sir Edward. At any rate the *Enigma Variations* came later in the programme.

Vaughan Williams's *Tallis Fantasia*, Delius's Violin Concerto, Strauss's *Bourgeois Gentilhomme* suite and Rakhmaninov's *Paganini Rhapsody* (which, having been composed in 1934, was still in its first brilliant flush of success) were among the works Barbirolli added to the orchestra's repertoire that season. Moiseiwitsch was pianist in the Rakhmaninov, as he was to be many times again, and the line-up of other soloists – Emanuel Feuermann in Dvořák's Cello Concerto, Jascha Heifetz in Brahms and Glazunov violin concertos, Egon Petri in the Brahms B flat, Alexander Kipnis in the 'Wahn' monologue from *Die Meistersinger* – gives an impression of the quality of talent Barbirolli was attracting to Scotland.

These, even in the nineteen-thirties, were expensive soloists. But the verve of Barbirolli's conducting, and the force of his personality, had hugely increased the size of the Glasgow audiences and, to a slightly lesser extent, those in Edinburgh. As a result, the orchestra was financially more stable than it had been for years. Only Elgar, a great composer about whom the Scots can still be curiously ambivalent, failed to draw the attendances he deserved. As an incomparable Elgarian, Barbirolli must have been hurt by this, but the management committee knew better than to interfere with his determination to keep on conducting the music he adored more than any other.

4

George Szell

In an article in *The Guardian* in 1935, Neville Cardus wrote that
what the Hallé Orchestra desperately needed was a conductor
of the calibre of George Szell. Standards in Manchester, after
Sir Hamilton Harty's resignation in 1933, had become erratic. Not
even Sir Thomas Beecham, as a regular visitor, could prevent the
playing from falling away 'astonishingly and alarmingly' – as the
Scottish Orchestra's had been prone to do in the nineteen-twenties
– when a lesser conductor was in charge. Szell, who at the time
was general music director of the Czech Philharmonic and of the
'German' Opera House in Prague, was in Cardus's opinion 'the
right man for the job'.

But in the end, from the winter of 1936 until the spring of 1939,
it was Scotland that won him. The fact that such a dauntingly
demanding Hungarian, who was destined from 1946 onwards to
build the Cleveland Orchestra into America's best, spent even a
small portion of his life licking the Scottish Orchestra into shape
may today seem strange – though no stranger perhaps than the
fact that Weingartner and Talich had already worked in Glasgow.

Strange, however, it undoubtedly was. Szell, by the time he
took up his Scottish appointment at the age of forty, had already
left a trail of destruction across Europe. He was a man, it was
said, who suffered nobody gladly. As John Culshaw, one of his
recording producers, put it, 'He had a notorious tongue and a
reputation for eating alive anyone who crossed his path.' When
he walked out of a production of *Tannhäuser* at the New York
Metropolitan in 1954, having fought with the producer, designer
and every member of the cast, someone remarked to Rudolf Bing
(founder of the Edinburgh Festival but by then the Met's general
manager) that Szell was his own worst enemy. 'Not while I am
alive', Bing trenchantly replied.

Loathed though he was, Szell got away with mayhem by being

an undeniably superb musician. What he did in Cleveland between 1946 and his death in 1970 was to transform the orchestra of a nondescript Ohio city – 'a deadly, dull, dead place,' as Henry Miller called it in *The Air-Conditioned Nightmare* – into an instrument superior to the New York Philharmonic, Boston Symphony and Chicago Symphony Orchestra. It is tantalising to think that he could have done the same in Glasgow, a city with things in common with Cleveland, had he not been considered, certainly by himself but also by the players (who continued at that time to keep their sights firmly fixed on Barbirolli, whom they preferred), simply an interim figure; and indeed, like other vagrant Middle Europeans, he prudently headed for America when war broke out.

Yet Szell, though he simultaneously held a post in The Hague, was no mere stopgap. Nor was he, as cynical people may suspect, the Scottish Orchestra's conductor only in name. Though Scottish concert seasons continued to be much shorter then than now, Szell stuck doggedly to his post throughout the bleak Scottish winter, rarely farming out his job to others (as most musical directors do today) and conducting at St Andrew's Hall even on Christmas Eve and Hogmanay. Perhaps seasonal celebrations, and domesticity in general, mattered less to him than to others. He never bought or rented a flat in Glasgow, and always stayed at Moore's Hotel (now a Strathclyde Council office block) in Elmbank Street, an easy walk from St Andrew's Hall.

Yet this supposedly ascetic Hungarian conductor could easily have been a Hungarian cook – admittedly another career that attracts martinets. His knowledge of cooking was reputedly compendious, his kitchen technique as precise as his stickwork. Among celebrated Hungarian chefs, perhaps only George Lang – owner of the old-world Café des Artistes near Lincoln Center in New York – could surpass him. Lang has written the most authoritative of books on Hungarian food, accessible to all in a fat Penguin edition. Szell, in contrast, guarded his kitchen secrets closely – so much so that when he uncharacteristically disclosed his personal recipe for goulash in one of those coffee-table cookbooks to which various celebrities are invited to contribute, people who knew him were amazed. But Szell, as usual, got the last harsh laugh. 'I left out the main ingredient,' he later explained.

Members of the Scottish Orchestra who survived the Szell years have confirmed the impression of a severe taskmaster for whom nothing was ever quite good enough and who, when things were going well, never produced more than a thin smile. A photograph of him in one of the Scottish programmes of the period showed the same mean mouth, the same pale, cold eyes staring through pale-rimmed glasses, as were to characterise him in old age.

One Scottish musician recalls him as being an expert in the art of personal humiliation, an act he performed in full view of the orchestra. Significantly, between his first Scottish season and his second, the orchestra's leader, Thomas Carter, resigned and was replaced by the Greenock-born Henri Temianka, a Polish Jew who evidently got on better with Szell. He appeared as soloist in the Beethoven and Mendelssohn concertos and gave the Scottish premiere of Victor Babin's *Conzertstück* before departing, at the same time as Szell, for America (where he recently died at the age of 85, having been leader of the Paganini Quartet and holder of various Californian teaching posts). Yet according to Hans Gál, a senior Edinburgh University lecturer who had been one of Szell's fellow students in Vienna, and whose friendship with him survived two world wars, Szell was the most completely gifted musician he ever met, whatever personality problems he revealed in front of an orchestra.

Gifted he certainly was. Though there are few left who can speak with authority about his Scottish years, Szell's visit to the Edinburgh Festival in 1967 with the Cleveland Orchestra at the peak of its achievement confirmed everything that has ever been said of his musicianship. The programmes, containing Mozart's Fortieth Symphony, Beethoven's *Eroica*, Sibelius's Second Symphony, Stravinsky's *Firebird* and *Pulcinella* suites and Walton's *Hindemith Variations*, were little different from those he had conducted with the Scottish Orchestra thirty years earlier. Not a note of modern American music was included in tribute to the land where Szell had won his highest fame. 'I do not believe,' he once declared, 'in the mass grave of an all-contemporary concert', though he was by no means opposed to infiltrating twentieth-century works of a conservative nature into classical programmes.

But the perfection of his musicianship, which he had been bestowing on his American players for twenty-one years, was never in doubt. At no time did he ever seem just another showman who manipulated the orchestra for his personal glory. Hovering, as one observer put it, like a motionless eagle over his players – just as he used to do in his Scottish Orchestra days – he was the obverse of the Bernstein school of conducting. He did not 'wow' the music of *The Firebird*, did not streamline it or glamorise it out of recognition, but ensured that every phrase, texture and rhythm glowed with life. Icy he may have been as a man, but the sounds he produced were invariably warm and unanimous in their clean-limbed yet singing tone. Pizzicato notes had a fullness and round-ness that denoted a conductor of the old school; it is a sound that the orchestra has begun to re-achieve today under its latest musical director, the Austrian Walter Weller.

A composer like Brahms, in Szell's hands, never lost his sense of struggle, of physical stress, of harmonic and rhythmic 'wrench,' of a journey undertaken. That is not how Brahms generally sounds in today's glossily predictable performances. Under Szell, Des-mond Shawe-Taylor once declared in the *Sunday Times*, Strauss's *Don Juan* 'leapt into the full lust and bloom of life' at the Usher Hall, Edinburgh, and retained its golden glory to the end. 'I was not', he added, 'the only listener who was irresistibly reminded of Toscanini.' No doubt Szell's Glasgow performance of *Till Eulenspiegel* in 1938, however more makeshift the orchestra, pul-sated with the same sort of ardour.

Paying tribute to Szell's early activities in Scotland, however, is not without an element of risk, as the Edinburgh Festival auth-orities discovered to their embarrassment in 1967. Szell's presence, it was proudly announced, carried a special significance that year, because he was one of the by then steadily shrinking handful of great musicians who had appeared at the very first Edinburgh Festival twenty-one years before. And sure enough, a glance at the vintage 1947 brochure would confirm that, as well as Bruno Walter's celebrated reunion with the Vienna Philharmonic, Glyndebourne Festival Opera had made its Edinburgh debut per-forming Verdi's *Macbeth* and Mozart's *Nozze di Figaro* with the Scottish Orchestra in the pit of the King's Theatre and with its one-time conductor, George Szell, in charge of both works.

At a press conference in Edinburgh, Peter Diamand, the Festi-val's director in 1967, drew attention to Szell's historic link with that epoch-making event; but in my report in *The Scotsman* the following morning I proved him wrong by revealing that in fact Szell had never appeared in 1947. As Spike Hughes explained in his published history of Glyndebourne, Szell during his rehearsals 'came to disagree strongly with the management over something or other and left'. Further details were not disclosed, and for the full story one needs to turn to Rudolf Bing's memoirs, *5000 Nights at the Opera*, which describe how Szell had been welcomed to Glyndebourne for rehearsals before the company moved north to Edinburgh for the performances at the King's Theatre.

To quote Bing: 'My wife and I tried our best to make Szell comfortable and happy, but the task proved beyond our resources; he was a nasty man, God rest his soul. I remember that on his second or third day we took him for a drive up the Downs in our lovely little Hillman, a car of which I was inordinately fond; and as we returned to the car from a walk to some scenic spot, I said, "Tell me – what would a car like this cost in America?" Szell replied with cruel scorn, "A car like this doesn't *exist* in America."'

The crunch, however, was still to come. With the Second World War only recently over, Glyndebourne had had difficulty finding a singer for the role of Susanna in *Figaro*, and was forced to settle for an American novice who arrived seriously unprepared. Szell, reported Bing, 'made a terrible scene, announced that he could not possibly work with an artist who didn't know her role, and to our amazement abandoned both productions. I always felt he had believed he was going to work with a London orchestra of the quality we had engaged for Glyndebourne before the war, and having heard some negative comments about the Scottish Orchestra that would be in the pit in Edinburgh he decided to seize on the soprano's failings as his excuse to quit.'

In the event, the nine performances of *Figaro* were conducted by Walter Susskind, who had become the Scottish Orchestra's conductor the previous year and had settled in Glasgow; and the nine of *Macbeth* by Berthold Goldschmidt, who was later to aid Deryck Cooke in preparing a performing edition of Mahler's Tenth Symphony. The total of eighteen Mozart and Verdi performances, at a time when opera had a higher profile in the Edinburgh Festival than it has now, won the Scottish Orchestra deserved acclaim, not least for its stamina. Within the same three weeks, the players also had to give an Usher Hall concert under Susskind, including performances of Dvořák's Eighth Symphony (a Susskind speciality), the four sea interludes from Britten's *Peter Grimes* and Ravel's G major Piano Concerto with Michelangeli as soloist. This meant that the orchestra was occupied for nineteen of the Festival's twenty-one nights.

Never since then have the players been so lavishly deployed in

Edinburgh, but their labours in the pit that year eventually had one important outcome: when Alexander Gibson set out to found Scottish Opera in the early nineteen-sixties, the willingness of the Scottish National Orchestra, as it had by then become, to return to the pit was a vital factor in his planning.

Yet if Szell was unwilling to work with his old orchestra in 1947, it was not – so far as one can tell – that he had been dissatisfied with it between 1936 and 1939. True, he once muttered something exceedingly rude in German which a member of the orchestra happened to understand and passed on to the other players. On the other hand, he was blessed by the horn section for bringing the modern horn to Scotland (after a series of fluff-ridden performances he insisted that a set of Lehmann compensating horns be sent from Czechoslovakia for the orchestra's use).

Szell's Scottish programmes, by his subsequent standards, were quite adventurous, and the distinguished international soloists to whom he had access ensured that Scottish audiences were given plenty to please them. True, his first half-season, between November 1936 and January 1937, possessed a somewhat improvised air, but that was because Barbirolli had originally been engaged as conductor and had backed out. The news of how Szell 'rescued' the Scottish Orchestra makes piquant reading today, but that was how – through force of circumstances – it actually was. Joseph Barnes's programme brochure of the period disclosed the circumstances as follows:-

'As announced at the close of last season, Mr John Barbirolli was appointed conductor of the orchestra for the season 1936–37 but, on his being offered the much coveted post of conductor of the New York Philharmonic in succession to Mr Arturo Toscanini . . . the committee readily agreed to release him from his engagement to the extent necessary to permit his accepting the offer. He will therefore officiate as conductor of the Scottish Orchestra only from 18 January 1937 to the end of the season. He also received a proposal from the Minneapolis Symphony Orchestra but preferred to decline this rather than request a further reduction in the period of his engagement as conductor of the Scottish Orchestra. During the preceding part of the season Mr George Szell will officiate as conductor. Mr Szell has already appeared as an orchestral conductor in London and Manchester with extraordinary success and comes with the very highest recommendation.'

Barnes's wording of his willingness to release Barbirolli from his Scottish responsibilities is nicely put. In fact Barbirolli gave Glasgow no choice. As for Szell, even before his two complete seasons as conductor, he was very definitely 'officiating' (a not inappropriate word) in Scotland. His first programme, at St Andrew's Hall on 17 November 1936, included a Mozart rarity with himself as solo pianist. This was the alternative rondo from the A major Piano Concerto, K414, which the Mozart specialist, Alfred Einstein, had pieced together two years previously out of fragments of manuscript that had turned up at a London auction.

Completed by Haydn's Symphony No 88 and Beethoven's *Eroica*, two Szell specialities that were to remain at the heart of his repertoire to the day he died, the concert must have given the conductor's Scottish listeners a clear taste of what they were in for. Szell's was always a crisp, keen-edged, strictly classical approach to Haydn, Mozart and Beethoven, which (even although he favoured a full string band) had more in common with today's 'authentic' school of conducting, as personified by Roger Norrington and John Eliot Gardiner, than with the luscious euphony of a Herbert von Karajan. On being told that his Mozart sounded too severe, Szell acidly replied: 'I cannot pour chocolate sauce over asparagus.'

His second concert, on 24 November 1936, had Scotland's most celebrated soloist, Frederick Lamond, as pianist in Beethoven's *Emperor* Concerto (Szell's last Scottish appearance, with the Cleveland Orchestra in August 1967, was destined to contain the same concerto, this time with Clifford Curzon as soloist). The rest of what looks today like a somewhat straggly programme included Mozart's *Figaro* overture and Beethoven's Fifth Symphony, with Lamond contributing solo piano pieces by Chopin and Liszt and forcing Szell to step down from the podium while he conducted his own *Overture from the Scottish Highlands*.

The rest of his programmes, before Barbirolli's return for the second half of the season, set the tone of the Szell repertoire for the next few years. Though twentieth-century works were to appear once he had established full control of the orchestra, the emphasis for the moment was more cautious, without being unimaginative. As early as December 1936 Szell paid tribute to his old friend Hans Gál – though Gál had not yet escaped from his native Austria to settle in Edinburgh – by giving the Scottish premiere of his *Ballet Suite* for small orchestra as centrepiece of a programme that ranged idiosyncratically from Beethoven's *Pastoral* symphony to Stravinsky's *Pastorale*, Bartók's *Three Hungarian Folksongs* and Auber's *Fra Diavolo* overture, in that order.

Ignaz Friedman and Benno Moiseiwitsch, Leschetitzky's two most sensational pupils, were the soloists in Chopin's E minor Piano Concerto and Rakhmaninov's C minor Piano Concerto – though Szell must have snarled at Friedman's famously free approach to the text of everything he played. Bronislav Huberman, who had performed Brahms's Violin Concerto to the composer's satisfaction in Vienna in 1896, chose the Beethoven Violin Concerto for his Scottish appearance with Szell, and Ria Ginster, hailed as 'a new Patti', sang the soprano solo in Mahler's Fourth Symphony, a work whose sunny sweetness may have seemed at odds with Szell's forbidding personality, but which, throughout his career, he conducted with delight.

Brahms's First Symphony, Schumann's Second, Tchaikovsky's Fifth and Dvořák's Eighth made up the rest of the repertoire, along with Reger's *Mozart Variations* (Szell had been a pupil of surly Reger), a Wagner programme, and a Handel oboe concerto featuring Barbirolli's future wife, Evelyn Rothwell, as soloist, with Szell directing the performance from the keyboard – a harpsichord or piano, one wonders?

In addition there was a topical novelty in the form of the prelude to Richard Strauss's *Die Schweigsame Frau*, which Szell conducted in Glasgow just two years after his old rival,' Karl Böhm, had unveiled the opera in Dresden. Though Böhm was already a Nazi sympathiser, and Strauss (in Hitler's opinion) the greatest German composer since Wagner, the Dresden performance was boycotted by both Hitler and Goebbels, whose seats in the theatre remained unoccupied because the librettist, Stefan Zweig, was a Jew.

Szell, who adored Strauss's music, did not let the Nazi contempt for Zweig stand in the way of his giving *Die Schweigsame Frau* its Czech premiere in Prague in 1936, and by a curious coincidence the first Austrian performance of the opera was given by one of the Scottish Orchestra's future conductors, Karl Rankl, who had not yet fled from the Anschluss. The work itself was generally hailed as a highly successful adaptation of Ben Jonson's *Epicoene*. Strauss, to his credit, championed his Jewish librettist; and though cynics may say he ran no great risk in doing so, at least he demonstrated that he was no Nazi toady.

Since in Germany the work was subsequently banned (or, as Strauss tactlessly put it, 'clapped into concentration camp') until the end of the war, Szell's conducting of the delicious overture in Scotland may have been politically motivated. Or else, just as probably, it was simply a statement of affection for his old colleague and mentor, who had encouraged him to become a conductor and upon whose meticulous, undemonstrative stick technique he had modelled his own conducting style.

Szell was a consummate Straussian. Recalling, in the nineteen-sixties, that it was an enthusiasm he had shared long ago in Vienna with his fellow-student, Hans Gál, he delighted his old pal by sending him his brand-new recording of the *Sinfonia Domestica* (an underrated work even today) all the way from Cleveland to Edinburgh. Gál, by then in his seventies and living in retirement, phoned me to tell me about it but said he had a problem. He could not play the disc because he did not possess anything as new-fangled as a stereo system. Would I be prepared to put at his disposal the record player that I, as music critic of *The Scotsman*, could be relied upon to own? I invited him home and in due course the slightly-built, stooping figure arrived at my door, listened intently to the performance, and afterwards reminisced affectionately about the man whose brief period in Scotland had preceded his own much longer one. What, I asked him, was Szell really like? Gál's tiny eyes twinkled behind his spectacles as he remarked that Szell had the sharpest mind and sharpest ears of any musician he had ever met. An infant prodigy who had made his debut at the age of eleven playing his own piano music, he could also, said Gál, have been a great pianist and a great composer. At the age of sixteen he had written a set of variations that went round all the German orchestras. By eighteen he was Strauss's protégé in Berlin, and by nineteen had produced his last work, because by then he knew his métier was to be conducting.

Yet the fairy who bestowed all these musical blessings upon him, said Gál, omitted one vital attribute. He was the 'only man without any human feelings or instincts' Gál had ever encountered. Evidently he did not allow this to stand in the way of their friendship. Though their careers were to go vastly different ways, they remained in each other's thoughts, even if their memories of each other were rooted perhaps in the one-upmanship games they had played together as students. These involved the sight-reading of orchestral scores in competition with each other at the piano, or else showing each other a page, a line, or even just a bar or a chord from some abstruse piece of music and challenging each other to identify it.

Neville Cardus, penning the conductor's obituary in *The Guardian* in 1970, said Szell had once at a party played the same game in his presence. Someone, hoping to catch Szell out, showed him a page of a symphony by, of all people, Charles Villiers Stanford. Naturally the great Straussian failed to recognise it, but his caustic voice could be heard remarking disparagingly that it looked to him like the work of some English composer of the eighteen-nineties.

Szell's own *Variations on an Original Theme*, the work that toured Germany in the nineteen-twenties, turned up in Scotland during his first complete season (1937–38), sharing a programme with Tchaikovsky's Fifth Symphony. The Tchaikovsky was repeated in the annual Plebiscite Concert, an excellent Scottish Orchestra tradition long ago abandoned, whereby concert-goers cast votes for those works which, heard earlier in the season, they would like to hear again in the final concert.

To some extent the system was subject to abuse on both sides of the house. Among the audience, champions of, say, Stravinsky could swing the vote in their hero's favour by filling in discarded forms on his behalf. Hugh Marshall, as the Glasgow Choral Union's young accompanist, recalls doing this in order to get a re-run of Skryabin's *Poem of Ecstasy*; but the management, for its part, could always retaliate by falsifying the ballot and programming the works which, perhaps, it had intended the orchestra to play all along.

In one of the last such concerts ever held – we are talking now of the nineteen-sixties and my period of personal experience of the orchestra – the public voted (or so I was informed by a mole in the orchestra's offices) for Bruckner's Third Symphony, which Jascha Horenstein had conducted to acclaim in one of his concerts as guest conductor. But as Horenstein was not available to conduct a repeat, and as the work was not in the repertoire of Alexander Gibson, who was in charge of the programme, Sibelius's Second Symphony was substituted.

Even if Szell's *Variations on an Original Theme* failed to win a repeat performance, it received 178 nominations, whereas (among the other works Szell had conducted that season) Debussy's *Three Nocturnes* scored only seventy-one, Mahler's *Das Lied von der Erde* (with Mary Jarred and Walter Widdop as soloists) a mere forty-

four, Shostakovich's First Symphony seventeen and Janáček's
Sinfonietta just one single vote. Tchaikovsky's tally was 663.

Would things today be so very different? Mahler and Janáček
would obviously fare better, because they are composers whom
modern audiences identify with. But in the nineteen-thirties in
Scotland they were still almost unknown territory, and Szell's
programmes must have seemed less conventional then than they
would have done later in his career.

Indeed, amid the Brahms and Beethoven performances he conducted during his two and a half years in Scotland, there was an
imposing list of Scottish premieres, even if such composers as
Schoenberg, Berg and Webern were conspicuous absentees. The
first Scottish performance of Shostakovich's First Symphony in
November 1937 formed part of a programme as adventurous as
any the orchestra had ever given – Stravinsky's *Pulcinella* and a
selection of Richard Strauss songs, with Dennis Noble as soloist,
formed the rest of the evening.

Four days earlier Szell had conducted Curt Mengelberg's Violin
Concerto (the composer, a nephew of the Dutch conductor, Wil-
lem Mengelberg, had organised a pioneering Concertgebouw
Mahler Festival in 1920, in which all Mahler's symphonies were
performed in nine concerts) along with Korngold's *Much Ado
About Nothing* suite and Sibelius's Fifth Symphony. Then, just
before Christmas, Paul Hindemith arrived to perform his own
Viola Concerto and the viola part in Berlioz's *Harold in Italy*.

Walton's First Symphony followed in January 1938. The popular belief that this abrasive product of the nineteen-thirties did
not receive its first Scottish performance until the Susskind era
probably stemmed from the fact that so many people noisily
walked out of Susskind's performance at the Usher Hall. Nobody,
one fancies, would have dared to walk out on Szell, who was a
long-term champion of Walton's music and later commissioned
the *Partita for Orchestra* for Cleveland. But his English repertoire
did not stop there. Whatever he felt about Stanford, he conducted
works by Bantock, Bax, Bliss, Delius, Elgar, Moeran and
Vaughan Williams in Scotland, though the young Britten seemed
not to have caught his attention and Tippett's orchestral music
still lay mostly in the future.

Nor was Scottish music ignored. The inclusion of works by
Erik Chisholm, Cedric Thorpe Davie, Francis George Scott and
Paul Kilburn – the orchestra's longest serving member, who

played viola and celesta, and whose death in the nineteen-fifties would be commemorated by Karl Rankl with a performance of Elgar's *Nimrod* – showed at least a willingness to dip a toe in Scottish waters. And the sequence of strathspeys and reels that Szell conducted on 2 January 1939 proved that the stern Hungarian could unbend when Scottish tradition inspired him.

In memory of Sir Landon Ronald – whose association with the orchestra had lasted, with varying degrees of intensity, from 1919 until 1933 – Szell himself conducted *Nimrod*. The two were old acquaintances, Szell having once appeared as solo pianist with Ronald as conductor. Artur Schnabel, who had engineered Szell's first London appearance, reunited with him in Scotland to perform Mozart's last piano concerto, the B flat major, K 595, along with Beethoven's G major in a single programme. Incredibly, the Mozart was receiving its Scottish premiere. With Szell at the helm, the orchestra's drawing power was reflected also in the appearance of Adolf Busch, Astra Desmond, Rudolf Firkušný, Egon Petri and Artur Rubinstein as soloists.

Szell's last two programmes as conductor of the Scottish Orchestra took place in February 1939. In one of them he conducted Elgar's Second Symphony, in the other the *Enigma Variations* (which he had also conducted on Hogmanay the previous year). Seven months later, Britain and Germany were at war and Szell was in New York. There, during the nineteen-forties, his conducting of Wagner and Richard Strauss won the highest praise.

To have persuaded him to stay longer in Scotland would have meant harder bargaining than Glasgow was capable of. Szell not only looked every inch a businessman – especially later in life when he had the air of a tall, broad-shouldered, unfoolable American bank manager – he was the son of a businessman and he behaved like a businessman. John Culshaw has related how he once outwitted Maurice Rosengarten, Decca's man in Switzerland, who was 'tiny, reserved and as sharp as a cut-throat razor'. But Szell, arriving to negotiate a new contract, proved sharper still. Wearing, for one of the few times in his life a broad grin, he paid tribute, said Culshaw, to Rosengarten's musical sensitivity and confessed himself to be no more than a simple businessman whose only interest was money. 'I shall therefore', he said, 'put forward proposals which, needless to say, are not subject to alteration.' Szell, needless to say, got what he wanted.

On his last visit to Scotland, in 1967, Szell strode into an

Edinburgh Festival press conference in much the same way. Imposing, confident, commanding, he had all the affability of someone who had just negotiated a successful deal – as, with Peter Diamand, the Festival director, he no doubt had. His answers to questions were open and friendly. He did not even squash the critic – the writer of this book – who asked him why he invariably cut a section out of the finale of Bartók's Concerto for Orchestra. The answer, delivered in a spirit of total bonhomie, was that he considered it musically unnecessary. It was obviously all an act, but it was brilliantly executed and the members of the orchestra who were in attendance supported him to the hilt. But one member of the Scottish Orchestra who survived to hear him conduct the Cleveland in Edinburgh had different feelings about him. He was nothing less than 'a holy terror'.

Certainly when Szell died three years later – by a curious coincidence on the same day as Sir John Barbirolli, his old rival in Scotland in the nineteen-thirties – even the Clevelanders said they never wanted another Szell. The days of the conductor as autocrat were over. Or were they? Had members of the Scottish Orchestra – who in the nineteen-fifties were to get the 'difficult' Karl Rankl – said the same about Szell in 1939? In the end, the Cleveland Orchestra got Lorin Maazel as Szell's successor, a conductor cast in a similar mould. The Scottish Orchestra, to start with, got the Australian, Aylmer Buesst, who had already appeared twice daily during the orchestra's performances at Glasgow's famous Empire Exhibition at Bellahouston Park in October 1937 (Szell evidently not being free) and who now had the dispiriting task of compiling a reduced season for a depleted orchestra during the first year of the war.

Of all the periods in the orchestra's history, Szell's and Barbirolli's are the ones I most regret not experiencing at first hand. Whatever the players thought of Szell as a man, he was one of the last representatives of a golden age of conductors – not a popular star but a star performer nevertheless.

5

The War Years

In Germany, during the Second World War, music remained a national pride and joy in a way unimaginable in Britain. The cost, in human and political terms, of that seemingly innocuous trait, has been written about often enough, though a reading of Fred K. Prieberg's Furtwängler biography, *Trial of Strength*, places it in better perspective than the average unresearched diatribe against Nazi music and musicians. There was a world of difference between a conductor such as Furtwängler, who remained in Germany because he was a German, who never considered doing otherwise and who (rightly or wrongly) believed his presence there might be a force for good, and opportunists like Herbert von Karajan and Karl Böhm for whom a career came first.

Yet the fact that, during the war, a Karajan (aged thirty-one in 1939) or a Böhm (aged forty-five) could think in terms of an ambitious musical career at all shows the difference in priorities between Germany and Britain at that time. The archives of the Deutsche Grammophon record company brim with recordings made between 1939 and 1945, and not at all makeshift do they tend to sound for their time (as a schoolboy during the war I was the happy owner of some 78 rpm shellac discs of Böhm conducting what the label described as the Saxon State Orchestra).

Whereas the Royal Opera House, Covent Garden, was transformed into a Palais-de-Danse by Mecca Cafés in 1940 – and nearly remained so in 1945, so determined was Mecca to cling to the property – the Deutsche Oper, Berlin, suffered no such downgrading. It stayed open through the worst air-raids and privations until it was destroyed by bombs in 1944. Even with Goebbels as its guiding spirit, it managed to provide musical nourishment for the people. A Covent Garden presided over by Churchill during the

blitz would have been unthinkable. Yet Bayreuth, with Hitler to
support it, kept going until 1944, while here in Britain the lunchtime concerts organised by Myra Hess at the National Gallery in
London have gone down in history simply because there was so
little else of importance to do so.

Certainly, in Scotland, Aylmer Buesst's period with the Scottish
Orchestra provided little to remember and Warwick Braithwaite's
not a great deal more. They were the conductors whose
unrewarding task it was to steer a diminished and dispirited
orchestra through a diminished and dispirited season of often
hackneyed programmes while people's minds were on other
things and many of the most gifted young orchestral players
were on active service. Yet through records and radio, many
people – myself as a schoolboy included – managed to learn
about music, without the help of a National Music Day or the
quantity of audience-seeking projects nowadays devised by our
musical organisations.

Buesst lasted only a single season with the Scottish Orchestra
before the New Zealand-born Braithwaite took over for the
remainder of the war. Both men had built their reputations in the
opera house rather than the concert hall, and though the Australian
Buesst had been (like Sir Adrian Boult) a pupil of Nikisch in
Leipzig, and had played a vital role in establishing the British
National Opera Company between the wars, he seems to have
brought no special insights or ambitions to his work with the
Scottish Orchestra.

As successor to Barbirolli and Szell, he inevitably represented a
downhill slide. Few books on conductors pay tribute to him,
and his name figures only in the most comprehensive of musical
dictionaries. The fifth (1954) edition of *Grove* devoted twenty-
seven lines to him, but ventured no opinion on his qualities. The
New Grove (1980), finding nothing fresh to say about him, was
content to repeat the earlier entry almost word for word, leaving
it to the *Concise Oxford Dictionary of Opera* to claim that he was
'particularly admired' for his Wagner interpretations and for his
'excellent' analysis of the *Ring*. These achievements, however,
were (or should have been) scarcely relevant to his work with the
Scottish Orchestra, no matter how valuable they may have been
to the by then defunct Beecham Opera Company and British
National Opera Company, both of which had specialised in
Wagner.

Though Buesst was surely aware of the powerful anti–German feeling aroused in London by Beecham's espousal of Wagner in 1914 (Wagner and Strauss were banned in Scotland at that time) he risked inserting – and evidently got away with it – the odd Wagner titbit into his Scottish programmes. Perhaps nobody told him it might seem tactless, or perhaps he thought that Glasgow was sufficiently far from London for it not to matter. At any rate, on 26 November 1939, making what was only his second appearance as the orchestra's official conductor, Buesst ended a 'Special Sunday Concert' at the Paramount Picture House, Renfield Street, with the *Flying Dutchman* overture. He programmed the prelude to *Parsifal* on Christmas Eve, excerpts from *Tristan* on 6 January 1940 and, even less tactfully, the *Ride of the Valkyries* on 13 January and the closing scene from *Götterdämmerung* (along with the *Meistersinger* overture) on 17 February. An audience in Germany at that time could hardly have hoped for more.

No doubt, had he been based in more war-conscious London, Buesst would not have been allowed to plan such provocative programmes, and it is true that he counterbalanced his Wagnerian leanings with performances of the French and British national anthems in a Hogmanay concert in aid of the Glasgow War Relief Fund, as well as with Ravel's *Bolero* on Christmas Eve. Nor, in the course of a season as predominantly Teutonic as any in the orchestra's history, could be have been accused of entirely neglecting new Scottish music.

The premiere of the Glasgow-born Erik Chisholm's Piano Concerto – a work deriving 'directly from Highland bagpipe music', incorporating (in the words of the programme note) a 'mood of Celtic vagueness' and ending with a lively reel – was clearly meant to rally its audience in the first grim winter of the war. Indeed, just in case anyone failed to get the message, the printed programme emphatically spelt it out. Chisholm's concerto, it proclaimed, embraced 'a nation whose history is a tale of war and sorrow but whose spirit no adverse fate can break'.

Only Glasgow, however, had the opportunity to be stirred, because only Glasgow heard the work performed. At a time when players habitually travelled by train, the threat of air raids caused the Edinburgh season to be cancelled not only in 1939 but for the following three years. And even in Glasgow, Buesst's one and only season was a more skeletal event than audiences had grown to expect from Szell and Barbirolli. 'It must have been universally regretted', declared the annual syllabus, 'that War Conditions compelled abandonment of the regular scheme of concerts proffered for the season 1939–40. In submitting a Modified Scheme, the Committee desire to convey the grateful thanks of the Union to all those who, by becoming Guarantors, have contributed to the maintenance of the Scheme hitherto.'

Nothing that happened in Scotland during the war could compare with Barbirolli's heroic return from New York in 1943 to become conductor of the Hallé Orchestra. If he had been wooed instead by Glasgow, scene of some of his most successful pre-war concerts, who knows how the Scottish Orchestra might have developed after the Second World War? But the Hallé's invitation to him, as Michael Kennedy has remarked in his history of the Manchester orchestra, came at just the right moment. Barbirolli, for a variety of reasons, had been longing to get back to Britain. His period with the New York Philharmonic had ended in disarray; he had refused a rival offer from the Los Angeles Philharmonic, even though he knew that Schoenberg and Stravinsky would be among his neighbours; and the telegram from the Hallé – though it might more easily have come from the Scottish Orchestra, if someone had thought of sending it – was just what he had been waiting for.

Though he discovered on arrival that the terms he had been offered were 'almost fraudulent', he soon recognised that his decision had been the right one. Among the players he induced to join the revamped Hallé at that time was Tommy Cheetham, a percussionist from the Scottish Orchestra who was later to be best man at his wedding to the Scottish Orchestra's oboist, Evelyn Rothwell; and within weeks of his opening concert in Manchester, he brought his new orchestra to Glasgow and Edinburgh for a series of concerts in each city, inspiring the music critic of *The Scotsman* – at that time Stewart Deas – to say that the performance of Elgar's *Enigma Variations* had 'touched perfection, something the playing of the Scottish Orchestra rarely did'.

Barbirolli brought the Hallé to Scotland often after that, usually for a week or two at a time and sometimes making a detour to Forfar, a town he had visited during his Scottish Orchestra tours, which had taken him as far north as Elgin. Later, when Rudolf Bing compiled a list of conductors and orchestras to appear alongside the Vienna Philharmonic at the first Edinburgh Festival,

Barbirolli and the Hallé were among them, and according to at least one Scottish critic they made a better showing (as at that time they were bound to) than the Scottish Orchestra.

A more recent comparison between the two orchestras would not have worked out in the Hallé's favour. But back in the nineteen-forties my own instinctive boyhood allegiance was certainly to Barbirolli and his annual Edinburgh visit. I even subscribed to the Hallé Magazine, in the absence then of a similar Scottish publication, and felt proud to see my name printed in it as winner of a competition to compile a season of programmes suitable for the Hallé to play.

Braithwaite's concerts with the Scottish Orchestra, mainly through my own ignorance, failed to attract me, whereas Barbirolli, with his huge scything beat and habit of conducting the first half of the National Anthem facing the audience, then twirling round at the halfway point, seemed the stuff of romance. Besides, the sort of music he brought to Scotland – the grand span of his Elgar, Sibelius's Second Symphony, Berlioz's *Symphonie Fantastique* (his recording of which took seven 78 rpm shellac discs to everyone else's six) and the drollery of Ibert's *Divertissement* – carried immense appeal.

Glancing in 1992 through Warwick Braithwaite's concert programmes, I realised that I had done him an injustice. They were not so bad. Indeed, though the quality of playing he drew from the Scottish Orchestra clearly left much to be desired, the concert programmes were notably good. He, too, conducted Berlioz and Sibelius at a time when, in Britain, it was still uncommon to do so. He championed British (if not specifically Scottish) music in a small but consistent way. One of his first Glasgow concerts in 1940 included the Fair Scene from Delius's *A Village Romeo and Juliet* – a rarity now, just as it was then. In others he conducted Elgar's two symphonies and *Falstaff*, Holst's *Beni Mora*, Vaughan Williams's Fifth Symphony, Walton's First Symphony and *Henry V* suite, Britten's *Sinfonia da Requiem* (this in 1943, two years before *Peter Grimes* restored Britten's war-tarnished name to British favour), Bliss's *Checkmate*, Moeran's Symphony in G minor and Delius's *Summer Night on the River*.

Such a tally of pieces, in a context of Falla's *Nights in the Gardens of Spain* (with a young Clifford Curzon as soloist), the Adagietto from Mahler's Fifth Symphony, Bloch's Violin Concerto, Khachaturian's Piano Concerto and Skryabin's *Poem of Ecstasy*, show

Braithwaite to have been a more progressive programme planner than I gave him credit for. Indeed, during the war, the Scottish Orchestra served its audience, increased by many servicemen and women, as rich a diet of music as it has done in many years since.

True, like Aylmer Buesst, Braithwaite displayed an untimely predilection for Wagner, and conducted the closing scene from *Götterdämmerung* (with the great Eva Turner as soloist) in the spring of 1940, but that was perhaps meant to have some symbolic reference to the outcome of the war at a time when spirits were low. He also, perhaps in the same frame of mind, conducted Strauss's *Death and Transfiguration* in the winter of 1943. But he counterbalanced these raids on the Nazi repertoire with an all-Russian programme, including Glazunov's *Stenka Razin*, Rimsky-Korsakov's *Ivan the Terrible* overture, Lyadov's *Eight Russian Folksongs* and the finale of *Petrushka*, in November 1941 when the Wehrmacht was advancing eastwards; and he added Christian Darnton's *Stalingrad* overture to the repertoire in 1944.

Darnton, more famed as a musical historian than a composer, cropped up more than once in Braithwaite's day, though by the time he wrote his *Jet Pilot* cantata in 1950 he had been dropped from the Scottish repertoire. Braithwaite himself, like several other of the orchestra's conductors, also had aspirations to be a composer, and in 1943 contrived to programme his own tone poem entitled *Ave*.

My early failure to recognise his qualities – I remember him later bringing a lively, gaudy Sadler's Wells production of Saint-Saëns's *Samson and Delilah* to Scotland, with Roderick Brydon, still a novice, clashing the cymbals – could be explained by the fact that so many of his concerts were confined to Glasgow and I was never there to hear him. That he achieved as much as he did was remarkable, considering that each season was launched with a gloomy statement by Joseph Barnes, filled with ponderous demands for money.

Thus, in 1940, he wrote, 'The Committee are deeply grateful to those who, by their Guarantees, have made the continuation of the concerts possible. They feel, however, that the financial burden should be shared by a still larger number and urgently invite all who appreciate the value of the Scheme to assist in the effort to enlist additional Guarantors.'

A year later there was an anxious appeal for 'the fullest measure of support' and 'frequent and regular attendance' at the Glasgow concerts, which were managing to maintain their traditional level of fourteen Saturday evening programmes and thirteen Sunday afternoon ones. All the more surprising, therefore, was the statement in 1943 that the committee had decided 'to enter upon the adventure of doubling the length of the concert season'. This, as Barnes put it with characteristic formality, would constitute 'an important epoch in the history of the Union and it is hoped that the general public by subscription for serial tickets will ensure that the committee's enterprise will be crowned with success'. Concert promotion today is a lot slicker.

The twenty-seven Saturday and twenty-six Sunday concerts given in Glasgow that season coincided with the centenary of the Glasgow Choral Union, which was celebrated with performances of *The Creation, The Dream of Gerontius* and an *Elijah* with Joan Hammond and the young Kathleen Ferrier among the soloists. The extended season was made possible 'only by the extreme generosity of Glasgow Corporation in donating £5,000' – an imposing sum at the time.

The development was successful enough to prompt the usually cautious Barnes to schedule the same number of concerts in 1945–46, and to re-engage Braithwaite as conductor – though Sir Thomas Beecham, who pepped up any Scottish Orchestra season he could be tempted to take part in, would be 'retained' as guest conductor for six concerts, a privilege for which single-ticket buyers had to pay extra money.

In fact the writing was on the wall for Braithwaite, who recognised (as Barnes was unwilling to) that the Scottish Orchestra could not go on disbanding its players each spring, and was outspoken enough to say so in public. 'Careless talk costs lives' was a wartime slogan still valid in 1946. Braithwaite's statement cost him his Scottish career. But even though his contract was not renewed, he had placed his finger on a running sore that was to continue to fester until, in 1950, the management finally gave in and admitted that the orchestra would never achieve credibility if it continued to disband its players each year. By 1952 the Edinburgh Festival was well established, and people knew that the Vienna Philharmonic, the Berlin Philharmonic and the Hamburg State Opera had all recovered quickly from the war, in a way that the Scottish Orchestra had not, and were striding into the future.

To give Barnes his due, he must have sensed this in 1946 when the first Edinburgh Festival was being planned under Glyndebourne auspices and the Scottish Orchestra was given its first opportunity to shine – or fall flat on its face – in an international context. No doubt he hoped the Festival would never happen or, if it did, it would never be repeated. Meanwhile he announced that the length of season would continue to be twenty-six weeks. He expressed the committee's 'gratification with the measure of support' and 'confidently' appealed for a 'still more intense and wider patronage during the coming season'. Walter Susskind, an admittedly enlightened choice, was invited to conduct the orchestra into the new age, with Eugene Goossens, Artur Rodzinski and Ian Whyte 'officiating' as guest conductors.

The appointment of Susskind marked a turning-point in the orchestra's history. He was not, like Szell, a disciplinarian. Indeed there was a laxness, some said a laziness, about his conducting that prevented the orchestra, during his six years in Scotland, from ever achieving the sort of technical expertise that was to come later. But this Czech émigré nevertheless possessed qualities that could not be measured in terms of orchestral virtuosity. He did not, in any case, have players at his disposal who in 1946 could have performed that way.

What he did have was a repertoire that stopped at nothing in terms of innovation, and a romantic nature that seemed just what was needed in the years of austerity after the war. In a Susskind performance of Musorgsky's *Pictures at an Exhibition*, the first trumpet was quite liable to crack its opening note; but the spirit of whatever Susskind conducted was indelibly fixed in the memories of people of my generation, who learnt the classics through him, and for whom, indeed, Susskind was school. All we could do was bless him for being in Scotland at that particular time.

6

Walter Susskind

Not everybody thought that the amiable, easy-going
Walter Susskind was the right conductor for the Scottish
Orchestra, and not everybody thought his programme
planning as imaginative as I did. Though stockily built, he was
the possessor of film-star good looks, and the way he used them
aroused suspicion. One of my music teachers said he could never
take seriously a conductor who wobbled his bottom, the way
Susskind did, on the viola triplet in the second bar of Wagner's
Siegfried Idyll.

When he returned in the nineteen-seventies as guest conductor
– he was now musical director of the St Louis Symphony Orchestra, a post he held until shortly before his death in 1980 – his
vanity was by then asserting itself in the form of a toupée and
platform shoes. Yet he remained the most musical of conductors,
who proved that he could bring all his old warmth to Brahms's
First Symphony, as well as to one of those picturesque tone poems
about Prague, composed by himself in the vein of Smetana and
of Suk, who had been one of his teachers.

When he succeeded Braithwaite in 1946, Susskind was only
twenty-eight, the youngest conductor – a fact he clearly savoured
– ever to be in charge of the Scottish Orchestra. In his native
Prague he had been, aptly enough, a pupil of George Szell, whose
assistant he became at the 'German' Opera House there, but whose
sarcasm he did not inherit. At the age of twenty, escaping Hey-
drich's clutches, he settled in Britain, first as a member of the
Czech Piano Trio, then as musical director of the Carl Rosa Opera
before landing his Scottish appointment.

As a teenager, seated each Friday in row 'D' of the organ gallery
in the Usher Hall, I idolised him. I used to wait, in high anticipa-
tion, for his 7.30 sprint on to the platform – in those days the
conductor emerged theatrically from beneath the organ rather than

from a side door – a dapper figure who seemed, I thought, everything a conductor should be. On reaching the rostrum, he would
immediately strike up the National Anthem – at that time the *de
rigueur* start to every concert – with an inimitably waggling beat
which, after the concert, I would try to copy in front of a mirror
at home. 'He had a beautiful beat', one of his old players told me
while I was researching this book, 'and he knew it.'

Once, as I tardily descended the steps from the organ gallery
after one of his concerts, I noted that the rostrum had already been
removed from the platform and was standing on a landing, with
Susskind's baton still stuck between the pages of the score of
whatever it was he had been conducting. I stood transfixed.
Should I filch it? Thoughts of what used to be done to Liszt's
property convinced me that it would be an act of adulation rather
than theft. But I resisted temptation. John Watt, the orchestra's
long-serving attendant, was standing watching.

A good memory being one of a music critic's primary assets, I
can still recall the first concert I heard Susskind conduct. Wagner's
Tannhäuser overture, providing (like the National Anthem) fascinating evidence of how Susskind beat 3/4 time, opened the programme, followed by the Forest Murmurs interlude from *Siegried*;
Gina Bachauer, grandly sounding the opening chords, was soloist
in Rakhmaninov's Second Piano Concerto; the symphony was
Brahms's Second.

By Susskind standards, it was not the most inventive of
evenings. Yet whenever I hear the Rakhmaninov today,
Bachauer's Electra-like face and imposing girth still loom before
my eyes. She seemed to knead the music like dough. The big
melodies, which I was hearing for the first time in a live performance, remained glued to my brain as I walked home. When, not
long afterwards, I encountered the same concerto while watching
a film – not *Brief Encounter*, which memorably used it to underpin
the romance between Celia Johnson and Trevor Howard, but
Immenzee, a German product of the same period – I sat through
it twice, revelling in a sentimental tale about an encounter between
a concert pianist and a conductor on the shores of an Alpine lake.

That the conductor could have been Susskind himself added to
my enjoyment. Had I learnt about orchestral music a decade earlier
via Szell, or a decade later via someone like Boulez, I wonder
whether, and in what ways, I would have become a different sort
of listener. Yet I recall getting little at the time out of Susskind's

Brahms. It was Mario Rossi, an Italian conductor who visited Scotland that same season with the Turin Symphony Orchestra, who did the trick with a performance of the Third Symphony, skilfully planted between Michelangeli playing the *Emperor* Concerto and the *Forza del Destino* overture as encore. My awakening critical faculties told me that Susskind could not compare, yet when he returned in the 1970s for that already-mentioned performance of the First Symphony, he conducted it with such unhesitating impulse and expressiveness that I realise I must originally have done him an injustice. But Brahms needs to be well performed and more probably by then the orchestra was simply a great deal better.

Just how bad it was after the war I was too inexperienced to realise, but at least one critic was under no delusions. Writing in the *Penguin Music Magazine*, a spirited but long defunct quarterly survey of the British musical scene, Maurice Lindsay lamented the orchestra's 'now undeniable decline' towards the state of little artistic consequence and financial instability that Barbirolli had tirelessly hauled it out of. 'In his more inspired moments,' Lindsay grudgingly admitted, 'Mr Susskind has managed to get good second-rate performances out of his players, but never more and usually less.' The fault, he conceded, was not Susskind's, whose considerable abilities were 'largely wasted on the hopeless material at his disposal'.

And why was the material hopeless? Because the management committee, still presided over by the Dickensian figure of Joseph Barnes, remained too timid to recruit a permanent orchestra. In 1947 the Edinburgh Festival had proved that there was now a use for a full-time Scottish Orchestra during the summer, but the challenge had been only half-heartedly met and nobody inside the organisation appeared to notice that the Hallé Orchestra and Liverpool Philharmonic, which appeared in Edinburgh alongside the Scottish Orchestra, were in much better shape.

But somebody noticed. Rudolf Bing noticed, and in 1948 he did not invite the Scottish Orchestra back. To accompany Glyndebourne's performances at the King's Theatre, he hired Sir Thomas Beecham's recently founded Royal Philharmonic Orchestra to play for Vittorio Gui and Rafael Kubelik; and at the Usher Hall he allotted two concerts to Ian Whyte and the BBC Scottish, one of them with Yehudi Menuhin as soloist, the other with Artur Schnabel. It was a slight of a sort the Scottish Orchestra would

not suffer again until 1989, when the (by then) BBC Scottish
Symphony Orchestra was invited to replace the (by then) Scottish
National Orchestra, after a spat between a different Festival direc-
tor and a different orchestral administrator.

Yet the orchestra's deficiencies were at least partly compensated
for by what the *New Grove* has described as Susskind's 'policy of
exploratory programme-building'. The sheer adventurousness of
Susskind's programmes escaped Maurice Lindsay, who grumbled
about 'safe romantic war-horses' and poked fun at Susskind's conducting of Gershwin's *Rhapsody in Blue* from the piano, 'spot-
lighted in a specially darkened hall', as part of a half-American
programme that also included Copland's *El Salón México* and
Barber's *School for Scandal* overture.

During his six years in Scotland, Susskind worked his way
through an enormous repertoire. He would conduct everything
that attracted him, the way you or I would sit down and read a
book. Sometimes the result would seem no more than a skim
through the music, yet it would be enough to convey the flavour
of whatever he had chosen. And sometimes the performances took
fire. I remember going, with misgivings, to hear him conduct
Mahler's First Symphony, a work I had never heard by a composer
upon whom, in Britain, it was then fashionable to pour contempt.
I listened elated, and wondered how Mahler could be, to Vaughan
Williams, no more than a 'tolerable imitation of a composer'.

Had Susskind done nothing else, that would have been enough.
But within a year of coming to Scotland he had conducted the
three concert excerpts from *Wozzeck*, though that was a time
when Berg, like Mahler, was anathema to the British establishment. And he also introduced his own orchestral transcription
of Bartók's *Allegro Barbaro*, Hindemith's *Nobilissima Visione* and
Busoni's Clarinet Concerto (with Thomas Young, the orchestra's
principal clarinet, as soloist).

These, however, were a mere preliminary. In succeeding
seasons, perhaps realising that he was not in Scotland for ever, he
grew more reckless. Carl Nielsen's tonally progressive *Sinfonia
Espansiva*, long before the Danish composer was a household name
in Glasgow or Edinburgh, was treated as if it were a classic symphony like any other. Unannounced works were added to programmes. Audiences were addressed as friends (Susskind loved to
chat to them from the platform) as well as listeners. And when,
in 1948–49, the Edinburgh Concert Society, which promoted the

orchestra's by now traditional Friday concerts at the Usher Hall, quarrelled with the orchestra's management committee, Susskind brought his players to Edinburgh on Wednesdays instead, while various English orchestras – the Hallé, the City of Birmingham and the newly-formed but sadly short-lived Yorkshire Symphony Orchestra under Maurice Miles – filled the Friday gap.

The 'special circumstances of the time', as Joseph Barnes put it in his introduction to the Scottish Orchestra's brochure that season, 'involves the Scheme in greater hazard than perhaps ever before'. But he could promise a 'list of soloists of unprecedented excellence', starting with Claudio Arrau in Brahms's D minor Piano Concerto.

Certainly, of all my boyhood seasons, this was the richest. Susskind, in his most devil-may-care mode, conducted the first Scottish performances of Hindemith's *Mathis der Mahler* symphony, Vaughan Williams's Sixth Symphony, Copland's Third Symphony, Constant Lambert's *Horoscope*, Bloch's *Symphonic Suite*, Kabalevsky's Second Symphony, Richard Strauss's Oboe Concerto with Evelyn Rothwell as soloist and Bartók's Third Piano Concerto with Louis Kentner. Interwoven with these, Ravel's G major Piano Concerto (originally to have been played by the magical but already dying Dinu Lipatti), Tchaikovsky's Second Piano Concerto, Kathleen Ferrier singing Mahler's *Kindertotenlieder*, Ida Haendel playing Elgar's Violin Concerto, Margherita Grandi singing the Sleepwalking Scene from Verdi's *Macbeth* and Susskind's cellist wife, Eleanor Warren, intoning Bloch's *Schelomo*, showed a conductor alive to all the possibilities of programme-compiling at that time.

Audiences dwindled. The Edinburgh Concert Society's more conservative orchestral programming, interwoven with star recitals by Elisabeth Schumann and Edwin Fischer, proved more popular, but anyone with any awareness that there would never again be such a double Edinburgh season must have seized the chance to attend both series. Happily, when things reverted to normal in the autumn of 1949, Susskind sustained his challenging programming, and Barnes, prattling of 'favourable auspices', appeared to acquiesce.

'All differences as to the further development of the Orchestra Scheme have been resolved in principle', he announced, 'and every part of Scotland is co-operating to ensure its success.' A new constitution, he promised, was in preparation, and Edinburgh was again on speaking terms with Glasgow. Moreover, Barbirolli had offered to conduct *The Dream of Gerontius* without fee as 'a mark of his affectionate regard for the scheme with which he was, for some years, so happily associated'.

As proof of his continuing boldness of policy, Susskind launched the season with the Glasgow premiere of Bartók's Concerto for Orchestra, a work Edinburgh had heard from Eduard van Beinum and the Concertgebouw Orchestra the previous year. Other premieres of one sort or another included Mahler's Ninth Symphony, Strauss's *Metamorphosen* (a work still banned at the time in Holland because of its Nazi associations), Respighi's *Concerto Gregoriano*, Barber's First Symphony, Ibert's Flute Concerto and Hans Gál's Piano Concerto. Otto Klemperer, not yet the monumental Beethovenian he was to become in London a decade later, made a guest appearance conducting Mozart's *Jupiter* symphony, Strauss's *Till Eulenspiegel* and two of Debussy's *Three Nocturnes*. Other works featured were Tchaikovsky's *Hamlet* overture, Liszt's *Prometheus* and Vaughan Williams's *Job*.

Meanwhile, faced with increasingly impatient demands from the newspapers for a full-time Scottish Orchestra, the management committee had continued to drag its feet. A polite request for Joseph Barnes's retirement had been ignored, along with a scheme, devised in Edinburgh, to split the orchestra in two, with a body of sixty-eight players based in Glasgow, and a chamber orchestra of thirty-four in Edinburgh. The capital city's desire for an orchestra of its own was nothing new. An ambitiously named Founders' Guild for an Edinburgh Symphony Orchestra had looked promising for a while, but soon was grounded on the bedrock of Edinburgh parsimony and inertia.

Then suddenly, on 8 July 1950, there was action in Glasgow. On that day a full-time Scottish National Orchestra grew out of the part-time Scottish Orchestra. The corporations of Glasgow, Edinburgh, Aberdeen and Dundee supplied a sum of £20,000. A further £15,000 came from elsewhere. An SNO Society was officially registered, membership being open to anyone guaranteeing a minimum of £1,000 per year, or subscribing a minimum of £500.

The terms offered to the players – an entitlement of just four free days per month, a four-week holiday period of which two weeks were to be unpaid, and severe restrictions on freelance work – could scarcely be called inviting. But at least the new orchestra was in business, and seventy-five players accepted the conditions.

In celebration, Susskind compiled a winter season that in no way played for safety. Bartók's Second Violin Concerto, one of the towering masterpieces of twentieth century music, received its belated Scottish premiere with Max Rostal as soloist. So also, after Maurice Lindsay's dismissal of his music as 'a spent force', did Stravinsky's Symphony in Three Movements.

Hindemith's Concerto for Wind Quartet showed Susskind's continuing enthusiasm for a composer nowadays widely neglected (though still, from time to time, championed by one of the orchestra's regular guest conductors, Matthias Bamert). His faith in English music was demonstrated by Vaughan Williams's Double Piano Concerto, and in American music by Copland's *Billy the Kid*.

The Edinburgh Festival, however, was not yet prepared to restore the orchestra to favour. In 1950 (as in 1948 and 1949) it was the BBC Scottish Orchestra that represented Scotland at the Usher Hall. Moreover the fact that Barbirolli and the Hallé were allotted no fewer than four programmes that year seemed a blatant insult to the newly-constituted SNO. Yet the truth was that a new name did not yet mean new standards of performance. Continuity had at last been established, but hard work was still needed to produce an orchestra worthy of its national identity.

Under Susskind, alas, that standard was never reached. The fresh energy that the orchestra's change of status might have been expected to give him did not materialise. Perhaps he was simply content to coast along, exploring whatever music attracted him, but neither aiming nor expecting to make things better. As Maurice Lindsay had written, 'the playing was, of course, erratic and uncertain'. And that was how it remained until Susskind resigned in 1952.

Yet (with Susskind there was always a 'yet') his explorations were worth sharing to the end. In 1951, back in favour with the Edinburgh Festival, he conducted the premiere of Karel Jírák's prize-winning Fifth Symphony at the Usher Hall. In those days, incredible as it may now seem, the Festival awarded an annual composition prize of £150, won on this occasion by William Wordsworth, with Jírák, as runner-up, receiving £75. Wordsworth's Second Symphony was premiered by Sir Adrian Boult and the London Philharmonic. Jîrák, being Czech, was reckoned the right composer for Susskind. Neither work, it has to be said, won a regular place in the repertoire.

To keep the orchestra active during the formerly empty summer months, sixteen concerts were given around Scotland (and another two in London) as part of the 1951 Festival of Britain. Then, in 1952, Susskind bade farewell with a performance of Suk's *Asrael* symphony at the Edinburgh Festival. Czech music loomed increasingly large in Susskind's concerts towards the end, just as Estonian music was to do later in Neeme Järvi's. Not all of it was relevant to a Scottish orchestra, but *Asrael*, a work of Mahlerian scale and intensity, clearly mattered to Susskind and might today be worthy of revival.

From Scotland, Susskind roamed first to Australia, then to Canada, before finally settling in Missouri. From the Toronto Symphony Orchestra he was ousted by the flashier, more dynamic Seiji Ozawa, just as Rafael Kubelik, his fellow Czech, was ousted from the Chicago Symphony Orchestra by the ferocious Fritz Reiner. Was there something too tolerant about these likeable Czech musicians? Whatever his shortcomings, Susskind was a lyricist, whose returns to Scotland were always welcomed.

Nothing summed up his musicality more vividly than when he brought the National Youth Orchestra of Canada, which he had founded in 1958, to the 1966 Edinburgh Festival. The moment he arrived he was told that there was an emergency. Could he take over the Stuttgart Opera's performance of Berg's *Wozzeck* without rehearsal at the King's Theatre that night? The temperamental Carlos Kleiber had just walked out, and Susskind, whose plane must have landed just as Kleiber's took off, was the only conductor in Britain at that moment who had practical experience of the opera and might be willing to conduct it.

The suggestion, in the end, proved unworkable. Had Susskind agreed to conduct *Wozzeck*, an opera of notorious complexity in a brand-new production which he had never seen, someone else would have been needed to conduct the National Youth Orchestra of Canada. Alexander Gibson, being resident in Scotland, was an obvious possibility, but the Festival management could not track him down in time. So *Wozzeck* was cancelled at the last moment, and the waiting audience – ironically including Alexander Gibson, who had no idea that people had been searching for him – was given the option of attending the National Youth Orchestra of Canada at the Usher Hall instead.

7

Viennese Nights

Conductors, in old age, enter their golden years. Conductors, through burn-out, generally deteriorate. Otto Klemperer provided the most famous confirmation of the first adage; André Previn has been cited, with sorrow, as an illustration of the other. As a critic, I have heard these statements made many times about one conductor or another, but have tried to avoid making them myself. There is, in any case, a third statement, equally valid, which says that most conductors stay the same.

After Susskind, whose qualities probably did not change much (he simply worked with increasingly good orchestras), the SNO was ruled by two Viennese conductors whose careers could be said to be in decline. That an orchestra with a new name, a new status and new ambition should have been saddled first with Karl Rankl, then with Hans Swarowsky, seems not merely bad luck but active carelessness.

The fourteenth child of an Austrian peasant, Rankl learnt conducting in the conventional Central European way – by working in minor opera houses before landing a job alongside Klemperer at the Kroll Opera in Berlin. Twice escaping Hitler's clutches. he settled in Britain at the age of forty, around the same time as Hans Gál. Not until after the war, however, did his moment come. Hired to rebuild the Covent Garden opera company from scratch, he did what is now generally agreed to have been a good job in difficult circumstances. Performing his often thankless task with tireless resourcefulness, he recruited British singers wherever possible, and persuaded Elisabeth Schwarzkopf and other international stars to learn their roles in English, the language he demanded of them as a matter of unexpectedly broad-minded policy.

An able Wagnerian, though hardly a Solti, Rankl regarded a new *Ring* cycle as high priority. He was willing to learn Britten's

Peter Grimes and – a less rewarding task – Bliss's new opera, *The Olympians*. He knew his Strauss and, if Covent Garden had desired him to conduct some Krenek, he could have offered the visionary *Karl V*, whose premiere he had given in Prague in 1938, at the time of the composer's escape to America.

Whatever Rankl thought about Strauss's (or Wagner's) politics, he reckoned that the music mattered more than the man. Of politically tainted conductors he was less tolerant, and when Clemens Krauss was invited by Covent Garden to conduct *Tristan and Isolde*, he vigorously objected. His prickly nature, indeed, was easily ruffled. Peter Brook, whose gifts as a producer were just beginning to win recognition, encountered it when he got Salvador Dali to design a *Salome* in which (among other atrocities) John the Baptist's head descended from the flies on a salver. 'I wish it were Rankl's head,' Brook is reported to have exclaimed in exasperation after the conductor had complained about almost every detail of the production. This was the man who, before long in Scotland, would be giving concerto soloists an equally hard time over matters of tempo and phrasing.

Meanwhile, in London, he had more serious problems. During rehearsals, Rankl and Brook communicated only in writing. It was one of the first major operatic battles between a conductor and a producer over who was boss, though who actually won is hard to say. Rankl, by refusing to take a curtain call on the first night, scored points; and Brook, whose contract was not renewed the following year, could be said to have lost in the end. But then, as things turned out, so did Rankl, in spite of Ernest Newman's public lamentation in the *Sunday Times*, which asked 'How much longer will the London opera public tolerate performances and productions which are for the most part an affront to their intelligence? How long, O Lord, how long?'

Little did Britain's most august music critic realise that, had he lived until 1992, the question would be still on his lips. But in the nineteen-forties, the irascible and insecure Rankl's days at Covent Garden were already numbered. When, behind his back, it was decided that it was time for him to go, a posting had to be found for faces (both his and the company's) to be saved. Susskind, by a piece of luck, had just resigned from the SNO. Rankl replaced him. What, at the time, was kept secret was the fact that the Arts Council had placed a pistol to the SNO administrator's head. If he wanted the SNO's grant to continue, he was told, he would have to accept Rankl as conductor. Since he was hardly in a position to argue, Rankl was duly announced as Susskind's successor. Joseph Barnes having at last stepped down, there were no ponderous pronouncements in the annual brochure. All it said, coolly and succinctly, was: 'The orchestra's new conductor, Karl Rankl, will conduct the majority of the concerts.'

Yet to anyone who did not know the truth, Rankl could have seemed a coup. A Viennese pupil of Schoenberg, and later of Anton Webern, he had impressive credentials. He had held the same post as George Szell in Prague. At the very least, if his Covent Garden achievement was anything to go by, he would be a good trainer, which was exactly what the orchestra needed at the time. Moreover, he was one of the first conductors to be invited – by Decca – to make records after the war, and to benefit from that company's much publicised 'full frequency range recordings'; and though that was before a relationship with a record company had become vital to every orchestra's credibility, it must nevertheless have been welcomed by an orchestra which until then had made no discs. But in fact, though nobody knew it at the time, Rankl's recording career was already over.

A more immediate area of doubt was his repertoire. His experience, until then, had been mostly operatic, but that – as the board of directors consoled themselves – could be said of many another German or Austrian conductor who had ultimately blossomed in the concert hall. What mattered, and gave hope for the future, was that the way he conducted his opening programme – a hefty German mixture of Weber, Beethoven and Strauss, with Clifford Curzon as soloist in Brahms's Second Piano Concerto – suggested that he was already imposing a new sonority and a new discipline on the orchestra. Later, alas, it was to become apparent that what the players had acquired was no more than (but at least no less than) a Kapellmeister in the most grumpily Teutonic mould. Whatever he had learnt from Schoenberg and Webern, it was not a progressive musical outlook.

What he could do, however, he did conscientiously. Beethoven's metronome markings were, by and large, meticulously observed at a time when other conductors considered them hopelessly misleading; and in that very opening programme his devotion to them resulted in a performance of the Eighth Symphony that nearly transformed the minuet into a one-in-the-bar scherzo. As a keen timekeeper himself, he demanded punctuality from his players. Arriving three minutes before the start of a rehearsal, he would place his watch on the music stand and say 'Good morning, let me begin.' Anyone who arrived late, for whatever reason, received a fearful dressing down.

The orchestra (as a picture in one of the brochures of the period confirms) was reseated by Rankl in the classic German platform layout, with the first and second violins to left and right of the podium, the cellos immediately in front and a phalanx of basses facing outwards behind the horns. Among British conductors, only Sir Adrian Boult persistently did the same, to sonorous advantage in terms of bass tone and with proper antiphonal differentiation between the upper strings. Rankl, presumably resentfully, later accepted the standard modern positioning, with first and second violins massed together to achieve greater unanimity of sound. Since he treated intonation as low priority at rehearsal, the change was doubtless beneficial.

But there were other, more unsettling, changes. Jean Rennie, the Glasgow violinist whom Susskind had boldly appointed leader of the orchestra, was demoted because Rankl, in the old European manner, disapproved of women players, especially if they held key positions. There was, as some former players recall, 'a lot of hiring and firing at this time'. Thomas Matthews, a more experienced leader than Rennie, with the smooth and somewhat shifty good looks of the film star Dan Duryea, was imported from England to replace her. Ostensibly this was because he had ambitions to be deputy conductor, but actually it was said to be because conductor and leader traditionally travelled together in a first class compartment on train journeys – as Barbirolli and McCallum had so usefully done – and Miss Rennie (though more probably Karl Rankl) might feel compromised by such proximity. This was not, at any rate, something that would have disconcerted the flirtatious Otto Klemperer. He, the story goes, once seized Rennie in his immense arms when the five-minute warning bell sounded before the second half of a concert he was conducting, and sang to her 'Give me five minutes more', a popular ditty of the time.

The repertoire, which had hugely expanded under Susskind, was steadily reduced by Rankl to the Germanic mainstream. Russian music was dismissed as 'silly' music; some former players recall a rehearsal of Tchaikovsky's Fourth Symphony in which the word 'silly' became a litany. French music was suspect, but a necessary evil. Sibelius and Nielsen were banned, being nothing but the 'scrapings of the Viennese masters'.

Not even Viennese music was sacrosanct, however. The slow movement of Schubert's Great C major Symphony was abbreviated because Rankl – a Viennese composer himself – thought it too long. All the same, during his five years in Scotland, he found time to conduct three of his own eight symphonies. Schumann's symphonies were performed in Mahler's arrangements, but Mahler's own symphonies, at least, were permitted to speak for themselves, a little warily at first – the two nocturnes from the Seventh Symphony were played but not the remainder of that structural minefield – though with increasing confidence. The Fifth Symphony was included in the 1954 Edinburgh Festival, and so was Schoenberg's gargantuan *Gurrelieder*, Rankl's most ambitious effort, in which the Edinburgh Royal Choral Union was augmented by the West Calder and District Male Choir. The work did not reappear in the orchestra's repertoire until Sir Alexander Gibson conducted it, with the veteran Hans Hotter as speaker, at the 1983 Edinburgh Festival.

In comparison, Vaughan Williams's picturesque *Sinfonia Antartica*, which received its Scottish premiere in the same year, must have seemed a snip. Rankl (like Neeme Järvi later) showed a predilection for Vaughan Williams's Englishness and he conducted the fourth, sixth and eighth symphonies with conviction, the last of these immediately after its Manchester premiere. Mainstream English composers – Walton, Berkeley, Rawsthorne, Gardner – he was able to take in his stride, along with Britten, but Tippett he would doubtless have regarded as silly.

In other respects, his rigidity of outlook proved increasingly a trial and ultimately an embarrassment. Soloists were expected to gear their performances to Rankl's accompaniments, and when they rebelled against this there could be trouble. After one cliff-hanging performance of Rakhmaninov's Third Piano Concerto by Cyril Smith, Rankl refused to return to the Usher Hall platform to share the applause.

Among his awkward foibles was a hatred for the harp, an instrument he would obsessively kick whenever he passed it. Only Sir Malcolm Sargent, who never allowed two harps to appear together on the platform and would rewrite Ravel's harp parts to prevent this happening, appeared to possess the same phobia in the same virulent form. Rankl's biggest insult to a wind player is

remembered as being, 'You sound like a brass harp.' A Covent
Garden harpist, chided by him right at the start of a rehearsal,
calmly covered over her harp and walked out. 'Do you mind if I
shout at you?', he once asked the SNO's harpist. 'You see, I hate
the harp.'

Insecurity, resulting in rudeness to individual players, was
judged to be Rankl's primary shortcoming. To ask a question
across the orchestra during a rehearsal was to court disaster. He
was capable of literally foaming at the mouth. To wait until later
was sensible. Then his eyes would twinkle behind his rimless
glasses, and he would look like an ageing Schubert.

Was he a good conductor? As one ex-player diplomatically puts
it, 'He was good at what he was good at.' Though he could cope
with *Gurrelieder*, the task of starting the finale of Schubert's Great
C major Symphony was apparently beyond him. When, one
season, his left arm stiffened and he was forced to depend solely
on his right, some players claimed that his conducting improved.
But Rankl tales were legion and, for all his barking and snarling,
he inspired a degree of affection, even if he was notably lacking
in humour. When, on his birthday, the players struck up 'Happy
Birthday to You,' a British orchestral tradition, he thought they
were poking fun at him. When it was explained to him that it was
a British joke, he spent the rest of the rehearsal muttering 'Bree-
teesh joke' whenever someone made a fluff.

Rankl worked hard, with that Germanic determination that
work was good. In 1954 his industry resulted in a series of 'Industrial Concerts' – a distinctly uninviting name for a scheme that
was meant to attract companies and businesses to take block bookings for members of their staff. In due course a future Scottish
conductor would become involved with the running of these,
initially on an administrative basis. His name, then quite unknown, was James Loughran – 'Jimmy' to members of the Glasgow staff – who would sit studying pocket scores during lulls in
his office duties.

At that time, we should remember, the chances of becoming an
established Scottish conductor were slight. Ian Whyte had done it
under the auspices of the BBC. Alexander Gibson had done it
in London. But Loughran still needed all the help he could get.
Promoting industrial concerts, with no hope of conducting them,
must have been frustrating for him, though he says he would have
swept the floor if necessary, just to be part of the SNO.

As a teenager with 'a burning ambition to conduct', he was given, he has told me, access to many of Walter Susskind's rehearsals, and been impressed by his 'fine technique and marvellous sense of gesture'. Then, at the subsequent concerts, he was fascinated, he said, by Susskind's ability to 'turn round and talk to the audience and make them enthusiastic about what they were going to hear'. Susskind, he recalls, was also a 'fabulous' pianist. 'I remember him playing the Ravel concerto and telling the audience that he'd been unable to get someone else to perform it so he'd just do it himself.'

Later, after National Service, Loughran's name was put forward to be an assistant conductor. Hugh Marshall, who was vice-chairman at the time, was supportive. But Joseph Barnes, who was still manager, said there was no scope for a young conductor and turned him down. Office duties were to be his *entrée*, and he recalls forming part of 'a wonderful team', with Jean Mearns (who, after marriage, became Jean Caldow) proving particularly valuable as concert administrator.

'She helped me', he says, 'in every conceivable way. She knew more about running the SNO than anybody. She was so precise. Nothing ever went wrong.' As for Rankl, 'He was a lovely musician in many ways, until he got sour about the whole profession.' The svelte Swarowsky, who succeeded him, proved more sophisticated. 'He was more authoritative than Rankl, who was much more of a peasant. But he was too smooth for comfort, with a lot of Viennese charm, and I was not attracted to study under him. I was put off by his dark glasses and suede shoes.'

Once Alexander Gibson, in turn, had been appointed as Swarowsky's successor, Loughran began to get chances to conduct. 'Alex offered to share a prom with me, and I did Tchaikovsky's *Romeo and Juliet* and Rimsky-Korsakov's *Capriccio Espagnole*. It was a wonderful occasion for me.' His career had begun. Soon John Pritchard invited him to prepare the orchestra for a Leeds Festival performance of Schoenberg's *Dance round the Golden Calf* and Alexander Goehr's *Sutter's Gold*. 'I was thrown in at the deep end, six hours a day for six consecutive days.' Step by step he proceeded, via more SNO dates, the winning of the Philharmonia's conducting competition (Giulini, who was present, addressed him as 'Maestro'), an assistant conductorship in Bournemouth, *Aida* at Covent Garden, *Acis and Galatea* at Aldeburgh, then major appointments with the BBC Scottish Symphony

Orchestra and, as crown of his career, the Hallé. Remembering his 'Industrial Concerts' with the SNO, he set up a similar concert series in Manchester, wisely changing the title to 'Opus One' in order to get rid, as he put it, of the 'boiler suit image'.

Though Rankl could hardly be said to have inspired Loughran's success, he helped to create a climate in which success was possible. Rankl's summer popular concerts, made feasible by the orchestra's new full-time status, also bore fruit, forming the basis of what in 1956 became fully-fledged prom seasons at St Andrew's Hall in Glasgow and in the more cramped surroundings of the Music Hall in Edinburgh. When, on one occasion, the sound of bagpipes threatened to disrupt a Music Hall concert – the rear of the building lies adjacent to the pubs of Rose Street – Rankl resourcefully paid the piper to abandon his tune.

But, as Loughran correctly diagnosed, Rankl was losing interest in conducting. He only did it, he told his players in a sad and candid moment, to earn money to compose. His rehearsals, though they continued to start punctually, had a way of ending earlier and earlier. His opera, *Deirdre of the Sorrows*, which in 1951 had won a Festival of Britain award, never received the Covent Garden performance he longed for. A return visit, as guest conductor, to Vienna made no great impact on the city of his youth.

How he must have felt when one of his own guest conductors – a fellow Viennese whose war years were less impeccable than Rankl's – supplanted him at the age of fifty-nine, one can only too readily imagine. It was the Covent Garden story all over again. Like Susskind before him, Rankl headed for Australia, where he found that the appointment he had been offered – the directorship of the Sydney Opera – was illusory, because the opera house was not yet built. Disillusioned, he returned to Europe to live quietly in retirement. Occasionally he was visible in the audience at Glyndebourne, if the opera was one he cared about. Only once was he seen again at Covent Garden, and that was when Solti conducted Schoenberg's *Moses and Aaron*. But in 1964, if only as stand-in for an indisposed Alexander Gibson, he reappeared with the SNO to conduct a hauntingly fragile, luminously beautiful performance of Mahler's *Das Lied von der Erde*. He died, aged seventy, in Salzburg in 1968.

Rankl could be difficult, but he was not a vain man. In spite of his maladroitness, his players respected him. His only small conceit was to wear velvet slippers while conducting, and maybe he simply found them more comfortable than evening shoes. Hans Swarowsky, his successor, possessed an ego more prominent. The epitome of a Viennese dandy, he wore the smartest suits, and on one single Glasgow shopping expedition to Forsyth's grand Gordon Street store (now closed) he bought eight expensive pairs of shoes. His hands were fastidiously manicured and he employed a finger sponge to help him to turn the pages of his score. Not, as he kept reminding his players, that he really required the printed text. 'I carry two hundred works in my head', he used to tell them. 'We soon found out that he didn't', one former hornist told me. 'He was very accident prone.'

But technically he was accomplished, more so than Rankl. His beat looked practised. When he reached the massive triple-forte chord at the climax of Beethoven's *Leonore No 3* overture, he would signal this blaring minor ninth by holding his baton in both hands, high above his head. 'He was', as one player put it, 'full of little Viennese tricks. Whenever he conducted Reznicek's *Donna Diana* overture, he would lay down his baton at a certain point and leave the orchestra to play by itself.'

The orchestra sometimes had to look after itself in other works also. 'He was a terrible accompanist', one former player recalls. 'For some reason he hated the pianist Shura Cherkassky, and there was once a very fraught rehearsal of Rakhmaninov's Second Piano Concerto which ended with Cherkassky slamming down the lid of the piano. It turned out that Swarowsky had never conducted it before. He didn't know any Russian works.

'He also had a row with the pianist Colin Horsley over how to perform Beethoven's Fourth Piano Concerto. He flung down his baton and told Horsley that that wasn't the way to play Beethoven. Then he said he would refuse to conduct. He had this habit of keeping his head down all the time when he was conducting, so that there was no eye contact. What he did do was sing. He sang his way through everything he conducted.' (Alceo Galliera, the Italian conductor, had impressed the same generation of SNO players by being able to sing tonic sol-fa faster than they could perform. He offered £100 to anyone who could outpace him, but nobody took him up).

Yet Swarowsky was the man who, at the Vienna Academy of Music, won renown as one of the greatest teachers, whose quantities of distinguished pupils included Claudio Abbado and Zubin Mehta (as well as our own Roderick Brydon) and who himself had been taught, like Karl Rankl, by Schoenberg and Webern, as well as by Weingartner and Richard Strauss. Though evidently no Nazi, he was equally evidently a wily survivor of the Hitler regime. The fact that he had a Jewish stepfather might have been a problem, but, as Zubin Mehta's American biographers have established, his tale that he was the illegitimate son of a Hapsburg Archduke apparently ensured his safety (he wore a signet ring of the Hapsburg dynasty).

But he was not, it seems, entirely above suspicion. Prevented from conducting in Germany during the war, he conducted in Cracow instead. He also did duty as an opera administrator in Munich and – his most bizarre appointment – joined Goebbels's Ministry of Propaganda, where (or so it was later claimed) he sent musically coded messages to the Allies. The same, from the opposite point of view, had been said of the Darmstadt-born Karl Muck when he was conductor of the Boston Symphony Orchestra during the First World War. As a result, the Americans imprisoned him as a spy.

When, in 1945, Herbert von Karajan's Nazi past caused him to be briefly banned from conducting at Salzburg, Swarowsky was one of those who were chosen to replace him (while Karajan, it is said, secretly directed the singers from the prompt box). As conductor of the SNO, however, Swarowsky was to find few friends. His skills, though erratic, were admired, but he as a person was not. According to one player, 'He was arrogant, and played to the gallery. His proficiency admittedly pleased some people after Rankl's awkward style, but he had no more humour than Rankl had. He was very smooth, but there was also something sleazy about him. He used to complain of back trouble, which he attributed to too much sex. And, in talking to female players, he would deliberately say breasts when he meant breaths.'

Uninfluenced by these aspects of his personality, I thought him a convincing, even if not greatly exciting, conductor in the Viennese tradition. Years of history seemed to flow through his performances of Brahms and Beethoven, not in the modern authentic manner of a Norrington or Eliot Gardiner, but simply through being in touch with players who had played for Brahms. He knew the score, even if he sometimes forgot it. But his repertoire was, if anything, even more restricted than Rankl's. For his first appearance at the Edinburgh Festival, in 1957, he chose nothing more daring than Hindemith's *Mathis der Maler* symphony and Blacher's

Variations on a Theme of Paganini, interwoven with Beethoven and Brahms. In 1958, Hindemith and Brahms still loomed large, with Iain Hamilton's *Bartholomew Fair* overture as a token tribute to his adopted country.

After five years of Rankl, two years of Swarowsky were quite sufficient. He would have liked to stay longer. Indeed, when his contract was terminated, he was taken by surprise. To soften the blow, he was told that a Scottish conductor needed to be given a chance. Alexander Gibson, who had made some successful guest appearances with the orchestra, was to be his heir. Swarowsky henceforward was to buy most of his shoes in Austria, where, like Rankl before him, he died in Salzburg, a week before his seventy-fifth birthday.

8

A Scot Takes Over

Sir Alexander Gibson's twenty-five uninterrupted years as principal conductor and musical director formed the longest reign in the orchestra's history. Nothing remotely like it had happened before, nothing similar seems likely to happen again. He arrived, like all great rulers, at exactly the right moment. After six years of claustrophobically narrow-minded Viennese rule, the players were demoralised. Programme planning had never been duller or more constricted. Karl Rankl, for four whole years, had virtually banned Sibelius, dismissed Tchaikovsky and been none too happy about Debussy's credentials. Hans Swarowsky, Karajan's predecessor at Aachen in the nineteen-thirties, had coasted along for a further two years on a handful of German classics. Into this area of musical scorched earth, Gibson arrived like a gulp of fresh Scottish air.

To remind his audiences what they had been missing, he programmed all seven Sibelius symphonies in his opening season – an artful stroke that won him instant acclaim, Scottish listeners being in tune with Sibelius and with nordic symphonies in general. It also revealed him to be an instinctively able and subtle conductor of these works, one of which (the Fifth Symphony) had formed his first major recording with the London Symphony Orchestra for RCA Victor.

True, at the age of thirty-three, he was deemed precociously young to be in charge of an institution as venerable as the SNO, and some sage Scottish heads nodded in dismay, fearing that it would all end in tears. To be old in Scotland in the nineteen-fifties was reckoned an asset, and even Walter Susskind, for all his foreign pedigree, had been considered suspiciously youthful.

William Fell, who had been administrator since Susskind's day, was said to be uncertain about offering Gibson the job. Rankl and Swarowsky – senior Viennese – had been Fell's men, even though the first of them had been forced on him, and a potentially trouble-some young Scot seemed not necessarily the happiest alternative to another Viennese, for whom Fell may well have been looking (he finally arrived, in 1992, in the person of Walter Weller).

But in 1959 the mood in Scotland was changing. People were becoming culturally and politically more self-aware, and one thing they were ready for was a native Scot on the rostrum. Now was the time, especially as the right person appeared to be available, to have a conductor tuned into the country's own music and needs. Gibson, born in Motherwell and trained – at least to begin with – in Glasgow, was clearly the man of the moment; moreover, having achieved early glory as musical director at Sadler's Wells, he was known to want an escape route from London, in order to develop his career away from the international glare of the metropolis.

It was a decision, once made, which must have lost him many an enticing invitation and many a lucrative contract, and perhaps the resident conductorship of an orchestra more famed than the SNO. In musical terms, apart from the Edinburgh Festival, Scot-land remained a backwater in 1959, and some would say, in the context of Vienna, Berlin, New York and London, that it still is. When Gibson returned home, Scotland's only two progressive composers, Iain Hamilton and Thea Musgrave, had already fled to work in more congenial American surroundings. Gibson wooed them – Hamilton sensationally so – with performances of their music, and made them Scottish names again.

In 1959, in international terms, the SNO lacked class, and a distinctive sound of its own. Gibson gave it these, and in 1967 took it on its first, by British standards belated, European tour, a three-week journey launched, not in some provincial town, but in Vienna's great Musikverein. He won it a proper, more fulfil-ling, role in the Edinburgh Festival, added London and other English cities to its regular itinerary, pioneered its output of recordings, vastly expanded its repertoire, captured for Glasgow the British premiere of Stockhausen's *Gruppen* (a seminal work of the period, which did not reach London till six years later) and – with the support of Glasgow University, a notion that would never have occurred to a Rankl or Swarowsky – encouraged living composers, some of them Scottish, by way of a short autumn festival entitled Musica Nova.

He did all this, moreover, with a modesty that won him instant appeal among his unflamboyant fellow countrymen. Gibson built up the SNO's audience in the four main Scottish cities to an unprecedented size and stability, but he did something else. Through the creation of Scottish Opera in 1962 he made Scotland musically self-sufficient in a way it had never been before. The founding of a national opera – an institution Scotland had never possessed – formed part of Gibson's musical strategy even before he had left Sadler's Wells. He had talked it over with singers, especially Scottish singers, resident in London. He had been invited by Richard Telfer, musical director of the Edinburgh Opera Company (an amateur but undoubtedly prophetic outfit) to conduct Verdi's *Nabucco* with David Ward, the Scottish bass and Scottish Opera's future Wotan in *The Ring*, as a member of the cast. For the occasion, the Usher Hall was transformed into an opera house. Those who, like me, experienced that production caught a glimpse, without realising that they were doing so, of Gibson's private vision. Though Scottish Opera was still a pipe-dream, it was very soon a reality.

But it would not have been a reality without the help of the SNO. It was the presence of the full-sized national orchestra, playing better than it had ever played before, in the King's Theatre, Glasgow, and the King's Theatre, Edinburgh, which gave the opera company its immediate chutzpah and made possible the productions of Debussy's *Pelléas et Mélisande*, Puccini's *Madama Butterfly* and Verdi's *Otello* that were its early glories. When the full orchestra flamboyantly spread itself out of the pit and into the stalls and side boxes of the Glasgow King's for *Götterdämmerung*, the climax of the *Ring* cycle, in 1971, Desmond Shawe-Taylor, music critic of the *Sunday Times*, who was sitting beside me, nudged my arm and said, 'Whaur's your Covent Garden noo?'

When, later in the decade, the SNO dropped out of Scottish Opera – whose seasons had grown too long and numerous for a busy symphony orchestra to cope with – something was lost that was never fully regained, either by the more recently-formed Scottish Chamber Orchestra, which bridged the gap until a full-time opera orchestra was founded, or by the latter when it was ultimately recruited.

Even the formation of the Scottish Chamber Orchestra, however, had been made possible by Gibson. True, he was never its conductor, except in the pit and as an occasional guest. But he created the musical climate in which it could burgeon, and in which it had become needed, just as he also provided fresh scope for the Scottish Baroque Ensemble, which was founded by the London-born violinist Leonard Friedman for performances at John Calder's Kinross-shire festival, Ledlanet Nights, but was soon swept into the complex musical network that Scottish Opera was already becoming. Add to this the formation of the Edinburgh Festival Chorus for the Scottish premiere of Mahler's Eighth Symphony by the SNO in 1965, and the benefit of having a Scot (admittedly an outstanding one) at the heart of Scotland's musical life becomes all the plainer.

Lord Harewood, by then in his final year as Festival director, had wanted to make the opening concert at the Usher Hall – traditionally a conservative occasion when civic dignitaries from Edinburgh and elsewhere, complete with medals, filled the grand tier of the auditorium – an event with a bit more oomph. His first thought was to present a great Handel oratorio or opera along the lines he had already explored at his other British festival, the Leeds Triennial. But whereas Leeds could boast a grandly sonorous Yorkshire choir (capable, in the nineteen-sixties, of tackling a scarifying full-length cantata by Hans Werner Henze) Edinburgh had only its by then somewhat ossified resident choral union, living on its memories of Bruno Walter conducting Brahms's German Requiem.

What was to be done? Harewood and Gibson between them hatched the idea of a brave new chorus, to be formed exclusively for the Festival, and Gibson and Richard Telfer between them came up with a name, Arthur Oldham, as the only possible chorusmaster. Oldham, who had been Benjamin Britten's sole composition pupil at Aldeburgh, had sunk into obscurity as music master at Scotus Academy, a Roman Catholic boys' school in Edinburgh, but it was a job that had one valuable by-product: the school choir, which sang at St Mary's Roman Catholic Cathedral in Leith Street, had begun to gain attention for the robust excellence of its singing, more 'Continental', it was said, than the traditional soft-grained English 'coo' of other British cathedral choirs.

Conductors such as Carlo Maria Giulini had made a point of attending services at St Mary's specially to hear it. Sir Georg Solti had employed its services in a Festival performance with the Orchestra of the Royal Opera House, Covent Garden, of Berlioz's *Damnation of Faust* (he offended Oldham by telling him later that the boys had sung flat). Oldham, with his dark beard and burning eyes, seemed to possess just the dynamism that the training of a grand new international festival chorus would require. Choosing him, no doubt, was no more than a hunch. A Wilhelm Pitz could easily have been hired from abroad. But the choice proved apt. Today, with a major chorus in Paris as well as his Scottish forces, Oldham is among the most distinguished and sought-after chorus-masters in the world, working regularly with all the leading conductors, including a now wholly admiring Sir Georg Solti.

If all this seemed marginal to the work of the SNO – which had at its disposal its own admirable Glasgow-based SNO Chorus, formed out of the old Glasgow Choral Union, and also now its SNO Junior Chorus – it is wholly relevant to Scotland's overall musical well-being, in which the SNO played a major part. Not until the formation of the Edinburgh Festival Chorus was there a vocal standard in Scotland to which other choruses could aspire. And in this, as in so much else, Gibson was the catalyst – a word used rather too freely nowadays, but in Gibson's case fully deserved.

Not until the formation of the Edinburgh Festival Chorus, indeed, did the SNO get its first opportunity to give the opening concert. Earlier in the Festival's history this would have been a risk. For all its conservatism the event carried immense prestige, and only a major orchestra was traditionally entrusted with it. 'So at last it has happened', I wrote in *The Scotsman* at the time; but what really mattered was that Gibson had not only persuaded Lord Harewood of the SNO's ability to rise to the occasion but had swung him away from the idea of Handel at the Usher Hall by proposing Mahler's Eighth Symphony instead. At once it became plain that this was to be the Festival's most ambitious opening concert ever; and even though Harewood quite rightly insisted on underplaying the gargantuan aspect of the symphony – what counted, as he pointed out, was that it was worth doing, not that it was some freakish 'Symphony of a Thousand' – this was bound to be a performance that would make Festival history. And it did. It was so successful that it was repeated the following year – the first and only time such a thing has happened in the Festival's musical history.

Yet Gibson's appointment as the SNO's musical director in 1959 had been by no means a foregone conclusion. William Fell, an administrator so set in his ways that he invariably used only a single London agent (Ibbs and Tillett) to supply him with soloists and guest conductors, thought that so radical a change in SNO tradition might be courting trouble. But in spite of Fell's caution, Gibson was approached informally in London by directors of the SNO when he was still musical director of Sadler's Wells Opera; and he had already been made aware, as a guest conductor with the orchestra during the Swarowsky period, of a strong move towards him, particularly among the orchestra's Glasgow-based directors, who clearly visualised him as Swarowsky's successor.

If this was to happen, however, a definite offer was necessary. Gibson had already resigned once from Sadler's Wells (after scarcely a year there) in order to become assistant conductor of the BBC Scottish Orchestra under Ian Whyte in 1952; and, having returned to Sadler's Wells, he was reluctant to resign again, at a time when his responsibilities with the opera company were increasing, along with his fame. A chance meeting with Lord Cameron, one of Scotland's senior law lords and a big influence at the time on Scottish artistic policy (he wielded enormous power over the Edinburgh Festival), gave Gibson the opportunity to say that he felt he needed to spend more time in opera in London and that he was not yet ready to take on the responsibility of the musical directorship of the SNO. 'Modesty,' replied Lord Cameron, driving Gibson round Charlotte Square in his Rolls-Royce, 'is an admirable quality in a conductor.' Two years later, while visiting Dundee with Sadler's Wells Opera, Gibson received a phone-call from Emmie Tillett, the London agent, asking him if he would like to be the SNO's next conductor.

Though Hans Swarowsky's contract still had a year to run, this was plainly no impediment. Gibson was now ready. His only pang of embarrassment came when, as conductor of a British youth orchestra at the Brussels Expo in 1958, he spotted, through the goldfish-bowl windows of the Austrian Pavilion, Swarowsky coaching young conductors and members of an Austrian youth orchestra. Gibson knew, as Swarowsky did not, that the Austrian's days in Scotland were numbered.

So, by then, were William Fell's. At the time of Gibson's appointment he had been running the orchestra for nine years, and – as Gibson has tactfully put it – was 'beginning to feel he'd done enough'. Though conductor and administrator got on reasonably well, it was a partnership only slightly easier than that between Bryden Thomson and Christopher Bishop thirty years later.

Gibson says he found Fell 'co-operative if idiosyncratic'. Fell's preference for a single London agent has already been mentioned. In my own experience he had a regimental approach to life, perhaps useful in the marshalling of an orchestra. In the orchestra's Hope Street offices he sat on a chair which his successor described as 'unbelievably uncomfortable'. He was a large, hale and hearty man who, I admit, had somewhat scared me when, having just left school, I asked (and happily received) his permission to attend SNO rehearsals at the Usher Hall in order to practise writing about them.

Fell's views on music were sound but insular. He saw nothing wrong with letting Karl Rankl conduct Brandenburg concertos when, even in the nineteen-fifties, a more worldly administrator might have expressed disapproval. He had inadvertently provoked Walter Susskind's resignation – which was imminent anyway – by slapping him jovially on the back and saying 'Have a go, old boy' just before, in a state of high nervous tension, Susskind was to go on to the platform to conduct Beethoven's Missa Solemnis for the first time in his career. And, in Gibson's time, he caused the orchestra to lose a foreign tour – including an appearance at the Concertgebouw, Amsterdam – because, at a crucial stage in negotiations, he confessed that he did not possess a passport.

Though dealing with two Viennese conductors in succession could not have been easy for him – Rankl was as testy with Fell as with everyone else – he may have found Gibson even more foreign. When Gibson proposed pepping up the SNO's programmes with Musica Viva concerts of the sort that John Pritchard had recently pioneered in Liverpool, the idea was anathema to Fell. Nevertheless he accepted the inevitable; and so Gibson's pilot season as SNO conductor included not only all the Sibelius symphonies that Rankl and Swarowsky had so conspicuously shunned but also something considerably more challenging in the form of eight Scottish premieres of major twentieth-century works, plus – on 29 April 1960 – Scotland's first stab at Musica Viva, an uncompromising but exhilarating evening at St Andrew's Hall when Iain Hamilton's Sinfonia for Two Orchestras, which had caused an outcry when Gibson conducted its world premiere at the 1959 Edinburgh Festival, was heard alongside Stravinsky's Ode and the British premiere of Schoenberg's Violin Concerto nearly a quarter of a century after it was written.

Fell, to give him his due, was good about Musica Viva. He also accepted another major project from which, when the time came, he really had no escape. When Gibson succeeded Swarowsky, one of the first things Fell had done was to show him a chart on the wall of the SNO offices in Hope Street. Dates between October and March were, as usual, well filled, but those between April and September displayed as usual an alarming amount of white space for an orchestra which, for the past nine years, had been operating full time. 'This, my boy, is what you're to do', said Fell. 'Fill these gaps.'

How Gibson filled them has gone down in history, even if it was different from how Fell expected. The first Musica Viva concert in April 1960 spawned three others the following season, two of them during the winter and the third – including the milestone performance of *Gruppen* – on May Day 1961. Never had prospects seemed fairer when, suddenly in 1962, disaster struck. With the winter season only just begun, and with more Musica Viva in preparation, there was a boxing match at St Andrew's Hall. Someone, or so it was later surmised, must have dropped a cigarette. A man and his dog raised the alarm. By morning, Britain's finest concert hall was gutted.

Why boxing matches were ever held in these unsurpassed acoustics is a question only Glasgow's city fathers could answer, but the reason is easy to guess. The people whom Maurice Lindsay had once described as square-toed philistines intent on making money needed something other than culture with which to justify this great hall's existence. Elsewhere in Europe the loss of a historic auditorium of this calibre would be considered a public tragedy. When Prague's National Theatre burned down, the front-page headline the following day exhorted 'Weep, City'. Funds were raised and soon the theatre was restored to its former glory.

In Glasgow no such thing occurred. For years James Sellars's marvellous building, erected in 1890 just before the naming of the Scottish Orchestra, remained an empty, dispiriting shell. Glasgow University offered its Bute Hall as a temporary refuge, but soon the orchestra was relegated, with a fine display of civic charity, to an abandoned cinema at the Charing Cross end of Argyle Street. This tatty building was hastily renamed the Glasgow Concert Hall and served for the next six years as the orchestra's home base. Thus did Glasgow treat the most valuable jewel in its artistic crown.

But 1962 was not all doom. Today, indeed, it is remembered

more for the birth of Scottish Opera than the death of St Andrew's Hall. Though founded ostensibly to give the SNO something to do in the spring, the company not only filled another of Fell's gaps but had far-reaching implications for Scotland that would swiftly emerge.

Nevertheless the loss of St Andrew's Hall could only have speeded Fell's decision to retire. His wife, spotting in a newspaper that the Gainsborough Museum Cottage in East Anglia required a curator, suggested that he apply. After *Gruppen* it must have seemed an idyllic prospect (he got the job). He had steered the SNO through a vital period in its history, had helped to establish it as the permanent orchestra it is now, and had presided for a while over the careers of four international conductors. Not a bad innings, as he himself might have said.

But before departing he delivered (as he put it in an interview with the author of this book) what he considered to be one important piece of advice: the fourth of these conductors, he said, would be well advised not to linger around too long with the SNO. Whether or not the same homily was delivered to the conductor himself, Gibson was by then too deeply involved in the development of Scottish Opera, as well as of the SNO, to heed the warning. Barbirolli had advised him to go for the job, and had recommended his appointment. No doubt Gibson saw himself as another Barbirolli, doing for Scotland over a long period what Barbirolli had been doing for Manchester over a similar time-span.

Meanwhile a new administrator had to be found, and the board of directors asked Gibson if he would approach – today we would say headhunt – Robert Ponsonby in London. It was a shrewd and, in the event, successful idea. Ponsonby had been languishing in a non-musical department of ITV after his resignation as director of the Edinburgh Festival in 1959. As he himself would be the first to admit, he had not been the happiest of Festival directors. Though he had gained experience as Ian Hunter's assistant earlier in the nineteen-fifties, he was elevated to the senior post before he was really ready for it. Musically he played for safety and for quality, but he proved himself the possessor of a notable operatic flair which, later in his career, he had scant chance to exploit except through broadcasting. It was Ponsonby who first brought the Stuttgart Opera to Edinburgh, thereby providing a rare opportunity to see Weber's *Euryanthe*; and it was Ponsonby who risked staging the Swedish sci-fi opera, Karl-Birger Blomdahl's *Aniara*, with its space-ship setting, thirty years before Michael Tippett explored the same theme in *New Year*.

But it was also Ponsonby who, on the drama side, staged *The Hidden King*, a theatrical disaster for which he was crucified by the critics. A sensitive and responsible man, he resigned soon after, moved unhappily to America, failed to settle there, returned – as he put it to me when I interviewed him while working on this book – with his 'tail between his legs', was invited by the British Council to be their man in Bangkok, turned down the offer ('if I'd accepted it, I would never have been taken seriously again') and joined ITV with the somewhat drab task of ensuring that sufficient minority-interest material got televised on the commercial channel. It was then that Alexander Gibson discreetly called on him and said: 'What about coming and living in Glasgow and running the SNO with me?'

Though he knew Edinburgh well enough, he knew almost nothing about Glasgow ('I thought it a bit uncouth'). But the idea attracted him and he sought out the chairman of ITV, Lord Hill, to say he might be quitting. Lord Hill gave him his blessing along with the advice, 'Never show the slightest twinge of loyalty to your current employer', and Ponsonby left for Scotland.

Though he had no previous experience of orchestral administration, it was the turning point in a career that was to lead ultimately to his being head of BBC music and a successful director of the London Proms during the difficult post-Glock period. Since his retirement from the BBC at the statutory age of sixty, he has been running the Musicians' Benevolent Fund in a pleasant office near Broadcasting House, and it was there, in his board room in March 1992, that I asked him about his eight years, from 1964 to 1972, with the SNO.

He said he had been very lucky, because it had been the most trouble-free time of his life. 'Those were the days', he reminded me, 'when the problem of sponsorship hardly existed.' Funds came quite straightforwardly from the Scottish Arts Council, the local authorities and the box-office. Whenever he or Gibson hit on an idea, there was nothing to prevent its being carried out. And the orchestra prospered. To celebrate his return to Scotland, Ponsonby proposed structuring each season around the works of a single composer and Gibson welcomed the challenge to find suitable candidates. Beethoven and Brahms, the obvious safe choices, were avoided, and it was not yet time for another round of Sibelius. So Schubert was chosen to launch the plan, with performances of all nine symphonies – music which suited the lyrical side of Gibson's nature, as did the Schumann and Dvořák surveys that came later.

Schumann, a composer far harder to perform than is popularly imagined, was a particularly thoughtful choice. Compared with Schubert, and even with Dvořák, he remains a neglected figure, still dismissed in some circles as an incompetent orchestrator, better at songs than symphonies. But all that is required is faith in him, and Gibson showed that, properly treated and given sufficient rehearsal time, his orchestral works, including the little-known *Overture, Scherzo and Finale*, could stand beside anyone else's. Other rarities, such as the incidental music for Byron's *Manfred*, were left to Jascha Horenstein, a Fell 'discovery' whom Ponsonby was rightly continuing to cultivate as guest conductor, and to Bryden Thomson, who drew what some people regarded as the short straw – the Violin Concerto, dating from the grim twilight of the composer's career.

Horenstein, an émigré Russian Jew once notorious for his evil temper – he was nicknamed 'Horrors' and had eyes, said Ponsonby, as 'black as Bartók's' – had entered a more mellow old age by the time the SNO got hold of him, though he could still scare the players. The only SNO performance I have ever heard break down was a *Freischütz* overture conducted by Horenstein at the Usher Hall. Having negotiated the two great detached chords that launch the coda, the orchestra was safely into the home straight when everything suddenly ground to a halt. Sam Bor, the leader, retrieved the situation by playing the theme all by himself for a few bars, until the rest of the orchestra resumed. At the end Horenstein remained standing, head bowed, his back to the audience, refusing to acknowledge the applause. The mishap was presumably his, and no doubt few listeners had noticed it, though one suspects there were recriminations afterwards.

Patience was not one of Horenstein's virtues. Though he could unfold a Bruckner symphony without haste, he once got cross in the Caledonian Hotel when I was interviewing him and his afternoon tea failed to arrive. Proceeding into the kitchen, he started shouting and banging things around. When he emerged, a waitress was at his heels.

As for Thomson's conducting of the Violin Concerto, this much-maligned score, with Franco Gulli as soloist, was largely

ALEXANDER GIBSON CONDUCTING AT THE LAST NIGHT OF THE GLASGOW PROMS, KELVIN HALL.

ALEXANDER GIBSON REHEARSING THE ORCHESTRA. (COURTESY THE HERALD)

SIR JOHN BARBIROLLI REHEARSING THE ORCHESTRA IN DALINTOBER HALL, 1969. (COURTESY THE HERALD)

GARY BERTINI, PRINCIPAL GUEST CONDUCTOR 1971-81. (COURTESY THE HERALD)

JAMES LOUGHRAN,
GUEST CONDUCTOR.
(COURTESY CONRAD WILSON)

KURT SANDERLING,
GUEST CONDUCTOR.

THE SNO CHORUS AT PRESTWICK AIRPORT EN ROUTE FOR TEL AVIV, 1972. (COURTESY THE HERALD)

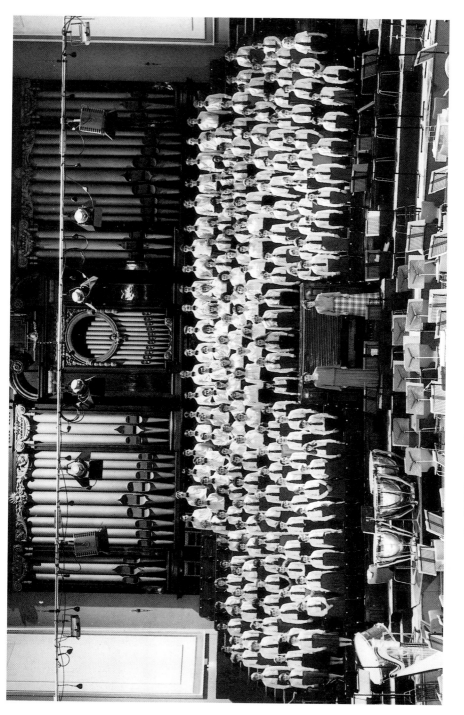

THE SNO YOUTH AND JUNIOR CHORUS IN THE USHER HALL, EDINBURGH.

Witold Lutoslawski,
Polish composer.
(Courtesy Conrad Wilson)

Iain Hamilton,
Scottish composer, 1981.

MUSICA NOVA 1987. LEFT TO RIGHT: *background* STEPHEN ARNOLD, DAVID MCKENZIE, JAMES MACMILLAN, RAY HERMAN, EDWARD MCGUIRE *foreground* CHARLES LYALL, GEOFFREY KING, WILLIAM SWEENEY, IAN WILLCOCK.

NEEME JÄRVI, MUSICAL DIRECTOR AND PRINCIPAL CONDUCTOR
OF THE SCOTTISH NATIONAL ORCHESTRA 1984-88.
MATTHIAS BAMERT, PRINCIPAL GUEST CONDUCTOR 1985-90.

SAM BOR,
LEADER OF THE ORCHESTRA 1959-74.

EDWIN PALING, LEADER OF THE ORCHESTRA 1976- .

BRYDEN THOMSON, MUSIC DIRECTOR AND PRINCIPAL CONDUCTOR 1988-91; NOVEMBER 1989.
JOHN CURRIE, CHORUSMASTER OF THE GLASGOW CHORAL UNION AND SNO CHORUS 1966-84.

The orchestra and Bryden Thomson in the Henry Wood Hall, Glasgow.

CHRISTOPHER BISHOP,
CHIEF EXECUTIVE OF THE ROYAL
SCOTTISH NATIONAL ORCHESTRA
1988- .

WALTER WELLER, PRINCIPAL CONDUCTOR OF THE ROYAL SCOTTISH NATIONAL ORCHESTRA 1992- .

The Caird Hall, Dundee

The orchestra and Sir Alexander Gibson in the Vienna Musikverein, September 1978.

vindicated and indeed, in recent years, has been successfully taken up by other performers.

A Mahler cycle, unhurriedly spread over several seasons, was launched, and a Henze cycle, similarly extended, was risked. That was a period, long before the Royal Festival Hall got round to the same idea, when thematic programme planning was rampant in Scotland and Lord Harewood had his 'featured composers' – Schoenberg, Shostakovich, Janáček, Berlioz, Boulez – at the Edinburgh Festival.

Ponsonby himself now looks back with amazed delight at the immense freedom he and Gibson were given to do just what they liked, and to take their audience with them as they went. Almost nothing seemed impossible. It was not that their board of directors, with Sir David Milne as chairman, was more enlightened than any other. Indeed, says Ponsonby, neither Milne nor the SNO Society's long-established secretary, G. K. V. Clarke, seemed particularly interested in music at all. They were there simply to keep an eye on the till.

Ponsonby thought this in some ways a pity. But there are times when an unmusical board, as this one seems to have been, can be better than one 'with musical ideas', in that it leaves the professionals to get on with their job. The opportunity to give the British premiere of Hans Werner Henze's Fourth Symphony in February 1966 (in a concert also containing Schumann's Fourth Symphony rather than some cynically chosen popular favourite as bait for the audience) was a case in point. Gibson not only seized the chance to teach it to the orchestra but used it as launching-pad for a Henze survey that stretched on for another four years until climaxing in Scottish Opera's memorable vindication (with the SNO in brilliant command of the luminous orchestral part) of Henze's early, until then maligned opera, *Elegy for Young Lovers*, at the 1970 Edinburgh Festival, with the composer himself as producer.

While it lasted, this was a remarkable period in SNO history, with its championing of a major European composer at a time when none of the London orchestras appeared to care. For the Glasgow and Edinburgh audiences, the abstractions of Henze's Fourth Symphony – with its complex single-movement structure devoid of clear-cut signposts – were undoubtedly a challenge, though Edinburgh, with all its Festival premieres, had had more experience of progressive modern music. But, through persistence, conductor and orchestra accustomed their listeners to Henze's sound world.

The British premiere of the Third Symphony (with Strauss's *Death and Transfiguration* as postlude) in 1967 and the performance of the Fifth Symphony (with *The Rite of Spring* as coupling) in 1968 were milestones on the route to the Second Piano Concerto, a work of ambitiously Brahmsian proportions with which the orchestra scored a considerable coup later that year. Commissioned by the town of Bielefeld for the opening of its new Kunsthaus, it had already created a scandal in Germany and had swept the young pianist, Christoph von Eschenbach, to fame. Again ahead of London, Ponsonby and Gibson were alert enough to grab the British premiere and invite Eschenbach to give it.

Their acumen proved justified. Even in what might have seemed a suicidal programme containing Stravinsky's neo-classical Symphony in C, and at the end of a chilly Scottish November, it did not prompt the orchestra's subscription audience to stay at home. Both in Glasgow and Edinburgh, listeners seemed riveted by the fiery argument of this huge autobiographical work, inspired by the Shakespeare sonnet 'The expense of spirit in a waste of shame' and considered by some to be a scarcely concealed expression of contempt for the Germany Henze had grown up in and escaped from.

London critics, making the pilgrimage to Glasgow to hear it, found their journey well worthwhile. For Andrew Porter, in the *Financial Times*, it proved 'a notable occasion'. Gibson, he declared, 'is a fine Henze conductor, for he combines precision with emotional warmth. The orchestra played well.'

Praise indeed, but this was a winter when English critics, and Porter in particular, were enamoured with what the SNO was achieving in Glasgow, where the players now, for the first time since the destruction of St Andrew's Hall, had a place worth performing in. The dilapidated cinema that had served as their home for six dismal years had at last been flattened by bulldozers. For some time the gradual demolishing of that end of Argyle Street had been audible during rehearsals – Gibson occasionally sent someone out to plead for silence – while simultaneously the construction of the flyovers and underpasses of Glasgow's controversial new road system around the Kingston Bridge was proving equally distracting. Like the nearby Buttery restaurant, one of the conductor's haunts at the time, the makeshift concert hall became marooned in a waste land of rubble and machinery. Audiences, fearing for their safety, dwindled. The restaurant happily survived; the demise of the concert hall was regretted by nobody.

When it became plain that the orchestra would again be homeless, the city fathers realised with dismay that they would have to do something about it. Having failed to rebuild St Andrew's Hall – though the insurance money would easily have enabled them to do so – and being unwilling to commit themselves to a much-mooted arts piazza near Queen Street Station, complete with custom-built auditoriums for Scottish Opera, the Citizens' Theatre and the SNO, they fell back on the idea of once more seeking a cheap, already existent auditorium for the orchestra.

But this time they struck lucky. Instead of converting another cinema or – as someone actually proposed – transferring the orchestra to the peril of Govan Town Hall, they decided to renovate the old City Hall in Candleriggs. It was a scheme they should have thought of sooner. True, at the time, the City Hall had surroundings almost as raffish as those of Argyle Street or Govan. The fact that it formed part of Glasgow's fruit market was not in itself a disadvantage – after all, the Royal Opera House, Covent Garden, was once similarly sited. But the neighbourhood as a whole, with its dilapidated buildings and scruffy pubs, was deemed a deterrent. That it would later be revitalised as Glasgow's 'Merchant City', with good restaurants and handsomely restored buildings, was not yet on the cards.

Why the City Hall had lain neglected for so long remains a mystery. It had been Glasgow's original Gewandhaus, built – like St Andrew's Hall, whose shell (to its shame) was acquired by the Mitchell Library as an extension to its adjoining premises – to the same design as Leipzig's. Today the grand façade of St Andrew's Hall stands afresh, and as one passes it, en route to the orchestra's new offices and rehearsal space at the other end of Berkeley Street, one can imagine the strains of all the music making – the splendour of Szell's Strauss and Barbirolli's Elgar, the revolving sonorities of *Gruppen* – that once went on there. But now, behind those walls, are books and silence.

The rediscovered City Hall provided a chance to make amends. It had been built, by George Murray, in 1841. Dickens and Thackeray had given readings there. Disraeli and Gladstone had argued politics. Sims Reeves had sung. But, more importantly, it had been the orchestra's first home, in the days when the players had no name of their own and were simply an appendage of the Choral Union. Its shoe-box shape – that of the other great halls mentioned above – promised good acoustics. Its coffered ceiling and narrow balcony were features – proven the world over – of good musical design. Behind the platform there was space for a Scandinavian-style restaurant (it soon closed). Beyond the first-floor foyer there was a roomy cafe-bar (unfortunately laid out in such a way that people formed long queues for their drinks).

Properly run, lovingly decorated, the place could have become one of the world's great concert halls. But Glasgow, sadly, did not know its luck. Though a splendid wooden colonnade remained at the back of the platform, the organ it had originally housed – and which had been reputedly sold for a song – was never replaced. The new plastic chairs were drably functional, and squeaked when you shifted position. The decor was dreary. The seating capacity – a mere 1,216 – was feared to be on the small side, even though audiences in the 2,000-seat Argyle Street hall had sometimes failed to reach a thousand.

Yet acoustically the City Hall was just the gem it was reputed to be. And the English critics who journeyed north for Gibson's opening programme on 10 October – Britten's overture *The Building of the House* (written for the opening of The Maltings at Snape), Haydn's B flat major Cello Concerto with Paul Tortelier as soloist, and Mahler's First Symphony – were exhilarated by what they heard.

'Acoustically,' declared Andrew Porter in the *Financial Times*, 'the Glasgow City Hall is super: in point of definition, blend, "singing tone," response, and placing the audience "in" the reverberation instead of somewhere outside it.' About the Mahler, he reported that he found the orchestra and their conductor in peak form. 'I was ravished, captivated, by the performance, moved by it as seldom since those early days of first discovering Mahler . . . The sound had much to do with it; but that I was not seduced solely by the splendidly warm acoustics, by the increasingly uncommon experience of hearing music in surroundings perfectly suited to it, was proved by a repeat performance in Edinburgh the next day.'

There, in the familiar surroundings of the Usher Hall, he found that the excellence of the Mahler was equally apparent. 'Gibson', he asserted, 'is a poet, a master of the broad span. Both the charm and the terror of the great symphony were vividly communicated. The detail was finely placed, but not fussed at. The shaping of the work as a whole was sure.'

Nevertheless it was Glasgow that won his keenest acclaim. In the sharp autumn sunlight, he said, it was a city to inspire euphoria, with architecture more exciting than any to be found on this scale outside Chicago. 'Why', he asked, 'did the Festival ever settle in Edinburgh?' Glasgow's hall, he added, was one which made him feel he would like to rediscover the classical repertory all over again in such acoustics.

Porter's praise is worth repeating. It is a Scottish habit that, when something is a success, forces of hatred gather against it. No sooner had the City Hall been extolled in London than performers and audiences began to find fault with it, complaining that it was too small for the heavyweight works performed there. Visiting orchestras, it was said, passed it by, because it did not hold enough people to make a concert financially viable. Well, perhaps: but even if it was on the small side for Shostakovich symphonies, or for the big vocal works that the SNO Chorus desired to sing, the classical repertoire up to Bruckner and Mahler sounded tremendous there. Moreover for chamber music – a series of Masterconcerts, with Elisabeth Schwarzkopf as first of a starry series of recitalists, was launched in 1968 but disappointingly abandoned – it was peerless. As Schwartzkopf said later, she would 'crawl on her hands and knees' to sing in the City Hall's acoustics, but 'would not cross the road' to sing in the Royal Festival Hall, London.

Since Glasgow now has its Royal Concert Hall – of which more in my final chapter – the City Hall is thought by some to have outlived its usefulness. Not so: for smaller-scale concerts, especially those of the Scottish Chamber Orchestra, it has never been more necessary, and threats to demolish it, or change its function, should be stoutly resisted. Sir Alexander Gibson has proclaimed himself passionately convinced that it must be preserved.

But were things really so good in 1968? People with long memories are forever citing the superior performances of yesteryear, the more adventurous programmes, the more thrilling range of soloists, the more meaningful summer proms. Yet it was surely not imagination. A glance through the old brochures does show that things were different then. During the Ponsonby period, guest conductors included not only Horenstein but Antal Dorati,

Sir Adrian Boult, Paul Kletzki, Aaron Copland – and Colin Davis, who has not appeared in Scotland since 1970.

And the array of soloists was tremendous indeed, with Daniel Barenboim, Jacqueline Du Pré, Alfred Brendel, Vladimir Ashkenazy, Henryk Szeryng, Janet Baker, Stephen Bishop-Kovacevich, Mstislav Rostropovich, Heinz Holliger, Kyung Wha Chung, Irmgard Seefried, Rudolf Firkušný, Leonard Rose, Clifford Curzon, Itzhak Perlman and Martha Argerich as people whom audiences had become accustomed to expect. But international star soloists and conductors now cost much more than they used to, and when they come to Britain – as they do sometimes no more than once or twice a year – they tend to perform in London only. As a result, the orchestra – in company with Scottish Opera and the Edinburgh Festival – has been forced to set its sights somewhat lower.

Yet when Ponsonby became administrator in 1964 the players themselves had little power. Though he had scant previous experience of orchestral administration, he was aware that they were poorly paid. The 'rank and file' salary (orchestral terminology for members of the orchestra who are not principals or sub-principals) had recently risen from £15 to £20 a week, but the players, says Ponsonby, 'were aware that they had little status in the community' and were 'pretty downtrodden members of society'. And because they felt this strongly, there was inevitably tension between them and the management.

Dealing with the Musicians' Union seems to have been neither easier nor harder then than now. As Ponsonby somewhat blandly explained to me, 'I wanted just as much as they did to give them more pay, but the money just wasn't there'. What he did give them, in the autumn of 1967, was their first foreign tour, which took them to Austria, Germany and Holland, and revealed that in these countries orchestral players had considerable status in the community – as one by no means elderly violinist noted to his amazement when people offered their seats to him on crowded trams.

The trip was organised with all the aplomb one could expect of an administrator whose background was Eton, Oxford and The Guards. Just as there was a Ponsonby at the Battle of Waterloo, so there was a Ponsonby to guide his musical troops from one victory to another between Vienna and Rotterdam. The logistics – and I, as music critic, was there to write about them – were deeply military. Before setting off each morning, the players stood by their buses as if on parade. The day's orders were announced. On one occasion, high in the Austrian Alps, someone nearly found himself on a charge for leaving – as Ponsonby said before departure next morning – his boots on the bed.

Yet to suggest that the tour was over-organised would be misleading. There was time between concerts (as there sometimes isn't nowadays) to escape from music, time to visit the Vienna State Opera, time to explore Salzburg, time to eat schnitzel, time to meet Murray Dickie, the Scottish tenor who had moved to Vienna early in his career and established himself as the leading exponent of that yodelling operetta, *Le Postillion de Longjumeau*. And, in spite of Ponsonby's scrupulous planning, there were the mishaps to which all orchestral trips are prone.

James Robertson, the former bassist who is now orchestral manager, recalls how the flight to Vienna (in an old four-engined slow-moving Brittania) nearly never happened because somebody forgot to book the buses to take the players to Glasgow Airport. They got there in a stream of taxis. Food poisoning struck between Vienna and Graz, but was successfully treated by the orchestra's doctor, nicknamed Killer McLean on account of the size of the pills he administered (a Mahler devotee, he claimed that he could have cured the dying composer of his heart disease).

In Linz, to everybody's horror, it was found that the hall lay beside a railway junction. But ever since Karajan had conducted there, and had complained, the trains were diverted during concerts. Listeners at Leverkusen, the massive Bayer aspirin complex between Cologne and Düsseldorf, lost their expected encore when Sam Bor – who abhorred German officialdom in all its manifestations – began to lead the players off the platform at the end of the concert and refused to be pushed back on to the stage by the hall's manager.

But such incidents did little to disrupt a tour in which almost everything that mattered went right. Good tours, as every player knows, depend not only on good music-making but on good halls, good accommodation and transport that runs on time. Ponsonby had found a German concert agent capable of getting dates for the orchestra in some of Europe's finest halls. Admittedly, the safest of repertoires had been insisted upon, with Brahms's Second, Sibelius's Second, Tchaikovsky's Fourth and Prokofiev's Fifth as the choice of symphonies, and Britten's *Sinfonia da Requiem* and *Young Person's Guide* as the only bits of modernity. Because audiences would expect to hear top British soloists, they were given Janet Baker, who sang Mahler's *Kindertotenlieder* and *Five Rückert Songs*, and Jacqueline Du Pré, who played the Dvořák and Elgar cello concertos. Charles Mackerras, who had been invited to share some of the conducting, dropped out during negotiations and in the end Gibson conducted all seventeen concerts.

On hearing what music had been chosen, a dumbfounded Cedric Thorpe Davie – whose works had won occasional performance from the orchestra – phoned me from St Andrews University to ask if it were really true that no Scottish pieces were being played. The Scottish branch of the Composers' Guild also expressed its feelings, but there was no hope, it seemed, even of *Land of the Mountain and Flood* as an encore. Ponsonby declared his hands to be tied and that 'Scottish music must wait'.

Whatever the dressy Viennese audience expected of the SNO on that opening night in that most sacrosanct of concert halls, the golden Musikverein, was not immediately plain. Britten and Dvořák were courteously received, but the applause for Tchaikovsky's Fourth Symphony seemed reserved. Yet for all its moderation, it failed to peter out. Instead of going home, many members of the audience advanced on the platform and sustained their tranquil clapping. In the end, Gibson realised that an encore was expected. But since none had been prepared, the only solution was – rather tamely – to repeat the symphony's scherzo. At the end, dislodged by the resonance of some chord or other, one of the organ pipes toppled on to the platform.

When, the following night, the same programme was presented in the same hall to a different audience, success was never in doubt. In place of the previous evening's reserve, there was eager enthusiasm. And this time, in the form of a Berlioz overture, there was an encore at the ready. The contrast between the two events was never satisfactorily explained. Perhaps Vienna's first nighters traditionally treat a 'new' orchestra – even one which had been advertised on a poster outside the hall as 'The Orchestra of the Edinburgh Festival' – with restraint. Or perhaps, in an auditorium where Karl Böhm regularly spread layers of Viennese warmth upon all the music he conducted, they simply found Scottish Tchaikovsky too cool for their taste.

Happily, nobody else did. The critics were favourable. At Graz, Brahms's Second Symphony – a risky work to take to Austria

– was acclaimed and the philosophical implications of Gibson's interpretation were analysed (favourably, it must be said). At Salzburg and Linz, the fine detail of the Mahler was thought ravishing. Nürnberg took less kindly to Sibelius (Gibson grumbled later about the audience 'sitting on its hands') but Munich seemed happy and so did Rotterdam.

Like all long tours, it placed hardships upon the players. Critics travelling abroad with orchestras – and this was the first, though certainly not the last, time I did so – learn that their own job is infinitely easier, at least in terms of tension. While the orchestra rehearses, and gets the feel of the next hall, the critic can explore, visit galleries, write reviews in congenial surroundings. Occasionally he can take a night off. At Bregenz, to escape Prokofiev's Fifth Symphony in a hall too cramped for it, I fled to a cinema to grapple with Michelangelo Antonioni's oblique movie, *Blow-Up*, dubbed into German. For an orchestral player there is no such escape.

Yet in the days before faxes and computers, critics had their problems too. Since major reviews were written 'on the night', I had to ensure that I could make contact with *The Scotsman* before my midnight deadline. Some hotels could provide a direct link with *The Scotsman*'s wire-room, though when they discovered that I wanted to send a thousand words they were displeased. Others forced me to fall back on the more expensive telephone, which sometimes entailed using a public phone-box in the hotel lobby to avoid excessive room charges. On one such occasion in Graz, Jacqueline Du Pré, spotting me at work, pressed her nose against the glass door of the box and pulled funny faces at me while I dictated my review.

Humour, on such tours, often erupts immediately after a concert. But sometimes it is the night *after* a major date, when the orchestra has finished with Munich or Nürnberg and reached somewhere like Aschaffenberg, that darker emotions can grow. It was on such a night that one of the cellists had to be persuaded not to resign, because, he thought, he had seriously fluffed the finale of the Prokofiev. But other players – such as the one whose phlegmatic ritual on arrival in every town was to head for the nearest launderette – seemed impervious to personal crisis.

Yet on the whole the orchestra – whose members are ruthless judges of the running of any tour – seemed satisfied with its first sortie outside Britain. There were, it was reckoned, no really duff dates of the sort that regularly get slipped into foreign concert itineraries (the Scottish Chamber Orchestra, on its first major tour in 1978, ended up one night in a salami town on the borders of Hungary and Romania). The three buses that are conventionally required to shift a symphony orchestra from place to place – the first two for non-smokers, the third for smokers, boozers and brass players – got everyone to their destinations on time. The third bus, though it sometimes lagged behind, never got lost.

The memorable halls – the ones which, as the players put it, they would have liked to take home with them – were those that framed the tour: the Vienna Musikverein, which they were to revisit in future years, and the brand-new Doelen in Rotterdam, whose comfort, spaciousness and good acoustics represented everything they lacked in Glasgow. Of the others, the marmoreal Hercules Hall in Munich had been admired (today's concerts are held in a less satisfactory new building) and Karajan's broad Festspielhaus in Salzburg had impressed but not been loved. Only claustrophobic Leverkusen had been found wanting.

Ironically, Prokofiev's Fifth Symphony was the first work they played in the dreary Glasgow Concert Hall after their long absence, during which, in Scotland, they had been replaced by other British orchestras. The Glasgow audience appeared not to notice they had been away, perhaps because *The Herald* had not covered the tour, as it would certainly have done now. Edinburgh's audience on the other hand – having been regaled with the progress reports I sent to *The Scotsman* – gave them heroes' welcomes, cheering them as they came on to the platform and being treated at the end to an encore in the form of the fugue from Britten's *Young Person's Guide*. Mid-season encores from the SNO were – still are – exceptionally rare, but Gibson had judged the mood to perfection.

9

Musica Nova

After 1967, foreign touring became part of SNO policy. For a while, scarcely a year went by without a trip of some sort. Sometimes it was just a quick dash to a single country – a couple of concerts, say, at the Bergen Festival in Norway. Sometimes it was considerably more complex. Ponsonby, cashing in on the success of the first big Euro tour, organised another of its kind which, though successful enough, seemed not quite such a hit – the players, complaining of their zigzag progress across Europe, said that it must have been planned with the map folded in two, concealing the number of detours.

Old hands in the orchestra, indeed, claim there have been only three tours that really mattered: the first European one, the first American one, and the first (so far the solitary) Japanese one. Though only one of these was Ponsonby's inspiration – the others were the work of his successors – the orchestra continued to benefit from his expertise for the remaining four years of his administration. Working with Gibson, he now says, was what supplied the impetus. He remembers Gibson then as being 'Absolutely in the prime of his ability, talent and energy – an extraordinarily elegant conductor. He never did anything ugly. He had a physical style one could recognise: firm, elegant, never brusque or harsh. The internal balance of his performances produced a luminous beauty. There was poetry, and a sense of line, in all he did. As Simon Rattle was later to prove in Birmingham, if you've got a conductor who imposes style, and if that style is always there, you can make a better orchestra than the material would suggest. Alex had that style.'

But Ponsonby, in his own sphere, had it too. Though I sometimes complained that his SNO prom programmes were uninventive – and on one occasion provoked him into an acrid correspondence that culminated in his banning me from them –

they were better than those of most of his successors. He regarded
them, he said, as the light-hearted summer obverse of Musica
Nova, the SNO's much tougher autumn festival of new music
which established itself in Ponsonby's time as a grand, brave
expansion of Musica Viva. The proms, as Ponsonby saw it, were
enjoyable escapism for orchestra and audience. And when I once
rudely dismissed them as 'mindless pap,' comparing them
unfavourably with London, he patiently replied that they were
not meant to be like London. The daring music was performed
during the winter season and in Musica Nova.

Though I refused to accept it at the time, he had a point. Ponsonby's proms never stooped so low as some of today's, and they
possessed, as Gerald Larner recently asserted in *The Guardian*, a
degree of creativity – 'capitalising on the popular favourites but
also offering the odd spectacular'. It was a period, which continued
for a while after Ponsonby departed, when a big Mahler symphony or Berlioz's Requiem might win its way into a concert.
Today that would be inconceivable, because, as Larner put it, there
is now 'little in the programmes outside the predictable routine of
repertoire, conductor, and soloist'.

But the SNO proms were never at any time as adventurous as
William Glock's at the Royal Albert Hall – which, ironically,
Ponsonby was soon to inherit and capitalise on. The real ingenuity
went into Musica Nova, which from the first had rigorous,
ambitious aims, and not only stuck to them but developed them.
If there was a problem, it was the predictable one of maintaining
the exceptionally high standards set during the Ponsonby years.
As his successors gradually discovered, there were simply not
enough top composers to keep Musica Nova supplied with new
works at an affordable price. But if the big names grew thin on
the ground, the level of interest did not dwindle and the aspirations
– at a time when much of British life was getting worse – remained
notably high.

Musica Nova's roots lay not only in Gibson's experiments with
Musica Viva but in his easily encouraged disposition to conduct
concerts of new music. Though he sometimes expressed reservations about isolating modern composers from their predecessors, he was aware that this was the only way that many
lesser-known composers would ever get a hearing. While Tippett's latest symphony could co-exist with Dvořák's Cello Concerto – as it did in one of Gibson's winter seasons, and I received an

angry mailbag for devoting the bulk of my review to the Tippett – less glamorous composers find it harder to get one of their works slotted into the conventional overture-concerto-symphony format of a popular subscription series.

For them, the future is more likely to lie in programmes devoted in their entirety to composers of their kind. At worst their audience will consist of critics, publishers – and other composers. But their music, with luck, will be reviewed, and one performance may lead to another, though not necessarily of the same piece. Gibson, recognising that he and the orchestra could act as a lifeline, had already in 1963 conducted in Glasgow what was claimed to be the first-ever programme of modern Scottish orchestral music. Not all the composers, it's true, were born in Scotland. But if, by Joyce McMillan's journalistic definition, a Scot is someone who lives in Scotland, then in 1963 all eight of the composers represented in the programme – Anthony Hedges, Gordon Lawson, Kenneth Leighton, Thea Musgrave, Robin Orr, John Purser, Thomas Wilson and William Wordsworth – were Scots.

One or two of them soon vanished without trace. But others, if they had not already established themselves, very soon did so. This was a different sort of event from Musica Viva, in that persuading a conventional audience to listen to new music was not its primary aim. Its intention, rather, was to cultivate composers and show them that, from time to time, the SNO could be their shop window – though admittedly four years passed before a similar programme was held in Edinburgh. There, in the Music Hall – George Street's classical edifice where the orchestra had once regularly played and where, in August and September, members of the Festival Club now daintily sipped afternoon tea – Gibson presented a 'Music Workshop' consisting of a further five Scottish pieces, this time by Martin Dalby, David Dorward, John Purser, Ronald Stevenson and Thomas Wilson. Though the Edinburgh Festival Guild sponsored the event (an experience it chose never to repeat) the real impetus came from Frederick Rimmer, Glasgow's progressive professor of music, who chaired a post-concert discussion.

It was Rimmer, too, who helped to pioneer Musica Nova in Glasgow at a time when no other British city would have taken such a risk. Though it could be argued that Latin names merely add to the ghetto-ising of modern music, at least nobody tried to call it a music workshop. But it took a visiting Englishman, John

Amis of the BBC, to hit on a Scottish title, 'Music the Noo', for a broadcast of the event. He was, naturally, accused of being patronising.

What was perfectly plain, however, was that the event was worth broadcasting, in England as well as Scotland. Sponsored not only by Glasgow University but by the Calouste Gulbenkian Foundation, it lasted six days and incorporated four major commissions, three of them from Scottish composers. Rehearsals took place in public, the composers took part in forums and seminars, and the closing concert, containing the four new works, had a fitting sense of climax. Astonishingly, critics and publishers did not seem to outnumber the general public.

The new Scottish works were Iain Hamilton's *Alastor*, Thea Musgrave's Horn Concerto and Thomas Wilson's *Sequentia Passionis*. Luciano Berio's *Bewegung* (which could mean 'Movement,' 'Exercise' or 'Emotion', depending on how you interpreted it) provided a sprinkling of continental spice. Douglas Young's *Departure*, winner of a prize in memory of Karl Rankl, was thrown in for good measure.

Only one of the works, Musgrave's Horn Concerto, went on to establish itself in the repertoire, its most recent Scottish performance being at the 1992 Edinburgh Festival. In the nineteen-seventies, on a return visit to the Vienna Musikverein, the orchestra played it with high success to that most conservative of audiences. Its popularity derived, then as now, from its theatricality and from the personality of Barry Tuckwell, the soloist for whom it was written. Like other Musgrave works of the period – the Concerto for Orchestra and the Clarinet Concerto, also championed by the SNO – it treated the players as characters in an abstract drama, requiring them to stand up and even at times move around the platform. A moment to savour in the Horn Concerto was when the orchestral horns, from different parts of the hall, all closed in on the soloist.

Yet Hamilton's Shelley-inspired tone poem, though dramatically more static and texturally a lot denser, was no less compelling. With its hallucinatory quotations from Chopin and other composers, it was Ponsonby's personal favourite of the works performed, and it was mine also. Hamilton, then living in New York, was at the age of 49 in his prime. That the music was 'dedicated to Mahler and those who died young' should have helped to ensure it a certain morbid success. That it was never revived suggests a failure of nerve on the part of the orchestra.

By the time Musica Nova recurred – the intention was to make it a triennial or (somewhat optimistically) biennial event – Ponsonby had returned to London and a new administrator, David Richardson, had taken over. To say that he left behind a satisfied orchestra would be to exaggerate. Orchestras – British ones anyway – are seldom satisfied, and improved conditions of the sort the SNO had begun to enjoy gave the players increased scope to express their dissatisfaction. This was simply in line with what was happening in London and elsewhere, where old-style conductors who ruled by terror had been largely phased out – not since Szell's day had the SNO thus suffered, though Rankl also knew how to humiliate – and the London tradition of orchestral self-government ensured that an unpopular conductor or administrator could always be removed.

With a board of directors which then contained not a single member of the orchestra, the SNO could hardly be said to possess that advantage. But at least the players could have reflected, had they so wished, that such orchestral power was not always wielded fruitfully. The London Symphony Orchestra, notorious for the abrasiveness of its players, had got rid of Ernest Fleischmann, arguably the most gifted of all its administrators (later, in charge of the Los Angeles Philharmonic, he was to go from strength to strength).

There was also a natural human tendency to choose conductors who would not get in the players' way but who, when they ceased to please, could be easily replaced. It was not a system which produced, within any one London orchestra, anything resembling a coherent artistic policy of the sort the SNO enjoyed – the repertoire at the Royal Festival Hall was conspicuously narrower than that in Glasgow and Edinburgh. Nor was there the kind of quality control which Szell bestowed on the Cleveland Orchestra and Karajan on the Berlin Philharmonic. But that was not the type of high-discipline music-making the London orchestras favoured. Famed for their ability to sight-read and work other wonders with far less rehearsal time than their European and American equivalents, they refused to be bullied and preferred to do the bullying. When Lorin Maazel, rehearsing Verdi's *Luisa Miller* at Covent Garden, told the orchestra it was playing badly and must pull itself together – or words to that effect – the players stood up and walked out on him.

Yet the SNO was not as docile as it once had been. James Robertson recalls how Sir Adrian Boult – a conductor who could rarely be accused of temperament – once strode from a Glasgow rehearsal because the players did not produce their pencils when he asked them to. It took all the leader's powers of persuasion to bring him back. Nor, more recently, on the two occasions he has appeared as guest conductor, has Simon Rattle struck the rapport with the SNO (or it with him) that has occurred elsewhere.

But confrontational problems seem largely to have passed Ponsonby by. There were the usual spats about pay, about whether players should receive special rates for playing the hair-raising solo parts in a work such as Berg's Chamber Concerto at the Edinburgh Festival, and about what freelance work they were allowed. Some players thought Ponsonby insensitive to such matters, yet the orchestra was notably stable at the time and Scottish Opera seemed less of a threat to its administration than it was to seem later.

Yet, with Gibson's eager connivance, the opera company was already a substantial cuckoo in Scotland's musical nest. Its spring seasons had expanded to take in not only Edinburgh but Aberdeen, Perth and Newcastle as well. The largest of masterpieces, including a complete production of Berlioz's *The Trojans*, a *Tristan and Isolde*, a *Ring* cycle and a *Rosenkavalier*, had been brilliantly tackled. And in all these works, each lasting five hours or more, the SNO had been automatically expected to play. That it had covered itself in glory was not, by the players, necessarily thought to be the point. The glory was reckoned to be merely reflected; a makeshift theatre pit was not as inviting as a concert platform; and with Sam Bor, an entrenched anti-Wagnerian, as leader, there were occasional mutterings of revolt.

Yet for Ponsonby, himself an opera man, the rapid growth of Scottish Opera presented less of a dilemma than it did to his orchestra. Part of him, as he admitted, loved to hear opera as well played as it was by the SNO under Gibson. Night after night he squeezed his long frame into a circle seat in the King's Theatre, Glasgow, and escaped into the world of Verdi's *Otello* and *Falstaff*, Beethoven's *Fidelio*, Mozart's *Cosi fan tutte*, Britten's *Peter Grimes*. Looking back, he says that Scottish Opera's first ten years were 'a development of such sure-footedness', and that Alexander Gibson, Peter Hemmings and Robin Orr, as conductor, administrator and chairman, were 'such a wise and efficient triumvirate', that hardly a single mistake was made.

It was for Ponsonby's successors that the opera company's expansion increasingly created problems and caused Gibson's allegiances to be, as some people saw it, increasingly torn between theatre and concert hall. Gibson himself, however, simply thought he was lucky to have two jobs in one city, unlike the growing number of conductors who jetted constantly between appointments in Europe and America.

Though Ponsonby escaped having to make an irrevocable decision about Scottish Opera, he considers that what finally happened – the creation of a full-time opera orchestra after other solutions had been tried without lasting success – was probably wrong. It resulted – and there are those now who would agree with him – in Scotland having too many orchestras. 'It was', he considers, 'never quite right that Scottish Opera should have its own orchestra.' And though he accepted that the SNO could not go on for ever doing all the work, he continues to believe, from his London vantage point, that the idea of sharing performances between several orchestras was never developed far enough.

In recent years, as the opera company has reeled from crisis to crisis, and a merger has been devised between the BBC SSO and the opera orchestra, Ponsonby's words have gained fresh significance. As a critic, I am aware of the value of the long view. All orchestras and opera companies have their ups and downs, their moments of glory and despair. But the late nineteen-sixties and early seventies were undoubtedly a special time for the SNO and Scottish Opera, and their relationship – which lasted, albeit sporadically, until Berg's *Wozzeck* and Janáček's *The Cunning Little Vixen* were performed at the Edinburgh Festival in the early eighties – was perhaps too hastily sundered. Nothing so good has replaced it, and I for one would trace some of Scottish Opera's troubles back to its split with the SNO.

For Gibson, whose ambition was always to transform the SNO into a Scottish version of the Vienna Philharmonic, serving concert hall and opera house, the split was a major disappointment. But the large pool of players he envisaged – a reservoir from which the two organisations could simultaneously draw – failed to win the enthusiasm of the Scottish Arts Council. Costs, it was feared, would escalate; an enlarged SNO would be swept into more and more performances of the *Ring* and other lavish projects, whereas the single complete cycle in December 1971 had been more than enough.

Nevertheless an idea so central to Gibson's philosophy did not just go away, and Ponsonby's successor, David Richardson, revived it in a different format. Rather than inflate the SNO into an outsize but divisible orchestra, it was now proposed that a second, smaller and separate orchestra be created under SNO auspices, with its own name (Scottish Sinfonietta was one suggestion) and identity.

The idea was, in fact, nothing new, even if the fine detail was more radical. In 1964 Lord Harewood had invented a 'Scottish National Chamber Orchestra' for a series of morning concerts conducted by Gibson at the Edinburgh Festival. The surprise announcement in the Festival brochure that year stirred me to inquire about the identity of the orchestra, what its links were with the SNO itself, and whether it would become a permanent body of players. Thus pressed, Harewood and the SNO disclosed that it was all semantics. The Scottish National Chamber Orchestra was simply a section of the SNO under a different name, with a brief to perform Haydn symphonies and works of similar scale from later periods.

Though the cotton-wool acoustics of Leith Town Hall, where the concerts were given, did the SNO's new offshoot no favours, the idea caught on. Had William Fell still been administrator, he would have seen that here was a way to fill still more gaps. And before long, indeed, towns and villages with halls too small for the full SNO began to receive visits from one or another of the two chamber orchestras carved from the parent body. While Gibson took one group of players to Orkney and the North to perform Haydn and Stravinsky (anticipating the sort of repertoire that the newly created full-time Scottish Chamber Orchestra would start playing a decade later), his associate, Bryden Thomson, took another group to Dumfries and the South.

But if these concerts worked, it was only after a fashion. Dividing a symphony orchestra in two did not, in fact, create two chamber orchestras. The strings, accustomed to playing *en masse*, simply sounded severed from each other. The wind failed to blend with the perfection one expects from a genuine chamber orchestra. There was a lack of real coherence. After a while the project was quietly dropped, though not before Raymond Leppard, as guest conductor, had taken one of the groups of players to the Hebrides, and had said, to the embarrassment of the players and their administrator, 'Sorry, it's not good enough'.

The plan for a Scottish Sinfonietta, which could give chamber concerts and accompany some of Scottish Opera's small-scale Mozart and Britten productions, seemed much more promising. Indeed, in the early nineteen-seventies, it seemed on the point of becoming a reality when it was scuppered by the Scottish Arts Council. A national symphony orchestra and chamber orchestra run by a single organisation, it was argued, could be dangerously monopolistic. If there was to be a full-time chamber orchestra – and, as Lord Harewood had already demonstrated, there was certainly scope for one – then it should have its own autonomy and be based in Edinburgh rather than Glasgow.

Accordingly, in 1974, the Scottish Chamber Orchestra was founded with the Scottish Arts Council's blessing. Its autonomy was not quite absolute, for it was linked with Leonard Friedman's already existent Scottish Baroque Ensemble beneath the umbrella of a somewhat nebulous organisation called the Scottish Philharmonia. In theory it would fill the various Scottish Opera theatre pits that were in the process of being vacated by the SNO. And in practice it did so – but only for a while. By an irony the Scottish Arts Council clearly did not expect, the newly-formed SCO was soon to do what the SNO had already done: withdraw its services from Scottish Opera and concentrate on giving concerts.

As a result, for the first time in history, the SNO would have competition which henceforward would have a bearing on its repertoire, its programme policy, its audience, its fund raising and the size of its Arts Council grant.

10

Halcyon Years

When the Scottish Chamber Orchestra was founded, David Richardson had been in charge of the SNO for two years. Strictly speaking, the two organisations were not straight rivals, for their repertoires were by no means identical, and chamber orchestras have never had the mass appeal of symphony orchestras. But in fact they soon found themselves competing for the same audience, often in the same halls.

In its ability to perform the heavyweight masterpieces of the nineteenth and twentieth centuries – a repertoire, roughly speaking, ranging from Beethoven's *Eroica* symphony to Bartók's Concerto for Orchestra – the SNO clearly had one advantage. But in its flair for Haydn and Mozart the SCO soon equally clearly had another. From now on, in common with symphony orchestras everywhere, the SNO would find its repertoire increasingly encroached upon.

As became apparent, there was some music, formerly the territory of symphony orchestras, which a good chamber orchestra could simply do better. When Richardson came to Scotland he expressed the hope that the SNO would perform all Haydn's symphonies – a tall order, for there are over a hundred of them – during his period as administrator. It was, as he now admits, a reckless statement. In the event, the SNO played very few Haydn symphonies, for the simple reason that its Haydn playing, by and large, was no longer viable.

Nevertheless Richardson proved a good and wise administrator during his decade in Glasgow. Though born in London, he had studied in Manchester and been a trumpeter in the Hallé and other orchestras in the North of England. But a performer's life was not what he really wanted. In 1966 he became a BBC producer in Manchester and in 1970 returned to London to be concerts manager with the New Philharmonia Orchestra. Two more SNO

administrators, Fiona Grant and Christopher Bishop, were subsequently to come from the same productive stable.

There were those who would have liked to see the appointment
go to a Scot. Not since Joseph Barnes had the orchestra had a local
man in charge. But Richardson, in compensation, could claim to
be the SNO's first administrator with practical orchestral experience. Six people were brought to Glasgow to be interviewed for
the post by a board including Dame Jean Roberts (a former Glasgow Lord Provost and by then the orchestra's latest chairman),
Michael Goldberg (of the department store of that name) and
Alexander Gibson. Richardson was told two days later that the
job was his.

Today Richardson is back in Manchester, as administrator of
the Hallé Orchestra, after the less than happy experience of running the Orchestra of St Paul, Minnesota, with the temperamental
Pinchas Zukerman, and a not wholly trouble-free period with the
Bournemouth Symphony Orchestra. In comparison, he acknowl-
edges, his SNO days were 'halcyon' ones. 'Looking back,' he said
when I visited him in the Hallé's offices in 1992, 'it was a fantastic
time. Life was simpler in those days, financially. That all changed
when the local authorities withdrew from funding the orchestra.
But I was very happy in Scotland. I had a good relationship with
Alex Gibson most of the time, and a good relationship also with
Gary Bertini, the principal guest conductor.'

Like Ponsonby, he could claim that most of the things he
wanted to do he had managed to do. True, his ambition to present
Messiaen's *Turangalîla* symphony was never realised – not for
another fifteen years would it receive its Scottish premiere, under
the baton of a subsequent principal guest conductor, Matthias
Bamert. But among his achievements was a high-profile concert
series coupling major works by Schoenberg with all five Beethoven piano concertos. Gary Bertini conducted. Vladimir Ashkenazy was soloist. The combination worked, and such potentially
daunting works as Schoenberg's Variations for Orchestra and his
monodrama *Erwartung* for once got the audience they deserved.

But Richardson's programmes were riddled with twentieth-
century masterpieces. Tippett's third and fourth symphonies,
Ives's *Three Places in New England*, Britten's touching valedictory
cantata, *Phaedra*, with Janet Baker as soloist, and Gerhard's Concerto for Orchestra were all performed during this period. Musica
Nova continued to flourish. Elgar's First Symphony, hardly a

new work but undoubtedly a twentieth-century masterpiece and certainly a Gibson speciality, was taken to Brussels with financial support from the SNO Endowment Fund and won acclaim in the glorious acoustics of the art deco Palais des Beaux-Arts. An Ian Whyte composition award, in memory of the pioneering Scottish conductor, was instated through an anonymous donor. Scottish and Scottish-based composers were actively encouraged. The repertoire broadened. Iain Hamilton's *Circus* for two trumpets, Ronald Stevenson's Second Piano Concerto, Kenneth Leighton's *Sinfonia Mistica*, John McLeod's *Lieder der Jugend*, Lyell Cresswell's *Salm* and Edward Harper's First Symphony all saw the light of day; and a tone poem, *Aurora*, was commissioned from Hamilton to be performed, along with his Violin Concerto, in the course of the orchestra's first American tour. In terms of programming, this was certainly an advance on the debut European tour of 1967.

Musica Nova likewise increased its scope. No doubt Richardson's first cycle, in 1973, was at least partly planned by Ponsonby before he left. It was, at any rate, a notable achievement. Peter Heyworth, comparing it with London's treatment of contemporary music at that time, wrote in *The Observer* that 'in Glasgow they set about these things more purposefully'.

Praising Gibson's track record in performing twentieth-century works that really mattered, and mentioning in particular how Schoenberg's Violin Concerto received its first hearing on this island not in London but in Scotland, he wrote, 'That is what I call artistic direction and it is a pity there is not more evidence of it elsewhere.' The works that lured Heyworth and other English critics to Glasgow in 1973 were Peter Maxwell Davies's *Stone Litany*, Gyorgy Ligeti's Double Concerto for Flute and Oboe, Luciano Berio's *Still* and a new Scottish work, Martin Dalby's *The Tower of Victory*. An opening chamber concert served *antipasto*-sized portions of music by all four composers, and twenty composition students from all over Britain attended the now established seminars and discussions.

Though there were complaints about superficial debates and Scottish meanness with copies of the scores – though surely the publishers were to blame for this – the pattern for the future was now effectively established. Inevitably the young Martin Dalby's music lacked the distinction of the other works, yet his short tone poem inspired by a Malaysian legend showed real feeling for dark instrumental timbres, underpinned from time to time by the uncommon sound of a double-bass clarinet – an instrument that was to cause more trouble than it was reckoned to be worth when Brian Ferneyhough some years later demanded one for a Musica Nova commission.

If 1973 stuck in the memory, however, it was principally for Davies's Orkney-inspired *Stone Litany*, subtitled *Runes from a House of the Dead* and inspired by the ancient tomb, Maes Howe, which sprouts like a green carbuncle on the landscape between Stromness and Kirkwall. Though Davies had not yet acquired his clifftop eyrie near the Old Man of Hoy, where he now produces the bulk of his prodigious output, the work provided an early taste of the music he was going to write there.

Among the inscriptions within the tomb was one that particularly fired the composer's imagination: 'Max the Mighty carved these runes.' Davies, familiarly known as Max, employed these words in his piece, which was written for the arching voice of the American singer, Jan DeGaetani, and an orchestra which made fastidious use of the sound of wine glasses stroked with moist fingers and the vibrancy of a flexatone, a species of musical saw. At the heart of the work, however, was an ominous orchestral seascape of the sort that was to reappear to striking effect in many of his later scores. The picturesque side of *Stone Litany* led one Scottish critic to dismiss it as just another *Hebrides* overture, but he missed the point of this intricate and desolate score, which could have been the slow movement of one of the vast symphonies Davies had yet to write.

Later, in New York, Pierre Boulez was to conduct *Stone Litany*, and in 1978 Gibson and the SNO were to take it to the Warsaw Autumn Festival along with the Polish premiere of Tippett's Fourth Symphony and Panufnik's *Sinfonia Sacra* – Panufnik, born in Warsaw in 1914, had been *persona non grata* in his homeland after escaping from his Communist overlords and settling in England. The SNO's performance of his symphony, for which special permission had to be sought, was an emotional occasion.

But then the whole Warsaw experience, which was the orchestra's first step into what was then Communist Europe, was an emotional and often disturbing one. As critic of *The Scotsman*, I was allotted a room in the Hotel Bristol, which had been used by the Gestapo during the Second World War. On arrival I was shaken to encounter fierce lights and Nazis in uniform in the corridors. I had not, as I feared, entered a time warp. A film was being made, but the drabness of my slit of a bedroom, with its rumpled, faded curtains and rusty sink, made me think of the horrors that might once have gone on there and I fled to the impersonal comfort of the newly-opened Intercontinental Hotel, where the orchestra was staying and where a room was available. But it was Malcolm Rayment of *The Herald*, adrift in the Hotel Metropol, who cheered everybody up when he quoted the printed request he had found, written in English, in his room: 'Cigarettes fag put the end on the ash-tray'. Waiters serving early morning tea along with a perpetual demand for US dollars proved less amusing.

In most of my trips with the SNO, I have enjoyed exploring cities and chronicling my adventures. Warsaw was depressing. Eighty-five per cent of it had been destroyed between 1939 and 1944. The immaculately rebuilt Old Town, upon which much praise has been heaped, seemed the most depressing place of all, because one was inevitably aware of what lay beneath. Seeking consolation in a restaurant famous for its duck, I found the premises shut; their supplies of duck (in a city where, at the time, I could buy a score of Szymanowski's *King Roger* for a handful of zlotys but could not track down a tube of toothpaste) had not been delivered, and since they served nothing but duck they had been forced to send the staff home.

Yet caviar and icy Polish vodka in a restaurant on the outskirts, with Witold Lutoslawski as guest, proved that not everything was in short supply. Nor, to judge by the dandified Poles who dined in the Intercontinental each night, was everybody short of cash. For the players, however, the contradictions of Warsaw were upsetting. Tippett's Fourth Symphony, an exceedingly tough work to perform, was dismissed as old-fashioned by the musically progressive Poles. But Tomasz Sikorski's ugly *Music in Twilight*, which the composer himself conducted, seemed squalidly unrewarding in comparison with Tippett's ardent, finely clinched symphony. A concert in industrial Katowice, where the German tanks had first crossed the Polish border, did nothing to lift the orchestra's spirits (nor did hotel bedrooms that stank of urine). Only old-world Cracow, where Bruckner's Sixth Symphony was played with Krzysztof Penderecki in the audience, provided respite.

But the sense of release that should have come with the ensuing visit to Vienna failed to materialise. The bus journey through

Czechoslovakia, though no distance on the map, proved arduous. Brno, where Janáček had written some of his most ecstatic music, looked grim. The border stops were endurance tests. The third bus got lost, and had to be waited for. The orchestral committee, which looks after the players' interests, insisted after a tense en route meeting that the following morning's rehearsal be cancelled, even though it was for a crucial concert in the Musikverein, with Thea Musgrave's Horn Concerto as the key work. It was held in the afternoon instead, which caused fresh displeasure, as did the fact that the hotel, near the Palace of Schönbrunn, was far from the city centre. Nobody, in fact, was in the mood for Vienna, or found its almost obscenely lavish window displays of expensive consumer goods an acceptable alternative to the poverty of Poland. Yet the concert itself, even if it lacked the exhilaration of 1967, went well enough.

To give the impression that foreign touring had become just another disagreeable task would be misleading, however. True, today it is not much liked by orchestral musicians. A long series of one-night stands, with a meagre amount of time off, can seem more trouble than they are worth. But players do accept that touring can be good for prestige, so long as they are not exploited in the process, and so long as conditions – hotels, travel arrangements, timing of rehearsals – are satisfactory enough to make it seem worth the effort.

From that point of view, the first visit to Canada and the United States, three years before the Polish one, had been a milestone in the orchestra's history, a triumph for Richardson as administrator and the highpoint of Gibson's quarter century as musical director. Like the first European tour back in 1967, it had the virtue of an almost faultless itinerary that began in Toronto and culminated in New York and the newly-opened Kennedy Center in Washington.

Andrew Porter, by then writing for the *New Yorker* magazine, attended the penultimate concert. 'As a critic who prefers warmth of interpretation to brilliance of execution, who admires the Berlin Philharmonic but loves the Czech Philharmonic, who would rather hear deeply serious music conducted by Bernard Haitink than by Karajan,' he declared, 'I have long counted among my favourite orchestras the Scottish National, moulded by its conductor, Alexander Gibson, into an eloquent and poetic if not, by Chicago standards, virtuoso ensemble.' In Carnegie Hall, the performances of Elgar's *Enigma Variations* and Mendelssohn's *Hebrides* overture elated him, and Iain Hamilton's *Aurora*, a twelve-minute piece of neo-Ravel, progressing from darkness into light (or from nocturne into scherzo), was hailed as a strongly-made, gripping composition.

In Toronto, the orchestra played in Massey Hall, a handsome, broad, classical building that had been allowed to run down – though it was acoustically finer than the gross new Roy Thomson Hall, where the orchestra was to appear on its second visit to Canada, seven years later. In Ottawa, the recently-opened National Arts Centre – fruit of Canada's country-wide developments during a period of cultural prosperity – seemed just another multi-purpose auditorium, for all the splendour of its facilities. I flew from Prestwick to join the players the night they reached New York, and checked into the Barbizon Plaza Hotel, South Central Park, just ahead of them. It was plain, as they poured into the lobby, that the tour had been going well. Though the previous day's concert had been in a high school auditorium in Pennsylvania, they arrived like star performers; and in the warm glow of Carnegie Hall the following night – still some years before its fine acoustics were damaged by renovations – they played like stars.

Good relations between orchestra and administrator continued during the rest of the Richardson regime. No doubt, as an ex-player himself, he was felt by at least some of the players to be 'one of them'; but, since British orchestras are seldom satisfied with their bosses, this was not necessarily something for which he was appreciated. As one ex-member of the orchestra has put it to me, 'Robert Ponsonby, for all his faults, was always a figure-head. David Richardson did not command that sort of respect. His dealings tended mostly to be in private. He was never close to the orchestra.' Yet clearly he had the orchestra's interests at heart. Indeed, some of the concessions he is reported to have made during union negotiations were to cause disharmony later, during leaner, cost-cutting, more managerial and determinedly Thatcherist years.

Yet even over the sunny landscape of the nineteen-seventies a few clouds were gathering. Though the orchestra, in Richardson's words, was in a healthy state, with strong, clearly defined audience support, not all the players were of the quality he desired. Under the previous administration the size of the orchestra, complete with quadruple woodwind and as many as ten double basses, had been increased to an official strength of ninety-six – the largest

ever – as part of Gibson's drive to turn it into a giant Scottish
Vienna Philharmonic. But in Richardson's view, the appointments
had been 'sometimes unwise – there were players with too little
experience, and some of the newcomers were simply not good
enough'.

So, by the fashionable device of not filling vacancies, the
numbers were gradually reduced to ninety-one, a figure Richardson thought more realistic. But with the continued expansion of
Scottish Opera – which in 1975 gained the Theatre Royal, Glasgow, as its base and, for the first time, the opportunity for full-
length seasons – tension between the two organisations was rising,
not least because Gibson continued to be musical director of
both.

There were by now, says Richardson, 'burgeoning jealousies'
on account of the Theatre Royal. 'Peter Hemmings [who was still
Scottish Opera's administrator] and I had to discuss what would
happen to our schedules. Peter started talking of short seasons and
of interrupting our concert series. I balked at that, and told him
and Alex Gibson that it wouldn't work. I said to Peter that it
would probably be the parting of the ways, though financially it
was quite an attractive proposition. My recommendation in the
end was that we should give notice to Scottish Opera that we
would stop playing for them.'

It was a tense time, and there was no doubt that eventually it
began to corrode the previously good relationship between
Richardson and Gibson. But not quite yet. Audiences continued
to expand. Stars continued to perform. Artur Rubinstein, at the
age of eighty-seven, played piano concertos by Chopin and Saint-
Saëns in a single concert. A year later he returned to play Beethoven and Grieg. On each occasion he held his hands aloft, with
a champion's gesture, to show that they were still supple. But the
sparkling first notes of the Saint-Saëns proved it anyway.

The summer proms, at one of which Gibson's conducting of
Mahler's Eighth Symphony was televised by STV, had by now
extended from Glasgow to Edinburgh, Aberdeen and Dundee.
Danny Newman, an endearingly eager American marketing man,
had been hired to revamp the annual programme brochure – previously a model of staidness and clarity – and, in Richardson's
words, 'beef up the subscriptions'. Gibson, as a result, was advertised as 'charismatic'. Hype ruled, clarity dwindled, but the
number of subscribers trebled. 'You did it again Glasgow',

trumpeted Danny's next brochure. 'More than 90 per cent of all seats were sold last season.'

There was expansion in other ways, too, because – for those who remember it – that was what life was like before Thatcherism began to grind down the arts. Cottage industries developed within the orchestra. Back in the nineteen-sixties, Sam Bor had set a precedent by forming a string quartet for occasional concerts featuring his wife, Dorothie, as second violin, and other members of the string section as viola and cello. But by 1973 there was a bigger, more ostentatious and, as some saw it, potentially more threatening development when Adrian Shepherd, the orchestra's principal cellist, created Cantilena, a conductorless chamber ensemble carved mostly from the SNO's strings and powered by Shepherd himself from the cello desk.

Having rehearsed privately for months, the group made a scintillating debut and proceeded to mount its own daytime concert series in Glasgow and Edinburgh, not entirely without opposition from the management, who regarded Cantilena as an asset to the orchestra only so long as it in no way interfered with concert schedules or with audience support for the orchestra itself. Cantilena's trump card and main self-justification, however, was simply its excellence. Interference with its activities would have seemed jealous and petty. Its repertoire skilfully mixed baroque and renaissance music for strings with forays into Haydn and Arne. It was one of the first British ensembles to recognise the catchiness of Pachelbel's now overexposed Canon.

Sonority, rather than style, was its priority. The players, sitting in a circle and gazing into each other's eyes, clearly savoured the rich sounds and textures that could be produced from a handful of strings, with occasional woodwind soloists to provide variety of timbre, and they communicated their keen enjoyment to their listeners. They did not play baroque instruments, and they were not the virtuoso 'authentic' ensemble Scotland still badly needs, but what they did they did conspicuously well. The quality of the recordings they made for Chandos rivalled those by the SNO itself. But the good times did not last. Money grew tighter and in the nineteen-eighties, after Gibson left the SNO, Shepherd fell out with Neeme Järvi, the conductor who succeeded him. People muttered in a Scottish way about chickens coming home to roost. Cantilena gradually showed signs of crumbling and, though Shepherd occasionally re-galvanises it from his new abode in

Sussex, it is no longer quite the exciting presence in Glasgow's and Edinburgh's concert life that it once was.

But other splinter groups surfaced and stayed the course. Sam Bor, who had retired as leader at the end of 1974, was briefly succeeded by Michael G. Davis from America (the middle initial differentiated him from the other Michael Davies, who has led various English orchestras) and then by Edwin Paling, who had served as assistant and associate leader before reaching the top rank at the age of twenty-six. Paling, a member of Cantilena, pursued his enthusiasm for chamber music in other groups also, including his own Allander Ensemble and a violin and piano duo he formed with his wife.

Chorally, too, there was expansion. In 1978 a much-needed SNO Junior Chorus was formed by Jean Kidd, music teacher at Bellahouston Academy, who recruited 150 pupils from schools in and around Glasgow and trained them to the level required by Britten's *Spring Symphony* and Mahler's Eighth, in both of which they sang at the Edinburgh Festival. As for the parent SNO Chorus, which had been gaining fresh strength and a new sense of purpose since ceasing to be the Glasgow Choral Union, it seemed intent on rivalling the SNO itself in the scope and ambition of its various foreign tours, the first it had ever undertaken, on which it embarked quite separately from the orchestra. With John Currie as the most visionary of chorusmasters, it raised through its own ingenuity the £16,000 it needed to visit Israel in 1972, and similarly financed its own trips to the United States in 1976 and 1980.

The singers, being enthusiastic amateurs, were prepared to rough it in a way that touchy professional orchestral musicians would not. And Israel at times was rough. Though I myself was allotted the semi-privacy of a small hotel in Tel Aviv, sharing a cramped, airless room with a fellow critic, the almost two hundred singers slept for ten nights in dormitories on the outskirts of town. While tummy bugs attacked without mercy, the chorus rehearsed in the summer heat for the startlingly doomladen, Mahlerlike performances of Brahms's German Requiem they were to give with the Israel Philharmonic under Daniel Barenboim in Jerusalem and Tel Aviv.

The same composer's *Song of Destiny* under a temporarily bearded Zubin Mehta (whose father, Mehli Mehta, had been a violinist in the SNO in Karl Rankl's day) drained less of the chorus's energy, though the gift of Scotch whisky with which they presented him in gratitude proved inapt: Mehta, as they discovered, does not drink.

There were also two lighter-weight concerts under Gary Bertini, the Israeli conductor who had helped to set up the tour and under whom the chorus had worked productively in Scotland. There was a recording session in a tiny Tel Aviv cinema where Currie led his singers into the dangerous waters of Handel's *Israel in Egypt*. And there was time off to visit the Sea of Galilee, climb Masada, have lunch in Sodom, and to hear Mehta conduct opera one sultry night in the open air at Caesarea. It was a lot more relaxed than an orchestral tour, and a lot more fun.

So, too, was the American Bicentennial tour in 1980, during which the singers again encountered Mehta, this time under the night sky at Hollywood Bowl, where they joined the Los Angeles Philharmonic in Beethoven's Ninth Symphony. Alexander Gibson flew from Glasgow to conduct one of his party pieces, Walton's *Belshazzar's Feast*, along with Bach's *Sleepers Awake* cantata (strange choice for Hollywood Bowl, strange choice for Gibson) and, more relevantly, a choral piece by Charles Ives.

Though Hollywood Boulevard was a sleazy disappointment, the Bowl was a fascinating piece of open-plan grandiosity, where Danny Kaye was apt to drop in during the morning to see who was rehearsing. Finding the SNO Chorus in full cry, he was invited to try his hand as conductor – and inimitably did so, to everyone's delight. In Hollywood, however, the real conductor was Ernest Fleischmann, the Los Angeles Philharmonic's Orson Wellesian administrator, who clearly saw himself as boss of the Bowl, verbally correcting Mehta's balancing of the chorus from his own control point, complete with loudspeakers, and reminding Gibson that, in these outsize surroundings, quick tempi in Bach were preferable to slow. Gibson, whatever his secret feelings on the matter, obeyed.

Two days later, having flown over a very visible Grand Canyon, the singers had two more open-air performances, this time at the Mississippi River Festival, outside St Louis, where Gibson conducted Haydn's *Creation* and Verdi's Requiem. Good orchestras – this time the St Louis Symphony, over which a former SNO conductor, Walter Susskind, had presided – were a feature of the tour. Later came performances of Beethoven's Ninth Symphony with Barenboim in Philadelphia, Mahler's Eighth

Symphony with Erich Leinsdorf in Cleveland, and another *Belshazzar*, this time with André Previn and the Chicago Symphony Orchestra. Currie himself, whose coaching of his singers in their strenuous repertoire earned high praise, seized the opportunity to conduct a concert of unaccompanied choral music at St Bartholomew's Church during a brief stopover in New York.

Ernest Fleischmann, who had been hugely impressed with the singing in Hollywood Bowl, was the trigger – and ultimately the saviour – of the next American trip, which was planned to start with a series of concerts in Cleveland before culminating in Hollywood, this time with Carlo Maria Giulini conducting Verdi's *Four Sacred Pieces*. But as the aircraft soared from Prestwick, Currie stood in the aisle and through a loudspeaker said in sombre tones, 'I have a disastrous announcement to make.'

With Goat Fell below, everybody feared the worst. But what Currie divulged was that the Cleveland Orchestra was on strike and that the concerts there had been cancelled. As a result the singers would be stuck in the Holiday Inn for several nights with nothing to do, until their next charter flight whisked them to Los Angeles. Psychologically, Currie's timing – whether intentionally or otherwise – was immaculate. Instead of reacting with outrage that their savings and precious holiday time would be squandered on a city in which they were no longer performing, they were relieved to learn that there was nothing wrong with the aircraft.

Thereafter, I sent daily reports of 165 choristers adrift in America, for there was no lack of news. Outside the Holiday Inn, two choristers narrowly escaped a mugging. Elsewhere, another chorister was threatened at gunpoint but clung to her handbag and fought off her assailant. In the end, however, it was Ernest Fleischmann, two thousand miles away, who came to the rescue and invited the chorus to fly immediately to Hollywood and he would find extra work for them. The work – mostly church concerts in and around Los Angeles – was admittedly nothing thrilling, but it was better than killing time (or being killed) in Cleveland.

In Hollywood, however, the assaults and near-assaults continued. The summer of 1980 was a bad time for choristers, but Giulini, as everybody agreed, made it all worthwhile, and even Martin Bernheimer, the sardonic music critic of the *Los Angeles Times*, seemed happy with the singing.

Whatever the occasional mishaps, the chorus's three big foreign

tours symbolised what was, on the whole, a carefree period in
SNO history. In the autumn of 1976 the third Musica Nova cycle
was as successful as its predecessors. This time the featured
composers were Harrison Birtwistle, David Dorward, Morton
Feldman and George Newsom, who at the time was occupying
Glasgow University's recently-created post of composer-in-
residence (Martin Dalby and Hugh Wood were others who filled
this role). Two other composers, Krzysztof Penderecki and Iain
Hamilton, were peripherally featured in a programme by the SNO
Chorus in Glasgow Cathedral, where the Polish composer conducted his own Magnificat and the Scottish one heard his own
Epitaph for This World and Time.

Of the new works, it was Birtwistle's *Melencolia 1* which
instantly stood out as something special. The title, with its booby-
trap spelling, was that of a Dürer engraving. The slow, mesmeris-
ing progress of the music was similar to that of *The Triumph of
Time*, in which Brueghel's allegorical painting of that title was
the source of Birtwistle's inspiration. But now, instead of a full
symphony orchestra, he required a quieter, quirkier line-up of
solo clarinet, harp and two sets of strings. The pace of the thirty-
minute piece was slow to the point of stagnancy; yet as a musical
'landscape' its effect never slackened. Gibson and his players, who
sustained it to perfection, later took it to the London proms and
rightly included it among the works performed at the Warsaw
Autumn Festival.

With two successful Musica Nova cycles to his credit, Richardson presented one more before departing in 1980 to America. Of
all the SNO's administrators, he was the one most faithful to the
cause of contemporary music, which he continued to champion
during the winter season as well as in the more arcane environment
of Musica Nova. Earlier – a risk none of his successors would
have dared to take – he had got Michael Tippett to conduct his
own Third Symphony at the 1974 Glasgow proms, and to return
the following season with *A Child of Our Time*. Heinz Holliger
appeared as solo oboist in his own *Siebengesang*. Krzysztof Penderecki conducted his Stabat Mater and other works.

Local composers were likewise encouraged. Ronald Stevenson's
Second Piano Concerto – in the composer's own unguarded words
'a trek through the musics of the continents, with all the struggle
of a piano pitted against an orchestra' – was featured in the Last
Night of the Proms, with the composer as soloist. 'It felt', as one

critic put it, 'rather like the Magic World Tour at Battersea Fun Fair, where a gaudy wooden boat bumps along a tiny canal through dimly lit, crudely painted scenes with cardboard props . . . Occasionally Mr Stevenson tucked his elbows under the piano lid, and once came out with a little glissando immediately echoed by harp; and that was pretty.'

A *Sinfonia Mistica* by Kenneth Leighton, Edinburgh University's professor of music, in memory of his mother, was not at all gaudy but characteristically sombre and self-tortured. Edward Harper, another member of Edinburgh University's music staff, wrote a First Symphony inspired (in a very abstract sort of way) by Elgar's Edwardian First Symphony, and dedicated it to Alexander Gibson, who conducted it. Lyell Cresswell, a Scottish-based New Zealander, won the Ian Whyte award with *Salm*, a work sonorously rooted in the psalm music of its idiosyncratically-spelt title. John McLeod, an industrious Edinburgh composer, conducted an orchestral version of his Mahler-inspired *Lieder der Jugend*, and John Currie, whose *String of Scottish Songs* (complete with an Alexander Gibson Reel) had been an asset to the Last Night of the Proms, produced a set of *Christmas Scenes*, with audience participation, to bring new zest to the orchestra's somewhat staid annual carol concert.

In promoting these works, the SNO recognised – in a way it subsequently ceased to do – the need to cultivate its own garden. Not all, perhaps indeed none, of them were music of international status; but all were worth doing by an orchestra calling itself the SNO. So, too, though in a different context, was Thea Musgrave's Clarinet Concerto, a work of real international stature, which brought musical distinction to an International Gathering of the Clans in Edinburgh in 1977, though the audience would doubtless have preferred a bagpipe concerto.

Richardson's third (and the orchestra's fourth) Musica Nova cycle, in the autumn of 1979, featured a further four composers, this time the potentially daunting Brian Ferneyhough from England via the Continent, Thomas Wilson from Glasgow, Robin Holloway from Cambridge and, from Switzerland, the exotically-named Tona Scherchen-Hsiao, daughter of the vanguard German conductor, Hermann Scherchen, and of the Chinese composer Hsiao Shu-sien.

On paper it looked a cleverly balanced quartet. In 1976, Peter Heyworth of *The Observer* had asked, rhetorically, 'Who is Brian

Ferneyhough?', and indeed at that time few people knew. Born in Coventry in 1943, he had been hailed by a Venetian critic as 'one of the great visionaries of our time'. Heyworth himself hailed him as an all-or-nothing man who 'makes enormous, even preposterous, demands of executants and listeners alike'. The SNO was soon to be made aware of the enormous and, as the players considered, preposterous demands of *La Terre est un Homme*, Ferneyhough's Musica Nova commission, which Alexander Gibson astutely passed on to Elgar Howarth to conduct.

Howarth, a Staffordshire-born trumpeter who had appeared with the SNO as soloist in Iain Hamilton's *Circus*, and later in the same concert had performed, with Philip Jones, the often omitted cornet parts in Debussy's *La Mer*, had recently taken up a new career as conductor and was soon to achieve international fame by giving the premiere of Ligeti's surrealist opera, *Le Grand Macabre*, in Stockholm. The dense textures and vast pile-up of instruments in Ferneyhough's *La Terre est un Homme* were an unrivalled preparation for anything that might befall him later.

For Peter Heyworth, Ferneyhough's music deluged the ear with a sea of sound. But on rehearing it, he claimed, one became aware of 'emergent shapes, and long sections that moved with a strong sense of consistent if complex purpose'. Players, engulfed by the deluge, found the sense of purpose harder to detect. So thick was the scoring that the composer's demands for the services of a double bass clarinet, at a moment of infinite complexity, were deemed an act of gilding the lily. Since the double bass clarinettist who had been hired to take part in Martin Dalby's *Tower of Victory* in a previous Musica Nova cycle proved unavailable this time, it was decided to omit a piece of instrumental colouring which, it was felt, would go unnoticed by everybody in the audience.

Everybody, that is, except the composer. Ferneyhough, on hearing that his music was to be vandalised, took a huff and walked out, and the performance was given without his blessing. It was as close as Musica Nova had steered to a scandal, and it made the good Scottish sense of Wilson's Third Symphony, the virtuosity of Holloway's Second Concerto for Orchestra and the delicate Takemitsu-like timbres of Scherchen-Hsiao's *L'invitation au voyage* (the composer, an authority on the p'i p'a, or Chinese lute, caused relief by not requesting its use in her piece) seem comparatively undemanding.

For Musica Nova, however, it marked a turning-point. The

performances, for the first time, took place in the small-scale surroundings of Trinity Church, Claremont Street, which had
recently been converted into rehearsal premises for the orchestra
and renamed the Henry Wood Hall and SNO Centre. Ironically
close to the old St Andrew's Hall, it had been built in 1863 but
was no longer used as a place of worship. With a modest amount
of ingenuity, the main body of the church could be converted into
an auditorium with recording facilities and room for an audience
of 350. Elsewhere in the building there was space for the orchestral
library, an instrument store, changing rooms and a staff canteen
to which the public could be given access. The price of all this
was to be £550,000, but grants from the Scottish Arts Council,
Scottish Television and the English-based Henry Wood Trust,
though they by no means covered the cost, helped the project to
go ahead.

At the opening ceremony, attended by Princess Margaret, the
SNO's latest chairman, Lord Polwarth, disclosed what the new
premises would mean. Until then, he said, the players had been
'literally wandering minstrels, traipsing around from one hall to
another'. But now at last their dream had come true. 'The players
have a home of their own.'

Well, not quite. What they had was a smart, albeit still churchy,
rehearsal hall with acoustics that would simply clutter the sound
of music such as Ferneyhough's *La Terre est un Homme*. As a
concert space it had severe limitations, and the decision to raise
money by hiring it out to other organisations, such as the BBC
Scottish Symphony Orchestra and the John Currie Singers, did
not necessarily do these groups a service.

As a recording studio, too, it had its shortcomings, as was
confirmed when the SNO later switched to the City Hall, Glasgow, and the Caird Hall, Dundee. But at least the SNO's offices,
which David Richardson had transferred from Hope Street to
airier rooms in LaBelle Place, were by 1990 skilfully rehoused in
brand-new premises tacked on to the back of the SNO Centre. In
this sense, at least, the orchestra at last had a home of sorts, though
why the city's long-awaited Royal Concert Hall, built in a flush
of civic pride in celebration of Glasgow 1990, did not become the
orchestra's true and deserved home is a question that will be raised
in a later chapter.

11

A New Administrator, A New Conductor

I n 1980, having run the orchestra for as long as Robert Ponsonby, David Richardson decided it was time to go. Peter Hemmings had already forsaken Scottish Opera for the Australian Opera in Sydney, and Peter Diamand's peaceful thirteen-year reign over the Edinburgh Festival had given way in 1979 to the high-profile abrasiveness of John Drummond. There was change in the air, but Alexander Gibson remained impervious to it, always finding – as he himself put it – something new that was worth doing in Scotland and that would retain him in his homeland, whatever the opportunities to conduct abroad.

The fact that Richardson's move to Minnesota, like Hemmings's to Sydney, was to end in tears no doubt convinced Gibson that he had done the right thing. But the climate of the nineteen-eighties in Scotland was to prove very different from that of the seventies. Under a succession of administrators, Scottish Opera was lurching between artistic crisis and financial crisis, its golden years a thing of the past. Gibson, less securely in control of the situation than he had been, seemed to lose some of his old momentum. Though there were things that were worth doing, Scottish Opera's dreadful *Turandot* and *Oberon*, artistic disasters that Gibson would at one time have averted, were not among them.

As Richardson's successor, Fiona Grant could at least claim to have inherited an orchestra in better shape than that. What she could not say – as Ponsonby and Richardson had been able to say – was that she had the scope to do almost anything she liked. Orchestral finance now took precedence over artistic decisions in a way it had never done before. As John Drummond was also finding in Edinburgh, the energy that used to be spent on genuine artistic direction now had to be devoted to tiresome things like fund-raising and finding sponsors.

This was what the Thatcher government had done to the arts, but Fiona Grant already had considerable experience in coping with it. Her credentials, indeed, looked excellent. For a start she was a Scot, the first since the nineteen-forties to be in charge of the orchestra. She had been, in a small way, a cellist and pianist, but more to the point was the fact that she had gained a post-graduate diploma in social administration at the London School of Economics, had worked for the British Council, had been Peter Diamand's personal assistant for six years, and (like Richardson before her and Christopher Bishop after her) had links with the Philharmonia Orchestra in London, for which she worked as assistant general manager and administrator. Moreover, as the daughter of a judge, the late Lord Grant, and with a parental home in Moray Place, poshest of Robert Louis Stevenson's 'draughty parallelograms' in Edinburgh's eighteenth-century New Town, she was of impeccable background.

But she was also a woman, the first ever to run a major British symphony orchestra. True, it was a less macho orchestra than it once had been, and only two out of every three players were nowadays men, but how would she cope? The question preoccupied at least one member of the panel who interviewed her for the job. When it came to entertaining performers, she was asked by a retired Glasgow professor who had been appointed to the board of directors, how would she deal with paying the dinner bill for Alfred Brendel?

Having replied satisfactorily, she was then asked whether she proposed to live in Edinburgh. This was a stock Glasgow question, which Robert Ponsonby – someone else with doubtful Edinburgh connections – had encountered sixteen years before. She said she planned to live in Glasgow. It was the right answer. She got the job.

To start with, all went well. True, she played safe in her programme planning and she played safe with the proms, but, as she put it when I visited her during my tour of the orchestra's former administrators in 1992, it was 'immensely rewarding to work with an orchestra that served its public in the way the SNO traditionally did – so different from the London scene where the orchestras are all desperately trying to create for themselves a particular image and audience, but can't succeed because there is so much going on'. The anonymous London relationship between orchestra and audience was something she remembered as being deeply frustrating, whereas the feeling of real personal commitment she found among Scottish audiences was rewarding and challenging. 'To be stopped in the middle of the Great Western Road in Glasgow and to be told by someone how enjoyable the previous night's concert had been was for me a novel experience.'

Yet to imply that she accepted things as they were, and was unprepared to take risks, would be to give a false impression of this astute and quietly determined young administrator. The orchestra, she was convinced, needed an injection of adrenalin, and when Gibson – who had by then received his knighthood along with a variety of other awards – announced after much self-debate that he would celebrate his twenty-fifth season with the orchestra by signing off, she was ready to capitalise on his decision by seeking a conductor of wholly different mould. Whether she was right or wrong to do so, only history will decide. But, in the short term – and, as things turned out, it was a very short term – the appointment of Neeme Järvi as Gibson's successor was as radical a choice as she could possibly have made.

Gibson, meanwhile, still had two years of his contract to run. Though his resignation came as a surprise – he informed the players of his decision while they were rehearsing at the SNO Centre with a guest conductor, Kurt Sanderling – it was obviously no hasty act. At the time of Richardson's departure, instinct must have told him that it was time for him to go, too. He had done more for music in Scotland than anyone else in history, and he had sacrificed an international career in order to do so. He had steered the SNO through a period of extraordinary development. He had taken it on its first trans-European and first North American tours, had established it as a recording orchestra, had extended its repertoire beyond recognition. He had founded Scottish Opera and, with Peter Hemmings, had given it an opera house (the converted Theatre Royal) to perform in, bringing it to the point where it was ready for the next chapter in its progress.

Having devoted so much of his life to the SNO and Scottish Opera, it must have been tempting to devote the rest of his life to it. That, after all, was what Barbirolli had done with the Hallé Orchestra, which he was still conducting at the time of his death in 1970. Gibson was not only one of Barbirolli's greatest admirers, but had been encouraged by him to keep concentrating on the

SNO at a time when he could have gone elsewhere. Was it a coincidence, therefore, that when he bade farewell to the SNO he chose Elgar, Barbirolli's favourite composer, as the theme of his twenty-fifth and final season?

Elgar had long been a Gibson favourite, too, of course. Where other conductors stuck to the *Enigma Variations* and a handful of shorter works, Gibson had been fanatical about the two symphonies even when their supposedly vainglorious posturing was still considered to represent the unacceptable face of the composer. Gibson knew – as Barbirolli also did, though in an entirely different way – that that was not what the music was really about. He understood, as he still does, the composer's black moods, the unease behind the pageantry, and what has been correctly called the poignant sense of lost happiness, upon which the emotional impact of all the major works depends. His feeling for *The Dream of Gerontius* once brought him close to persuading Peter Diamand to let him open the Edinburgh Festival with it. But though, perhaps inevitably, he failed in that ambition, he later recorded *The Dream* with the SNO and SNO Chorus, and with Robert Tear, Benjamin Luxon and the much missed Alfreda Hodgson as soloists, in a way that revealed the skull beneath the skin of that profoundly disturbing score.

In lighter yet still serious vein, it had been entirely characteristic of him to announce that he would conduct *Land of Hope and Glory* on the last night of the SNO proms in the year that his old rival, Colin Davis, proposed dropping it from the London ones. That Elgar himself had confused feelings about the piece was entirely in keeping with his complex personality. But Gibson knew that the last night required that particular ritual, whether in England or in Scotland; he also knew it to be, in Elgar's own words, music that would 'knock 'em flat'.

But if Elgar was to be the composer with whom Gibson signed off, he meanwhile had two more seasons before doing so, and some would say they were two seasons too many. The relationship between a conductor and an orchestra has often been compared with marriage. The honeymoon period, when neither conductor nor players can do anything wrong, may lead to a long and comfortable partnership but may equally well cool into contempt and hatred. The most famous of all partnerships, Karajan's with the Berlin Philharmonic, ended in disenchantment, likewise Haitink's with the Concertgebouw and, more predictably

124 PLAYING FOR SCOTLAND

perhaps, Previn's with the LSO. If Gibson's with the SNO did not degenerate into marital mayhem, it was nevertheless perhaps a mistake to announce the separation then go on living in the house for another two years.

The coda of Gibson's quarter century with the orchestra was unpredictable in its progress. A vast tour of the British Isles, sponsored by General Accident Assurance in 1981 and connected with a new recording of Mahler's Fourth Symphony, was an undoubted success. Of the performance of that work in Perth City Hall, Malcolm Rayment of *The Herald* said that he could not imagine hearing it better done. But in spite of the presence of the wonderful Witold Lutoslawski, or because of the presence of Milton Babbitt, Musica Nova that autumn proved more indigestible than usual, and the orchestra's second major North American tour, a year later, lacked the impact of the first.

On paper it had looked promising. An itinerary including Philadelphia, Chicago, Ottawa, Toronto, Washington, New York and the World Fair at Knoxville, Tennessee, smacked of assiduous planning. But when, chronicling part of the tour as usual for *The Scotsman*, I joined the orchestra in Chicago, I detected tension in the air. Perhaps, I thought, it was because the Chicago Symphony Orchestra was on strike and its hall might not be available to the SNO that night. But the threat was lifted, the concert took place, and Gibson's conducting of Sibelius had all its old aplomb.

Then the orchestra headed into the Deep South and I, opting out of that section of the tour, rejoined it some days later in Canada. The mood, once again, seemed prickly. Mahler's Fourth Symphony in Ottawa's National Arts Centre failed to please the local critic, who claimed that the SNO had deteriorated since he had last heard it, five years before. Sibelius's Fifth Symphony, in Toronto's gleaming new Roy Thomson Hall, went better – so much so that people started applauding before the last of the work's six crashing but widely detached final chords had struck home. Gibson, who had reason to feel cross, instead complimented the audience on the quality of the auditorium, adding that he and the orchestra would like to take it back to Glasgow with them, 'lock, stock and barrel'. (In fact its acoustics were to prove as tricky, and as clinically cold, as those of any other modern hall, and were one reason for Andrew Davis's resignation from the conductorship of the Toronto Symphony Orchestra a year or two later).

In a packed Carnegie Hall, on the last night of the tour, emotion ran high. Gibson, visibly moved, conducted Sibelius's Second Symphony as if he knew from note to note that this would be his last New York appearance with the orchestra whose musical director he had been for so long. The fact that the soloist, the octogenarian Claudio Arrau, was now too old and frail to articulate the great chords of Brahms's D minor Piano Concerto – a work he had performed with Gibson more than once before – undoubtedly added to the tension of the occasion.

But there was more to it than that, though it was not until I talked to Fiona Grant in London ten years later that I realised how potentially incendiary these fifteen transatlantic days – by courtesy of a subsidy of £125,000 from General Accident – had been. In retrospect, she says, it marked a turning-point in her relationship with the players – even though her great coup, the appointment of Neeme Järvi as Gibson's successor, still lay ahead.

Shepherding a symphony orchestra on foreign tour is a hazardous undertaking, and many are the tales that come back about members of London orchestras falling through windows, losing their flight tickets and behaving like hyperactive children. No doubt many of these are exaggerated by aghast managers, yet it is true that the tension of a series of one-night stands in a foreign land does lead regularly to a sense of post-concert release that can take many forms.

With an early departure next morning, and a rehearsal soon after arrival in the next town, seasoned orchestral players know that they have only a short time each day to relax and enjoy themselves. They may go to bed and read a book. They may, in groups, go out for a late-night supper or booze-up during which grievances get aired. As John Boyden, a former managing director of the London Symphony Orchestra, put it to *The Guardian* in a now notorious interview during a one-hour stopover in Alaska on the way back from Japan, 'A lot of orchestral players will complain about everything and anything in a quite indiscriminate fashion. When people are working under pressure they naturally attack something: they get frustrated and attack what they consider to be the organisation or lack of it. This is one of the things I have grown to accept, it just washes off my back because complaints are always – well, let's say ninety per cent of the time – unnecessary and based on ignorance.'

Boyden, though his contract still had a long way to run, left the LSO a few days later. His comments had undoubtedly been tactless, but they referred to situations which, with the SNO seven years later, Fiona Grant also encountered. Being thinner skinned, she found that they did not wash off her back. By 1992, long after her resignation, they were still sticking there.

The SNO she took to America in 1982 was not, or only partly, the orchestra Ponsonby had taken round Europe in 1967. Though some of the old hands remained, it was in general a younger, more acerbic orchestra, less willing to accept the status quo or to look on touring as being in any sense a perk. Traditional differences between players and management are more likely to be exposed than resolved at such a time. Even Ponsonby, though generally respected by the players, was repaid for what was perceived by some to be his haughtiness when it was discovered that he spoke German less fluently than a number of members of the orchestra. 'There were times on that tour', one former player recently told me, 'when we could have helped him out but we didn't. We felt we didn't owe him anything. He had sometimes been extremely unhelpful to us. So we took a certain relish in watching him shoot himself in the foot.'

For Fiona Grant, the American tour was quite simply 'a nightmare'. As she put it to me: 'It wasn't that I lacked experience. I had done twenty-five tours with the Philharmonia Orchestra. Touring was my big thing. But I was totally put off by the attitude of the SNO. I said I was not prepared to tour with them under these circumstances ever again. I'll never forget the pettiness of it all. They wanted a bed and breakfast allowance simply for sitting on a plane, and a meal allowance even although they were served an in-flight meal. Then, they had to be paid according to how many hours they had sat in a bus. I've never known such unpleasant negotiations. We were in America for three weeks, with important concerts from beginning to end. But just because I flew back to Britain at one point to do some business, I was asked when I rejoined them if I'd enjoyed my holiday. It was all far more hassle than it was worth.'

Yet should there not be some compensating factor, financial or otherwise, for being away from home for so long, for the exhausting schedules and the fact that a foreign tour, which requires adjusting to different acoustics every night, can fracture any player's nerves? Flying across the Atlantic, doctors say, can alter the ear-drums for days at a time. Even a commuter flight can have such an effect, and swallowing aspirin can temporarily cut response to high frequencies. But no orchestral schedules make allowances for this. A day without a concert is a day wasted, and performances sometimes begin within an hour or so of arrival at an airport. When the New York Philharmonic performed at the Edinburgh Festival in the nineteen-fifties it came by sea and played only in Edinburgh. Humane touring of that sort would today be prohibitively expensive.

Fiona Grant's touring criteria, she says, were based on what she considered to be satisfactory and long-established London practices. These, admittedly, may not have worked particularly well for John Boyden and the LSO, but they had worked for her with the Philharmonia. 'We simply sat down and looked at the figures and said, "Shall we go or shan't we?"'

The SNO, in her opinion, simply failed to grasp the reality of touring. 'They did not understand that they could not make the same demands abroad as the Philharmonia or the LSO, both of which had invested heavily in touring over the years, in a way that the SNO had not. Their attitude was blinkered. They were like children.'

But if she saw her players as children, they for their part saw her as an irksome, non-comprehending head prefect whose authority had to be challenged. It was not a happy relationship. Indeed, she says, 'it was so strange that perhaps, as I now sometimes think, I didn't deal with it very well. From the very beginning I was disturbed by the lack of communication between players and management. I just hoped that truth and honesty would prevail. But it was difficult on every level. Every time I made a suggestion to the office staff, I was told that it had been tried twenty-five years ago and that it hadn't worked. I got tired of bickering. I got tired full-stop.'

What kept her going for three years beyond the American fracas was undoubtedly the pursuit of Neeme Järvi – a splendid piece of big game for any hunter to bag – and her final netting of him in Birmingham, where he had been acting as Simon Rattle's principal guest conductor in the same way as, in Scotland, Paavo Berglund was acting as Alexander Gibson's.

As soon as Gibson announced his intention to leave, speculation became rife about a successor. With two players – a flautist and a hornist – now on the board of directors, the orchestra had more say in the matter than formerly. But in any case, with good democratic integrity, Fiona Grant canvassed all the players to discover their views.

Though there were ample possibilities, the field soon narrowed. The left-handed Berglund was deemed too Finnish, with an unpredictable nordic temperament, a reputedly mean temper and a repertoire that was, in any case, too akin to Gibson's. Gary Bertini, a previous guest conductor with a good track record, had talked too much at rehearsal and was, so far as the orchestra was concerned, one of yesterday's men. James Loughran, on the brink of severing his links with the Hallé Orchestra, might be OK if another Scot was thought desirable. Kurt Sanderling, who had been making some impressive guest appearances, was worth considering in the short term, but was felt to be over-critical, too humourlessly Teutonic and, being already in his seventies, arguably too old. David Atherton, who had broken away from the London Sinfonietta to conduct larger orchestras in a more romantic repertoire, was another contender, but was considered too cold. Andrew Davis, who had worked as one of the BBC Scottish Symphony Orchestra's astounding chain of gifted assistant conductors (Alexander Gibson, Colin Davis and Simon Rattle were others), might be tempted back to Scotland from his state of disillusionment in Canada, but had appeared seldom with the SNO and was something of an unknown quantity.

The one name, as Fiona Grant noted, which kept recurring was that of Neeme Järvi, the maverick Estonian who had first conducted the orchestra back in the nineteen-sixties and had made some inspiring reappearances. Would he be available? The two players who were members of the board thought she should find out.

'We put her in a cleft stick', one of them recently said to me. 'She had to be seen by the Scottish Arts Council to be making a rational appointment and doing things in the right way. But she couldn't afford to delay. She knew that she had to snap him up. We kept our fingers crossed.'

So feelers were discreetly extended. 'I remember flying down to Birmingham to talk to him,' Grant recalls. 'He seemed very surprised, but reacted positively. The next stage was to meet him and his agent [the mysterious and secretive American, Ronald Wilford, president of Columbia Artists Management] together in Amsterdam, where Järvi was conducting the Concertgebouw. We agreed on a contract. It was remarkably painless.'

In fact the SNO nabbed Järvi at just the right moment. A month earlier, or a month later, and the deal might have been off. A pupil of Mravinsky in Leningrad, he was then in his middle forties and had just broken free from the Soviet Union, where, in retribution, his name had been stripped from all the recordings he had made. Even before his appointment, his bond with the SNO had been immediate. The main, perhaps the only, condition he now laid down was that he wanted to record.

'Record, record, record' soon became his catchphrase. If there was a psychological reason for this frenzied desire to make discs, and to regard them as more important than public concerts, it surely lay in his Soviet background and the loss, when he left, of everything he had previously achieved. Well, not quite everything. There was still his musical experience. His conducting technique was brilliant. The young British conductor, Sian Edwards, who encountered him in Leningrad, is reported to have asked him how he learnt it. His reply: 'I practise five hours a day, with an orchestra or in front of a mirror.'

When I first interviewed him in Birmingham, just after his SNO appointment had been announced, he was recovering from a performance of Mahler's Third Symphony he had conducted with the City of Birmingham Symphony Orchestra the previous night, with Simon Rattle in the audience. It had not gone well, and he openly admitted that more rehearsal time had been spent on the vast first movement ('a structural failure' in Deryck Cooke's controversial opinion) than on the rest of the work. The first movement had, indeed, been wonderful, and so utterly convincing that the uncertainty of the rest of the performance had been doubly disappointing.

So willing was Järvi to admit the fact, so seemingly lacking in the usual sort of conductorial vanity, that one warmed to him at once. We turned to more general matters and he explained to me, in ropy English, how to conduct the opening of Strauss's *Don Juan*. His words were barely comprehensible (they soon improved) but his gestures supplied the necessary information. The crucial beat came from his upper arm. 'Never the hand, never the wrist', he said. He thumped his arm in emphasis. Then he thumped mine. At the Edinburgh Festival a few weeks later I saw a rival Russian give the same beat with his wrist. It was a flabby performance.

Järvi could be flabby, too, particularly in the German classics.

In Mozart symphonies, in which he liked to employ a biggish orchestra, he was prone to slow up for second subjects, the way Bruno Walter used to do. The end of a movement would be signalled by a mighty rallentando. It was all very old fashioned. Brahms symphonies likewise limped from one tempo change to another, so that by the end of, say, the first movement of the Third Symphony the music was devoid of energy.

But it was not for German music that the SNO went chasing Järvi, and certainly not for his way with Handel's *Messiah*, of which, as guest conductor in 1983, he gave an Easter performance at Glasgow City Hall in which Part One lasted an astonishing sixty-five minutes. Conductors with a sense of Handelian style and a feeling for Handelian rhythm nowadays get it down to fifty. Järvi made it sound like the thicker-textured Mozart arrangement of *Messiah* rearranged by Brahms. 'This won't do,' Fiona Grant is reputed to have said to him afterwards.

Yet the fact that, as a guest conductor, he was willing to do *Messiah* at all provided the first clue, as I remarked in *The Scotsman* at the time, that he might just conceivably be about to become the SNO's next musical director. Who else, I speculated, would possibly be willing to take on such an unrewarding assignment as performing *Messiah* with a symphony orchestra and large chorus? This was a period when there was much speculation. But in the end (the assiduous Michael Tumelty not yet having joined *The Herald*) it was Andrew Clark, a Swiss-based radio journalist writing in the London-based *Classical Music Fortnightly*, who broke the news. Clark, a Scot, tracked down the secret meeting between Järvi, Grant and Wilford in Amsterdam, and made his own deductions.

As was obvious even before he took over the musical directorship, Järvi could inspire thrillingly spontaneous playing from the orchestra. As guest conductor, touring Tchaikovsky's Fifth Symphony round Aberdeen, Dundee, Edinburgh and Glasgow, he had proved that nothing he did was predetermined. The music was never the same way twice. As a result, there were fluffs and rough edges. The mercurial tempi constantly courted disaster, but on each occasion the performance stayed on the rails. It was an object-lesson in creative risk-taking. The stuff of Tchaikovsky's genius was there.

In another concert the inclusion of Tchaikovsky's *Mozartiana* suite showed Järvi's flair for highlighting the peripheries of the repertoire. Ultimately this could prove exasperating, when he was prone to rediscover Svendsen, or champion minor Estonian composers, at the expense of music that mattered. Järvi, even more perhaps than other conductors, put his own needs before those of the orchestra, and when Chandos issued an SNO disc entitled 'Music from Estonia No 1', one fervently hoped there would not be a No 2.

His desire to record was unquenchable. If Gibson had already built up the SNO as a recording orchestra with his impressive tally of Sibelius and Elgar performances, and a valuable Stravinsky box, Järvi went very much farther in an incredibly short space of time. Vast areas of Prokofiev and Shostakovich were quarried. All Dvořák's symphonies and symphonic poems were recorded. An undeserved amount of Glazunov and Khachaturian was marketed. Skryabin was resuscitated and a Mahler cycle launched. Often these recordings were ends in themselves. Very few of the Prokofiev discs were backed up by concert performances.

For those who would have welcomed a live Prokofiev cycle, this was frustrating. But Shostakovich, at least, was well served, with public performances of the fourth and seventh symphonies, in particular, which searingly vindicated these vast and still controversial works. Nobody, on hearing Järvi conduct them, could doubt that they were masterpieces of the first order. Even if doubts set in afterwards, Järvi had made them live for the moment. The Fourth Symphony, a work of epic sweep and variety, received what could only be hailed as a historic performance, unfailing in its intensity of utterance, and making the SNO seem as fine an orchestra as any in the world. As for the Seventh Symphony, with its pictures of a beleaguered Leningrad, the clamorous emptiness of the first movement was transformed by Järvi's alchemy into an asset, the obscenity of the Nazi advance made glaringly explicit. In these and other performances – even the familiar Fifth Symphony took on a new and more ominous colouring when Järvi conducted it – he went some way towards establishing Shostakovich as a symphonist with a Mahlerian ability to speak of soul-searing things to a large and appreciative audience. Had he done nothing else, he would thereby have justified his four years as the SNO's musical director.

But what else did he do? He did works by Eduard Tubin, Wilhelm Stenhammar and Arvo Pärt, which, though not without interest, hardly compensated for his lack of interest in the twentieth-century music he should have been doing. Pärt's *Canto in Memory of Benjamin Britten* was a simple, touching elegy, but it would have been more rewarding to hear Britten's own Cello Symphony, or *Spring Symphony*, or *Sinfonia da Requiem*, or *Frank Bridge Variations* – pieces Järvi might have conducted to admiration. Vaughan Williams's *Sea Symphony* was one inert tribute he did pay to British music, and he alarmed Fiona Grant by saying that Parry was next in line. Happily, the promise was not kept.

For Fiona Grant, as administrator, Järvi's lack of interest in contemporary music was understandable but regrettable. 'He could have been extremely good at it if he'd wished, and as he once or twice very tantalisingly demonstrated. One project he did want to do was the music of Alfred Shnitke, which would certainly have been topical. But he really preferred to champion unknown repertoire of a previous era. Whenever he offered me something by a contemporary of Brahms, the question would have to be asked: was it great music or was it just like Brahms, only not so good?'

This, of course, was Järvi's escape route from modernity, which he continues to pursue in Detroit, where he is now based. Doing Stenhammar absolves him from doing Stockhausen. But since, as Fiona Grant was fully aware, 'Järvi was not likely to involve himself in Musica Nova', she had to find someone who was more willing. So she consulted Howard Hartog, the London agent and editor of a pioneering, window-opening book on twentieth-century European music, which made history in the nineteen-fifties by establishing for British readers that Sibelius was not the only composer of his period who mattered. Since Paavo Berglund's tenure as principal guest conductor was drawing to a close, she asked Hartog if he could suggest a replacement who might be willing to do the things Järvi refused to do.

Hartog proposed Matthias Bamert, a Swiss conductor then in his early forties and with a reputation still to be made in Britain, though he had galvanised the Aberdeen Festival of Youth Orchestras a few years previously. She accepted Hartog's advice. 'I always respected Howard,' she said. 'He was one of the few great big men of music.' What she needed immediately was somebody to do the Fauré Requiem with the SNO Chorus and eventually some Messiaen, because 'the repertoire was lacking some French flavour at the time'.

Bamert filled the bill, even to the extent of taking command of

Musica Nova as well, though he demanded as his reward the opportunity to conduct Dvořák's *New World* symphony, Tchaikovsky's *Pathétique* and other popular pieces – inside him, as with many another advocate of new music, there was a romantic screaming to get out. Though some found him somewhat cool and clinical in the familiar repertoire (he knocked about twenty minutes off Leonard Bernstein's self-indulgent running-time for the Tchaikovsky) the sharp rhythms and lucid textures of his performances gave the music a fresh gleam.

Nevertheless it was as Järvi's obverse – or, as Fiona Grant put it, 'as an excellent foil' – that he had been engaged, and it was in the ticktock precision of Messiaen's *Chronochromie* that he soon made his mark. Every time he conducted, the shrewd though by then frail figure of Howard Hartog could be seen in the audience, monitoring the impact of each performance. An astute old impresario, who looked as though he had a cigar between his lips even when he hadn't, Hartog lived in Kensington but had worked in German and Austrian broadcasting after the war, as well as for Schott's the music publishers, and always exuded an air of Middle European expertise. Once, after a Bamert concert with the SNO in a new hall in Nottingham, he drove me to London in his stately vintage car. When I arrived I was a better-informed critic than when I set out.

With Bamert as adviser, Musica Nova was in safe hands for the next few years. The players appreciated his Swiss exactitude – especially when they had the music of Elliott Carter to contend with, as they had in 1984 and at the London proms the following year – but it was Järvi they loved. He had the ability to turn almost every concert into an event, and his few failures seemed a small price to pay for his many successes. He also had the personality to generate excitement the moment he walked on to the platform. It was not that he looked specially romantic – indeed he looked simply large and burly, with a short neck and what could have been an Estonian farmer's face – but the latent electricity was indisputable. Although, shortly before his appointment, Scottish audiences still regarded him as a fairly unknown quantity, and some kept forgetting his name, that was a state of affairs that very soon changed.

Järvi's qualities were ones on which Fiona Grant and the orchestra quickly capitalised. His sheer unpredictability as an interpreter was one of his major assets. At an Aberdeen concert I attended, the first three movements of Beethoven's Seventh Symphony passed by so uneventfully that I wondered why I had bothered to make the journey. The finale changed my opinion. Taken at a tempo that bore no relation to the rest of the performance, or to any performance I had ever heard, it erupted with energy. It was Järvi's way of springing surprises, or of rescuing at the last minute a performance that had been going nowhere.

Upon big choral works – such as Mahler's Eighth Symphony at the Edinburgh Festival – he flung himself like a force of nature. This was, as Gerald Larner remarked in *The Guardian*, 'the musical event to obliterate all others during the last few days'. Why then, instead of congratulating Fiona Grant for bringing them Järvi, had the players earlier rallied against her with – of all things – a vote of no confidence?

As one of them explained to me in 1992, 'It seems very ironic now, but it was because we felt that she wasn't finding us enough work. If we'd known what was going to happen later, and known more about what she was in fact doing for us, I don't think we would have voted that way. Speaking to her office staff long after she left, we gathered that she had actually been working extremely hard. But she wasn't very good at communicating, she didn't talk very well to the players, she didn't like telling the orchestra what was going on. Yet the orchestra couldn't be accused of a sustained vindictive campaign against her. I think it was sheer frustration. Things didn't seem to be going well at that time.'

Fiona Grant, who herself had spoken to me about lack of communication, survived the vote and remained in charge for another two years until her resignation in 1985. Through her fund-raising acumen she had set out to raise a million pounds to keep the orchestra secure, and she came close to that figure before she left. But damage had been done to her relationship with the orchestra. In 1992 I asked her if she had felt personally damaged by what had occurred. 'It upset me greatly', she replied. 'I couldn't believe that a relationship could deteriorate like that. As far as I was concerned, things were going well for the orchestra. They voted one hundred per cent to renew Järvi's contract, which suggested that they thought I was working on the right lines. They were making records which were winning prizes. I'd got them a good lot of sponsorship. Finances were relatively healthy. They were being better paid and they had good working conditions – better than anyone in London.'

When, finally fed up, Fiona Grant left the SNO, she swore that she would never run a symphony orchestra again. She has been true to her word. She now lives in London, working as a part-time guide for the British Museum and doing a little freelance chamber music administration. She is, she says, a good deal happier. But as Raymond Williamson, who was chairman at the time of her departure, sees it: 'They said she was aloof, and so they broke her. It was one of the tragedies that they did this to a person of such ability. Such a combination of talents coincide in one person on such rare occasions.'

12

Stephen Carpenter

Before quitting Glasgow, Fiona Grant began to organise one more foreign tour for the orchestra, though by then she had no intention of taking part in it herself. Her successor, Stephen Carpenter, fell heir to the plans and saw them through to completion. Perhaps, at the time, he wondered why his predecessor had backed out. With Järvi as conductor, Felicity Lott and the Labèque Sisters as soloists, and Vienna and Berlin among the destinations, it was a trip that could hardly fail. And indeed, supervised by Steve, as everybody called him, it turned out to be one of the orchestra's major successes. But as for why Fiona Grant had backed out, Carpenter soon began to learn.

True, things began happily for him. His appointment, at the age of twenty-eight, perhaps surprised him as much as anyone else. Never before had the SNO appointed someone so young as its general administrator. But, having already worked for the Scottish Chamber Orchestra, he had the managerial experience and, having studied the cello at Edinburgh University and been soloist in a student performance of Elgar's Cello Concerto, he had the musical experience to back it up. Ironically, it was a background not unlike Fiona Grant's. But she, beforehand, had had more managerial power and had learnt a great deal about handling money. Carpenter had still to learn about that, and the mistakes he made in doing so were soon to be used against him.

Meanwhile the sun was smiling on the Dorset-born boy who, so far, represented no threat to the players. In 1981, after graduating, he had written to every arts organisation in the country in the hope of finding a job. Michael Storrs, vigilant boss of the Scottish Chamber Orchestra, was the first to reply. With the SCO, Carpenter learnt his trade the fundamental way – shifting pianos and music stands around the platform, and driving the orchestra's van around Scotland. But he thereby discovered how an orchestra – and, more importantly, orchestral players – functioned. Before long he could be trusted to play the role of acting general manager. He took part in innumerable SCO tours in one capacity or another, including a difficult one to Hong Kong and Taiwan where, backstage, he relaxed by playing tough computer chess with himself. A knowledge of moves and gambits would stand him in good stead when he got round to running the SNO. But orchestras, however mechanical their reactions, are not computers. Sadly for him, it was a game he finally lost.

When the SNO administration fell vacant in the spring of 1985, Carpenter was still too young and obscure to be headhunted. Not since Ponsonby's time had that happened, and not until Christopher Bishop's would it happen again. But he was ready to apply for the post, because running his own orchestra had become his main ambition. So he wrote off in the usual way, and soon was interviewed by the usual sort of committee asking the usual sort of questions. An additional feature was an attitude test, involving yes or no answers to a series of psychological probes intended to reveal the interviewee's strengths and weaknesses. Carpenter recalls being asked whether, in group discussions, he liked to take the lead, and whether, if an orchestral player had problems, he would lend a sympathetic ear.

'I knew I gave a good account of myself', he told me when I met him for coffee near his present office in the City of London during my 1992 tour of the orchestra's former administrators. 'For one thing, I knew Scotland well, which gave me an advantage over some of the other applicants. There were two rounds of interviews, involving seven or eight members of the board along with the chairman, Raymond Williamson, and Christie Duncan, music director of the Scottish Arts Council, though not Neeme Järvi. At the second interview, held in the SNO Centre, I was surprised that no effort was made to conceal the short-listed candidates from each other – we could see exactly who we were up against.'

Whether rightly or wrongly, Carpenter perceived himself to be Raymond Williamson's appointment. 'He was supportive until the end.' But it was the opportunity to work with Neeme Järvi that sustained him through his increasingly troubled year and a half in Glasgow, and it was the tour of Japan – an organisational triumph – that gave him his greatest piece of job satisfaction.

'Planning programmes with Neeme was highly rewarding,' he

remembers, 'though it has to be said that ideas which seemed quite firm one week would change entirely a fortnight later owing to the dictates of Neeme's recording plans.'

But since Järvi's Glasgow flat – which he treated more like a hotel than a home – was almost next door to Carpenter's, decisions could be made, and altered, without too much pain. 'On Sunday afternoons I'd go round and plan with him for two or three hours on end, and very enjoyable it was, too.' In that way the fine detail of the 1986 European tour came into focus, the 1987 Japanese tour was planned from scratch, and one recording after another was scheduled to satisfy the conductor's belief that that was where the future lay.

But since, for much of the time, Järvi was an absentee musical director, a great many policy decisions were left to Carpenter, who had to convince both the board and the orchestra that his administrative philosophy was correct. Like Fiona Grant, he was convinced that changes needed to be made. But how, bearing in mind the things he had been asked in his attitude test, would he push them through?

First, there were the summer proms which, in terms of quality and programme content, had been deteriorating alarmingly. Not daring to do too much to their established format in 1986, he was content simply to change their Glasgow venue from the traditionally popular but acoustically ill-focused surroundings of the Kelvin Hall, with its awkward layout and stale circus smells, to the newly-built but acoustically by no means proven Scottish Exhibition and Conference Centre on the banks of the Clyde.

It was a move forced on him by the Kelvin Hall's temporary closure, but no doubt he hoped the orchestra might be able to benefit from it on the basis that any change would be a change for the better. Already one concert had been held at the SECC, a gala event featuring the by then sixty-year-old Jon Vickers as solo singer. Carpenter would remember it well, because his appointment as administrator was announced during the morning rehearsal. But the place's shortcomings soon established themselves. The site was inaccessible, the acoustics worse than the Kelvin Hall's, and the rain drummed audibly on the roof.

Only Pavarotti and the Bolshoy Opera in 1990 could persuade the public to tolerate it, and then only because the product was so hugely attractive. Failing to come up with anything so obviously alluring, Carpenter decided in 1987 (the Kelvin Hall remaining unavailable) to appeal to the audience's imagination and intelligence. This time, to give the proms a greater sense of purpose – but disastrously failing to recognise that their one and only purpose now was to make money – he prepared a thematic programme series entitled 'Rain, Steam and Speed', and illustrated the cover of the brochure with a reproduction of Turner's evocative painting of the same name.

For the occasion, Douglas Young was commissioned to compose an orchestral piece with that as its title. Rain, in isolation, was represented in another concert by MacCunn's overture, *Land of the Mountain and Flood*, and steam by Honegger's *Pacific 231*, Villa-Lobos's *Little Train of the Caipira* and Richard Rodney Bennett's film score for *Murder on the Orient Express* (curiously, the Strauss family's delectable railway music got forgotten about). Other programmes seemed compiled to demonstrate that, for the first time in many years, the SNO proms were proms with brains. Matthias Bamert conducted Mendelssohn's *Erste Walpurgisnacht* as part of a musical witches' brew, with season-ticket holders being given the opportunity, a month beforehand, to choose the concert's other ingredients. Neeme Järvi conducted, all in one evening, Stravinsky's *The Soldier's Tale*, Martinů's culinary tone poem, *La Revue de Cuisine* and Mozart's *Musical Joke*. Other Järvi concerts mixed Glinka with Glazunov, Leo Weiner with Prokofiev. It was all, as Carpenter realised to his cost, too clever by half. As he admitted later, 'I simply didn't take account of the fact that every concert should have been one hundred per cent shamelessly popular'. Instead of making their usual and much-needed profit, the proms lost £20,000 and, as Carpenter put it, 'the finger of blame was pointed at me'.

It was pointed at him again when Musica Nova 1987, though certainly not expected to make a profit, made a more than usually colossal loss. Once more it seemed that the programmes were over-ambitious, extending the range of previous cycles, and presenting no fewer than a dozen works by the fashionable Japanese composer, Toru Takemitsu, among them a pair of fanfares entitled *Day* and *Night* in a concert sponsored by the Scottish Post Office during a period of impressive artistic largesse.

With a retrospective of the music of the German composer, Bernd Alois Zimmermann (who had killed himself in 1970), with commissioned works from James Dillon and Mark-Anthony

Turnage, and with special emphasis on electronic music, it seemed plain that Carpenter had bitten off more than he could chew. Perhaps he was lulled into a false sense of security by the quantity of sponsors, who this time included the Calouste Gulbenkian Foundation, the Japanese Foundation of London and the Japan-Scotland Society, in addition to the Scottish Arts Council and other old faithfuls. At any rate – 'due to unforeseen circumstances', as Carpenter himself delicately worded it, but at least partly because of the large number of extra fees that were demanded by members of the orchestra for playing unusual instruments and awkward solos – an event budgeted to lose £20,000 eventually lost three times that sum.

Yet as he himself rightly said, it was 'an artistic success and well worth doing', though Gerald Larner in *The Guardian* suggested that mixing Takemitsu with Dillon and Zimmermann risked 'some unpredictable chemical reactions'. One unpredictable reaction was perhaps the mild case of food poisoning Takemitsu suffered after I had invited him for a seafood lunch in a Glasgow restaurant, thereby nearly depriving Musica Nova of his presence.

Japanese dreams – whether represented by Takemitsu's *To the Edge of Dream* for guitar and orchestra or by his atmospheric *A Flock Descends into the Pentagonal Garden* – were powerfully counterbalanced by the reality of Turnage's *Gross Intrusion*, which was just as hard-edged as its title implied, and Dillon's *Helle Nacht*, which proved that a Glasgow-born composer could write music as progressive and arresting as anybody in the world.

Indeed this was quite the most densely textured work to have been heard at Musica Nova since Brian Ferneyhough's *La Terre est un Homme*. The title, meaning 'Bright Night', may have been ironically intended, since, as Gerald Larner pointed out, what emerged to the ear was 'thick black sound'. But then, that was perhaps not how the composer heard it, and Larner was prepared to give him the benefit of the doubt by adding that the music's undulating and wriggling surface did deflect such light as there was in all directions.

But it was the deceased Zimmerman, whose music had been productively promoted before by the SNO, as well as by the Edinburgh Festival in the British premiere of his opera *Die Soldaten*, who set the standard by which the rest of this consignment of Musica Nova had to be judged. As a result, it was generally agreed that Takemitsu's frail and beautiful Japanese sonorities had been overexposed and that greater concentration on Zimmermann might have been more to the point, if the quality of his Cello Concerto – an 'amazingly original work', according to Michael Tumelty of *The Herald* – was anything to go by.

What Musica Nova did achieve this time, however much it cost in financial terms, was a genuine popular success of the sort that seemed within its grasp in the days when Luciano Berio, Peter Maxwell Davies and Gyorgy Ligeti were featured composers. For some years it had been failing to attract anything but the most specialised of audiences, and had been content – to quote Tumelty again – to steam away in an internalised, hothouse atmosphere. For Matthias Bamert, whose subsequent ambitions for Musica Nova were only partly realised, it was a triumph; and it proved that, if Carpenter's success as an administrator had depended only on his ability to bring out the best in conductors, his career in Glasgow might have lasted a good deal longer.

Carpenter, indeed, knew exactly how to balance Järvi against Bamert to the advantage of each of them, and was able to exploit their contrasted abilities as conductors. Järvi having decided that Richard Strauss would form an agreeable extension of his recording activities, *Also sprach Zarathustra* was included in the 1986–87 season along with the *Alpine Symphony*, an even more marvellously monstrous piece of orchestral kitsch. The fact that 1986 was the centenary of Liszt's death provided a reason for Bamert to programme the *Dante Symphony*, and Järvi (for once showing more restraint) to conduct *Les Préludes* and the First Piano Concerto, with the steel-fingered Cécile Ousset as soloist.

To Järvi's performance of Shostakovich's Tenth Symphony, Bamert replied with Schoenberg's *Pelleas und Melisande*. To Järvi's performance of Sibelius's *Pélleas et Melisande*, Bamert replied with Messiaen's *Turangalîla* symphony. To what extent there was rivalry, or some degree of one-upmanship, between them is hard to say. Since Järvi took his duties as musical director fairly lightly, in that he was uninterested in overseeing what other conductors were doing, it is probable that most of the correlating was done by Carpenter. The result, which included Järvi performances of Kalinnikov's First Symphony, Enescu's First Symphony and Act Two of Tchaikovsky's *Nutcracker*, counterbalanced by an imaginative Bamert coupling of Mozart's Requiem with a concert performance of Rimsky-Korsakov's opera, *Mozart and Salieri*, was a notably rewarding season, even if Scottish music was represented

only by the faded charms of *The Passing of Beatrice* by William
Wallace.

Carpenter's second and – as things turned out – final season was
similarly structured. Järvi conducted Dvořák's Requiem with the
SNO Chorus; Bamert, in Swiss mode, chose Honegger's *Christmas Cantata*. Järvi conducted Shostakovich's *Leningrad* symphony,
Bamert a complete *Daphnis et Chloé*. Järvi did an Elgar programme; Bamert cleverly coupled Boulez's *Rituel* with Stravinsky's *Rite*. Interlaced with these programmes were ones
featuring two future musical directors of the orchestra – Bryden
Thomson, who championed (as he had previously done and was
to do again) the music of the Glasgow composer, Thomas Wilson,
and Walter Weller, who brought from Vienna a gigantic visiting
card in the form of Bruckner's Eighth Symphony.

One of England's young hopes, Jan Latham-Koenig, appeared
with an interesting programme of Shostakovich's First Symphony
(a perhaps risky invasion of Järvi territory), Tchaikovsky's splendid but much-abused Second Piano Concerto and a work with the
Tippettian title of *Moving into Aquarius*, jointly composed by Thea
Musgrave and Richard Rodney Bennett. The players reacted in a
way that suggested they were unimpressed with Koenig. At any
rate he was not invited back, and went on to pursue a more
rewarding career abroad. A young East German conductor, Claus
Peter Flor, also appeared, choosing an enterprising French programme (Fauré's Requiem and *Cantique de Jean Racine*, Saint-
Saëns's Third Symphony) for his Scottish debut. He was soon to
become principal guest conductor of the Philharmonia Orchestra
in London and to return to Scotland with his own orchestra, the
Berlin Symphony, for concerts at the Edinburgh Festival.

All this was the sort of programme planning one expected of a
young and alert new administrator who had feelers out everywhere. Indeed, on the strength of winter seasons as thoughtful
as these, and with two greatly successful foreign tours (the first
admittedly drafted by Fiona Grant before she resigned) to his
credit, you would think that the SNO would have given him the
scope to develop his ideas further, and to learn more about what
a symphony orchestra can afford to do and what it can't. All he
needed was the right sort of support, and perhaps the occasional
helping hand.

But it was not to be. In the distance there was discernible a
cloud no bigger than a man's hand, but soon to grow. During the

first tour the only threat from the skies – though it was a grave one and it threatened more than Carpenter – came from the Chernobyl disaster, which occurred after the orchestra had visited Spain, Austria and Liechtenstein but before it reached Berlin, which was intended to be the summit of the trip. In radioactive terms, Berlin was a lot nearer the site of the explosion than Düsseldorf, where the players had spent the previous night. Should they proceed with the tour? The English National Ballet had already cancelled a Berlin date, and reassurances from the British Embassy and Foreign Office were not necessarily to be trusted. 'So we discussed it', says Carpenter, 'and decided to go on. Neeme seemed relaxed, though it has to be said that he had a tendency to say yes to every offer.'

Certainly the concert – which was to take place in the Philharmonie, home of the Berlin Philharmonic and the best of all modern concert halls – carried maximum prestige, but its cancellation would have been understandable. The determination to go ahead brought its reward at the end of the evening in an audience response so tumultuous that four encores were given, including one of Malcolm Arnold's *Scottish Dances* – not genuine Scottish music, but as close as Järvi generally got to the real thing. Coming after a characteristically spontaneous, unpredictable performance of Tchaikovsky's Fifth Symphony ('whipped into an experience of quite extraordinary intensity', according to Michael Tumelty, who was present) it brought the large audience to its feet, and if the Berliners had known 'Will ye no' come back again?' they would doubtless have sung it.

But the earlier part of the tour must have been almost as exhilarating, whatever strain it placed on the orchestra's van drivers, who had first of all to transport the heavier instruments all the way from Glasgow to Madrid through dreadful weather with temperamental windscreen wipers, arriving just in time for the first rehearsal. After two concerts in Madrid and one in Barcelona's marvellous Palace of Music, an art nouveau extravaganza worthy of Gaudi, the players reached Vienna for the only night of the tour I personally attended, *The Scotsman* being on one of its increasingly frequent economy drives at the time. Sadly the concert took place not in the golden Musikverein but in the larger, more nondescript surroundings of the Konzerthaus, whose brasher acoustics suited the performance of Poulenc's Concerto for Two Pianos by the Labèque Sisters better than it suited Felicity Lott's luminous singing of Britten's *Les Illuminations*, included in honour of a British Festival being promoted in Vienna at the time by the British Council. Nevertheless, as the *Wiener Zeitung* pointed out, 'the Scots took Vienna by storm'.

The next big tour, which took the orchestra for the first time to Japan, was no less triumphant. Being organised by Carpenter in conjunction with the Mitsukoshi chain of department stores, it should have sealed his administrative success. In fact, with the fatefulness of a classical tragedy, it coincided – for quite other reasons – with his downfall.

The preparations went smoothly. 'For a start,' says Carpenter, 'they *wanted* us. In February 1987 I had learnt through Ibbs and Tillett that Mitsukoshi were celebrating twenty years of trading with Britain, and were interested in taking a British orchestra on tour, to be paid for entirely by them. It's rare that the real costs of a tour are met in this way. Though the big London orchestras can command big fees, the payments to regional orchestras usually don't nearly cover the cost, so funding from other sources has also to be found.

'This tour was very well organised, with excellent hotels. It meant revamping a bit of our winter season, but that was a small price to pay. I found myself negotiating with a nice bloke called Matsuyama, a Mitsukoshi representative who came to Glasgow in May 1987. To my surprise, he arrived with a complete schedule, right down to platform numbers for the train journeys. He really took it seriously. I went out and did a dummy run to see that all was well. I remember having a very difficult conversation with the players' committee around that time. They wanted the best conditions, but they got them. There were no complaints.'

As for the Japanese, their only stipulation was that they wanted a popular repertoire. 'So we gave them Saint-Saëns's Organ Symphony, a lot of performances of Rimsky-Korsakov's *Sheherazade*, Dvořák's Fourth Symphony (not such a well-known work, but extremely useful, because it was to be our next recording) and Elgar's first *Pomp and Circumstance* march, complete with organ. I flew out with Neeme three days ahead of the orchestra. We were all treated excellently, players and management alike.'

So what went wrong? Certainly not the concerts, three of which were given in Tokyo's brand-new Suntory Hall. 'Järvi's approach to his absolutely sterling orchestra', said Paul Driver in the *Financial Times*, 'was powerfully engaging . . . the repeated programmes allowed one to observe how excellently unmechanical and unfixed Järvi's readings were.'

In Hiroshima, the conductor and some of his players took time off to teach a local school orchestra the overture to *Die Fledermaus*. Järvi, a family man with three gifted children of his own, was always at ease on such occasions. After an Edinburgh concert, Carpenter recalls, a father brought his musical son round to the conductor's room. Järvi grabbed the child's hands and taught him how to conduct the opening of Mozart's fortieth symphony. Järvi: 'What's the first thing you do with your arms?' Boy: 'You move them up for the upbeat.' Järvi: 'No, even for an upbeat, you go *down* first.' Paavo, one of Järvi's own sons, conducted an Edinburgh lunchtime programme of Mozart wind serenades for the increasingly active Friends of the SNO at the Scottish National Gallery of Modern Art, and later recorded them, along with the great B flat major serenade for thirteen wind instruments, for Chandos. These, says Carpenter, were happy times.

To say that everything changed during the seventeen-hour flight that took the orchestra via Alaska to Japan would be too simplistic, yet there is something about long flights and Anchorage stopovers that can cause trouble, as John Boyden had learnt to his cost on his tour with the LSO. Grievances, at such times, are nursed and explosive situations duly explode. 'On the flight out,' says Carpenter, 'the gulf that was opening between me and the players over some major changes I was making to the Glasgow concert schedules was communicated to Michael Tumelty of the *Glasgow Herald*, and reported by him in his newspaper while we were in Japan.'

I myself, having already accepted a rival invitation to visit Japan with the Scottish Chamber Orchestra that same year, did not go on the SNO trip. But as Tumelty informed me later, 'A lot of talking can take place in seventeen hours. Even after we got off the plane, the players were more or less queuing up to give me their views on the proposed structural changes that would affect future Glasgow concerts though not the Edinburgh ones. At Tokyo I asked Steve if I could speak to him about it, and it was done in a perfectly straightforward manner.'

From the other side of the world, it gave Tumelty a Glasgow news story that outweighed the events of the Japanese tour itself. Carpenter's side of it, in his own opinion at any rate, was simple: 'With the prospect of a big new concert hall opening in Glasgow within three years, I wanted to alter the orchestra's concert pattern in order to be ready for this. In conversation with the board of directors, I said I wanted to get round the problem of giving certain programmes in Glasgow twice in a single week. In order to avoid the Thursday and Saturday repeat sequence [at this point in the orchestra's history occurring eight times per season] I planned to reduce the number of Saturday concerts, and to do Tuesday concerts, with an entirely different programme, instead.'

Since Glasgow's Thursday concerts, which benefited from *Herald* sponsorship, had been devised in the first place because the City Hall was so small, and thus gave people a choice of days for the same programme, Carpenter argued that they would no longer be necessary in the more capacious new hall. Indeed he feared that seats might prove hard to sell if the old concert pattern prevailed. A revamp seemed necessary, and he decided that the answer lay in altering the Glasgow pattern while leaving Edinburgh's Friday night concerts unaffected.

But orchestras, like other people, object when someone proposes changing working conditions that seem to them perfectly satisfactory. 'The players', Carpenter told me, 'were up in arms that I was interfering with long-standing traditions. Yet the management of the City of Birmingham Symphony Orchestra did the same thing when the new Birmingham Symphony Hall was in prospect. The players hated the idea, but it worked fine ultimately. In Glasgow, on the other hand, the eighty-seven voices of the players were sufficient to stop the experiment.'

By ventilating Stephen Carpenter's proposals in *The Herald*, Michael Tumelty soon established that the public, too, were against the idea. As a result, Carpenter was accused of not properly testing the market beforehand. Though again he could claim that the same happened in Birmingham, it was plain that his scheme was stillborn. Moreover, having recklessly presented it to the orchestra as a *fait accompli* at a time when it had yet to be finally accepted by the board of directors, he found himself in a vulnerably exposed position that left him ultimately with no option but to resign. As Raymond Williamson, the chairman of the board, bluntly put it to the players: 'Yesterday I invited Mr Carpenter into my office for a talk. As a result of that talk, he has tendered his resignation which we have accepted.'

For Williamson, who had shown faith in Carpenter from the beginning, it must have seemed a sad but inevitable outcome for what had undoubtedly been a promising and imaginative appointment. But Carpenter's abilities were soon reaffirmed when he became administrator of the thriving young City of London Sinfonia, whose programmes – recently filled with works by John Adams, Nigel Osborne, Robin Holloway, Michael Berkeley and Judith Weir – clearly reflect his tastes.

Persuading him, for the purposes of this book, to talk to me about his experiences with the SNO proved difficult. Of the four former administrators I interviewed, he was the only one who initially refused. His memories, he said, were too bitter, and he wanted to put them behind him. That he made mistakes he readily admits. His adventurous prom programmes, he now recognises, might have been better as part of the winter season. But working with Järvi was something he would hate to have missed.

Did he have any unfulfilled plans? 'No,' he replied, 'not really. I was too preoccupied with the problems. Since I left, in terms of fund-raising, I've had successes. I would like to think I could have done something to get the SNO an incentive funding award, which the City of London Sinfonia got and which the Scottish Chamber Orchestra got. I'd have gone for that, if the players had given me time to do it. But when, rightly or wrongly, they force their administrator into endless meetings to negotiate what, to them, may be important points, the result is that he may spend fifty per cent of his time concentrating on these points to the exclusion of arguably more important matters such as sponsorship. My experience since leaving the SNO is that I spend no time whatsoever arguing over small negotiating details, so why did it happen with the SNO?'

Well, the reduction of the Saturday concerts in Glasgow was hardly a minor detail. But those who stated that they were sacrosanct – or, as the then concert manager, Erik Knussen, put it, 'written in stone' – were not quite right. In 1967, Robert Ponsonby had switched them to Thursday evenings for two entire seasons, and for exactly the same reason as Carpenter twenty years later: the orchestra was moving to a different hall – in Ponsonby's time the City Hall – and a new strategy seemed desirable. Although in 1969 Ponsonby reverted to Saturdays (he says in retrospect that the public did seem to prefer concerts on that night) the weekly Thursday concerts worked well enough. They were not a box-office disaster, and they gave the players their Saturday

evenings free. Perhaps they would have established themselves –
and even been written in stone – had Ponsonby decided to continue
with them. Carpenter was not given that opportunity.

previous page
THE SCOTTISH ORCHESTRA
IN FRONT OF THE TEMPORARY
INDUSTRIAL HALL AT THE GLASGOW
INTERNATIONAL EXHIBITION, 1901.

FREDERIC COWEN IS IN THE FRONT
ROW, 9TH FROM LEFT.

WILLEM KES,
PRINCIPAL CONDUCTOR OF THE
SCOTTISH ORCHESTRA 1895-98.

FREDERIC COWEN,
PRINCIPAL CONDUCTOR OF THE
SCOTTISH ORCHESTRA 1900-11.

PAYMENTS TO ORCHESTRA.

SEASON 1913-1914.

1ˢᵗ Week ending   15ᵗʰ November 1913

NAME.			SALARY.	ALLOWANCE.	EMPLOYEE'S INSURANCE.	TOTAL.
ALEXANDRA, J. H.,	...	1st Bassoon,	6	- 2		6 - 2
ALLAN, M.,	...	Violoncello,	3	- 2		3 - 2
ANGLISS, E.,		Violoncello,	4	- 2		4 - 2
ARNOLD, ADOLF,	...	Viola,	3 - 5	- 2		3 - 7
ARNOLD, ALBERT,	...	Viola,	3	- 2		3 - 2
ALLAN, W. D.,	...	Double Bass,	2 - 10	- 2		2 - 12
BATESON, H.,	...	Viola,	3 - 5	- 2		3 - 7
BROWN, P. W.,	...	1st Violin,	3 - 10	- 2		3 - 12
BURGESS, REGINALD,	...	Viola, &c.,	4	- 2		4 - 2
BROUGH, L.,	...	1st Clarinet,	6 - 10	- 2		6 - 12
BEEARLEY, A.,	...	Viola,	3	- 2		3 - 2
CLAXTON, W. J.,	...	Violoncello,	4	- 2		4 - 2
CHEVREAU, JEANNE,	...	Harp,	6	- 2		6 - 2
COLE, F. G.,	...	Double Bass,	4	- 2		4 - 2
COLE, H. W.,	...	1st Violin,	3 - 10	- 2		3 - 12
CONNABEER, L. A.,	...	2nd Violin,	3 - 15	- 2		3 - 2
DARELITZ, R.,	...	Principal 2nd Violin,	6	- 2		6 - 2
DALY, JOHN,	...	2nd Violin,	4	- 2		4 - 2
DEICHEN, O.,	...	4th Horn,	4 - 5	- 2		4 - 7
DIXON, FRED.,	...	2nd Violin,	2 - 10	- 2		2 - 12
DIXON, J. B.,	...	Violoncello,	2 - 10	- 2		2 - 12
DRUMMOND, T.,	...	2nd Bassoon,	4	- 2		4 - 2
DE CONISCE, GEO.,	...	3rd Trombone,	4	- 2		4 - 2
EDGAR, J.,	...	1st Violin,	3 - 15	- 2		3 - 17
EIPER, T.,	...	Double Bass,	5	- 2		5 - 2
FAWCETT, H.,	...	2nd Violin,	4 - 10	- 2		4 - 12
FAWCETT, M.,	...	2nd Clarinet,	4 - 5	- 2		4 - 7
FAWCETT, W.,	...	Double Bass,	3 - 5	- 2		3 - 7
FLETCHER, A.,	...	1st Violin,	3 - 5	- 2		3 - 7
FREEMAN, C. E.,	...	2nd Trumpet,	4	- 2		4 - 2
FREEDMAN, M.,	...	1st Violin,	3 - 15	- 2		3 - 17
FLEMING, S.,	...	2nd Violin,	2 - 10	- 2		2 - 12
Forward,	...	...£	124	3 - 4		127 - 4

LIST OF PAYMENTS TO THE ORCHESTRA, NOVEMBER 1913.

Mdme. Agnes Nicholls. Mr. Ben Davies.
Miss Helen Blain. Mr. Robert Radford.
SATURDAY, 1st January, 1916, at 12 noon.
MESSIAH
(Annual Performance).
Glasgow Choral Union. The Scottish Orchestra.
Conductor—Mr. Warren T. Clemens.
Tickets—7/6, 5/ (Reserved), at Paterson's, 152 Buchanan St.
Prospective Concert Announcements.
Second Popular Concert.
ST. ANDREW'S HALL,
Saturday Evening, 13th November, 1915, at 7.30.
SOLO PIANIST—
MR. ARTHUR RUBINSTEIN
SYMPHONY, in C minor (No. 9 of B. & H. Ed.), - HAYDN.
CONCERTO for Pianoforte and Orchestra, - TSCHAIKOWSKY.
PRELUDE to "Parsifal," - WAGNER.
PIANOFORTE SOLO, "Les Djinns," - FRANCK.
SYMPHONIC POEM, "Le Rouet d'Omphale," - SAINT-SAËNS.
SLAVONIC DANCE, - DVOŘÁK.
THE SCOTTISH ORCHESTRA.
Conductor—Mr. EMIL MLYNARSKI.
TICKETS—BALCONIES, 3/, 2/ (Reserved); Early Door for Area, North or Platform Balcony (Unreserved), 6.30 to 7, 1/6—at PATERSON'S, 152 Buchanan Street.
ADMISSION AFTER 7 P.M., ONE SHILLING.
Second Tuesday Concert.
ST. ANDREW'S HALL,
Tuesday Evening, 16th November, 1915, at 8.
SOLO PIANIST—
Mr. LEONARD BORWICK.
OVERTURE to "The Magic Flute," - MOZART.
CONCERTO for Pianoforte and Orchestra, No. 2, in B flat, - BRAHMS.
RHAPSODY No. 4, in A minor (Op. 141), - STANFORD.
("The Fisherman of Lough Neagh and what he saw.")
(First time at these Concerts.)
PIANOFORTE SOLOS, (a) Three Études, - SCRIABINE.
(b) "Conte Légendaire," - MEDTNER.
INTRODUCTION to Act III., "Lohengrin," - WAGNER.
THE SCOTTISH ORCHESTRA.
Conductor—Mr. EMIL MLYNARSKI.
FRONT AREA, 7/; BALCONY, 4/ (Reserved). AREA, NORTH or PLATFORM BALCONY (Unreserved), 2/—at PATERSON'S, 152 Buchanan Street. ADMISSION ONE SHILLING.

Poster for Arthur Rubinstein's debut concert with the Scottish Orchestra, 13 November 1915.

FELIX WEINGARTNER
REHEARSING THE LONDON
SYMPHONY ORCHESTRA,
2 FEBRUARY 1938.
(COURTESY THE HERALD)

SIR LANDON RONALD,
PRINCIPAL CONDUCTOR OF THE
SCOTTISH ORCHESTRA 1919-23.

CLIFFORD CURZON
(COURTESY THE HERALD)

GEORGE SZELL, PRINCIPAL CONDUCTOR 1936-39.

Sir John Barbirolli

with members of the Scottish Orchestra on his arrival in Glasgow after returning from America, 1943.

THE ORCHESTRA AND WALTER SUSSKIND IN ST ANDREW'S HALL, GLASGOW, 1950. THE LEADER IS JEAN POUGNET.

WARWICK BRAITHWAITE,
PRINCIPAL CONDUCTOR OF THE SCOTTISH
ORCHESTRA 1940-45.

WALTER SUSSKIND,
PRINCIPAL CONDUCTOR 1946-52,
REHEARSING THE ORCHESTRA IN THE
USHER HALL, EDINBURGH.

(COURTESY THE HERALD)

KARL RANKL,
PRINCIPAL CONDUCTOR 1952-56,
REHEARSING THE SCOTTISH
NATIONAL ORCHESTRA,
4 OCTOBER 1952.
(COURTESY THE HERALD)

HANS SWAROWSKY,
PRINCIPAL CONDUCTOR 1957-59
(COURTESY THE HERALD)

The Scottish National Orchestra and Karl Rankl playing *Til Eulenspiegel* at the Edinburgh Festival, 1953.

previous page St Andrew's Hall, Glasgow

St Andrew's Hall, Interior (destroyed by fire, 1962).

The Orchestra recording in the City Hall, Glasgow.

13

Bryden Thomson

F our months after Stephen Carpenter's resignation, Neeme
Järvi resigned also – but not, it seemed, in sympathy. Resignation was simply in the air. Järvi had his own reasons for
doing so, mostly concerned with cash, with his growing fame
around the world, and with his eagerness to extend still further
his recording career, though no doubt Columbia Artists Management, that 'vast warehouse of talent' as it has been called, was
lurking in the background, ready to advise him and shape his
future life.

Järvi had always been in demand, but his steadily increasing
output of discs – not only with the SNO but with the Royal
Concertgebouw in Amsterdam, the Gothenburg Symphony
Orchestra and the London Philharmonic – made him an ever more
attractive prospect. Gradually he had whittled down the quantity
of his Scottish appearances to the point where he might simply
have been principal guest conductor rather than musical director.
By 1987 he was conducting just six programmes per season, compared with Karl Rankl's seventeen-or-so in the nineteen-fifties.
But the days when musical directors were expected to be in residence for most of the season were long since past. Even Sir Alexander Gibson, the only SNO conductor ever to make his home
in Glasgow, had reduced his schedule to a dozen programmes
per season by the end of his regime. In committing himself to eight
programmes in the 1992–93 season, Walter Weller, the orchestra's
latest musical director, seems quite generous.

Järvi's departure being as sudden as Carpenter's, people began
to wonder what was going on. To lose a general administrator
and a musical director at one and the same time did look a bit like
carelessness. Erik Knussen, a former bassist and tuba player,
whose brother Stuart had been the SNO's principal bass before
moving to the LSO, suddenly found himself elevated from the

role of orchestral manager to acting administrator. Playing for safety, he adjusted some of the more controversial aspects of Carpenter's programming and announced: 'We've got to keep on the traditional lines that have worked well.' Raymond Williamson who, as chairman, was now in charge of all major decisions, played down whatever backstage dramas were then in progress. Asked by me, on behalf of *The Scotsman*, if the orchestra was not seriously adrift, he replied that the ship was on course and there was no cause for alarm.

In fact, as he admitted to me long after it happened, Williamson saw Järvi's resignation coming. There were hints on the Japanese tour, and even earlier, that Järvi's mind was elsewhere. Had it been possible to bribe him with still more recordings, perhaps he would have extended his stay. But in fact his recordings, for all their sales figures, were costing the SNO a fortune. Because he had discovered, to his surprise, that the Caird Hall, Dundee, possessed acoustics that suited him, Järvi had insisted on making many of his discs there, rather than in Glasgow or Edinburgh. But naturally it added considerably to the expense of recordings whose manufacture was being subsidised by the SNO rather than the other way around.

As Raymond Williamson has pointed out, the SNO did not grudge the money. Järvi, as everyone agreed, was wonderful to work with, and he recognised in a keenly prophetic way that it was in recording that his and the orchestra's prospects lay. His output of discs within so short a space of time was phenomenal by any standards, but it was also financially draining. The process that Sir Alexander Gibson had started in the nineteen-sixties had accelerated out of control. 'What tended to happen', says Williamson, 'is that you started off with a project for recording Brahms's symphonies and suddenly found that it had turned into Richard Strauss's tone poems. This was obviously a very expensive thing, but it was also a good thing, though perhaps the record company should have picked up the tab. Yet it has to be said that Chandos continued to make marvellous recordings.'

I asked Williamson if he thought there was an air of unreality in going on recording with Järvi as if there were no tomorrow. Shostakovich's enormous Seventh Symphony in Dundee, for instance, had been said to cost a bomb, though Chandos did in the end pay towards this. Williamson said that he preferred not to see it as 'a ludicrous indulgence of Järvi's whims'. Järvi, he said, 'perceived that the best way of presenting the orchestra at that stage was through recordings. Indeed the standing of the orchestra was hugely assisted by that project. I was not critical of the philosophy behind Järvi's aspirations. The problem lay in managerial cost control.'

Ludicrous indulgence or not, the orchestra's financial resources were dwindling in other ways also; they were even raided for a time by an accountant who, it was discovered, had embezzled £16,000 (he was imprisoned for it). It was not a large sum by orchestral standards but was symptomatic of the SNO's financial malaise. But, to quote Williamson again, 'the core element of the whole financial equation was quite simply the fall in support from local authorities.' In the good days of Ponsonby and Richardson, this had amounted to about one-third of the orchestra's budget. It now rested at a dismal seven per cent, 'and *that*', says Williamson, 'remains basically the problem'.

No matter how an astute administrator such as Fiona Grant had been able to raise private subsidies and launch successful appeals, running a full-time symphony orchestra was proving an increasingly expensive business, not helped, in Williamson's opinion, by the behaviour of the players. 'Orchestras throughout the world have a totally unrealistic expectation of what general administrators ought to be able to do for them. They think the administrator's job is a doddle. All that's necessary is to wave a magic wand. They want power without responsibility, and the current business [he was referring to the latest tensions between orchestra and management, of which more in the next chapter] is a demonstration of their philosophy.'

As soon as Williamson began to suspect that Järvi might resign before his contract had expired – 'nothing was actually said, but I felt it in my bones' – he acted like the astute lawyer he is and formed a private sub-committee from members of the board and the orchestra to look, as he put it, at the issue of 'what if'. At that point, Williamson recalls, he thought it might happen in about eighteen months. 'The committee met on a number of occasions and reviewed all possible courses. These were very private discussions, because Järvi himself had said nothing so far.'

Williamson's instinctive solution was that Järvi and Bamert should simply swap jobs, which would maintain the status quo and might even work better. Järvi, after all, had always been by nature more of a principal guest conductor than a musical director, whereas Bamert quite clearly had the capacity and perhaps also the inclination to become a musical director. But so logical a solution had no possibility of being accepted in the complex world of orchestral machinations. As soon, says Williamson, as the players got a hint of what was on his mind, 'the lynching mob was out'. Bamert may have been OK for Musica Nova and the occasional guest appearance, but there was no way the players would have him as their musical director.

Discarding that idea, Williamson and his committee floated another one: Bryden Thomson was their man. He was a good conductor; he had worked often with the orchestra and was generally liked; he had an enormous repertoire and had made recordings with a variety of orchestras; he was, like Gibson before him, a Scot; and, though he lived in Dublin, he was within easy flying distance of Glasgow. Moreover he was probably available. So why had nobody thought of him before?

The answer lay more in Thomson's thrawn and prickly personality than in any musical failings. He was, as people agreed, a supremely well-balanced Scot – 'he had a chip on both his shoulders'. Anyway there was no time to procrastinate. Williamson's prediction that they had eighteen months in which to find a successor to Järvi fell far wide of the mark. No sooner had the committee agreed that Thomson, in Williamson's words, was 'somebody who had the capacity admirably to fulfil the role of musical director' than a telex arrived from Columbia Artists Management in America saying that Järvi was terminating his contract. Williamson's hopes that they might get one more season out of him were dashed. Only six months had passed since he had had his accurate hunch.

It could not, as the phrase has it, have happened at a worse moment. Carpenter had already departed, leaving a cloud of mystery and unsettlement behind him. Rumours were even more rife than usual in orchestral circles. Erik Knussen was keeping the press at bay with a few bland statements. Williamson rapidly recalled his committee to see if it still agreed about Thomson – who, by a happy coincidence, was due to appear as guest conductor a fortnight later. It was ascertained that he was willing to talk.

Meanwhile the board of directors was worried about the demoralising effect on the orchestra that any delay in finding a new administrator and conductor might have. It was decided that, if Thomson was available, they should act fast to 'prevent insidious rumours getting around'. Williamson, whose words these were, had strong views on rumours. 'I may say', he told me with heavy emphasis, 'that the players who were on the committee were *particularly concerned* about that aspect.'

The haste with which Thomson was appointed, however, left a fair amount of fine detail unresolved. Dealing with his awkward temperament, it was agreed, would have to be left to chance. But the general feeling was that 'after the jubilant, whirlwind excitement of working with Järvi, the orchestra might welcome a period of less hectic excitement, with a conductor who would be around more and would do more concerts'. With luck, thought Williamson, they would have the sort of set-up that Simon Rattle had developed in Birmingham.

But this was purely wishful thinking. Bryden Thomson was not Simon Rattle. At the age of almost sixty, he was older, touchier, more cynical and by no means keen to do what was imagined of him. Though nobody, it seems, expected that he would quit Dublin – where his wife was an established teacher and where the previously nomadic Thomson found the lifestyle to his liking – it had been hoped that he would spend more time in his homeland than he actually did. As things turned out, he was prone to take the last possible plane from Dublin to Glasgow and the first possible one back after he had fulfilled his conducting duties. In Rattle-like developments, or simply in the nitty-gritty of musical directorship, he was simply not interested.

Whether he was already ill at this point, nobody has been able to say. If he was already suffering from the cancer that was to kill him only a few years later, then his eagerness to spend as much time as possible with his wife would be understandable. But initially there was no evidence of this. He was his usual abrasive self, making his usual insulting (and, let it be said, often hilariously funny) comments to all and sundry, and conducting with all the precision for which he was famed. He possessed, as Neville Garden remarked in *Scotland on Sunday*, the 'clearest beat in the business'. This, in itself, endeared him to the orchestra. If he behaved outrageously – practising golf strokes on the podium during rehearsals, pulling funny faces behind the back of a celebrated young violinist whom he despised (but forgetting that, in Edinburgh and Glasgow, members of the audience seated behind the orchestra could see him) – so much the better. Compared with most conductors, he was a breath of bracing air.

But was he a fine conductor, and was he right for the SNO? He was certainly a good technician, and he knew how to cut through the layers of – as he saw it – unnecessary expressiveness with which other conductors distorted some of his favourite music. He was always to the point. But, just because of that, his performances could seem somewhat cold and functional. Rakhmaninov's Second Symphony, conducted by him, was never the warm bath of sound the audience expected it to be, and that Sir Alexander Gibson had made it.

The music, and the composer, always mattered to him. If the applause for a performance seemed insufficient, he would hold up his copy of the score to the audience and cup his hand round his ear. The device usually worked, but he did it too often and it irritated some people (me included, I have to say). He was, in Williamson's diagnosis, his own worst enemy – to the point, at times, of being self-destructive. Just because certain things were expected of him, he chose to withhold them. 'There is no doubt that at times we felt short-changed by him. He hardly came once to Glasgow when he didn't have to, he never once listened to the orchestra with someone else conducting – yet he, after all, was the music director.'

The riches of his repertoire, too, turned out to be a treasure-house into which he was unwilling to dip. All those Bax symphonies and similar rarities which he had been at such pains to record, as well as perform with his previous orchestras in Manchester, Cardiff, Belfast and Dublin, were part of his past. Like Järvi's, his recordings tended to be an end in themselves. What the man with one of the biggest symphonic repertoires in the world now wanted to do was extend it into areas – such as the Mahler symphonies – that had previously been unattainable. Since the SNO was already doing a Mahler cycle with Järvi, this desire of Thomson's was presumably unexpected; but it did result in a refreshingly clear and unexaggerated account of the great Eighth Symphony in celebration of the opening of Glasgow's Royal Concert Hall in 1990. By then, however, he was ill – a stool had been placed on the podium for him to rest on – and his plans to conduct Mahler remained largely unfulfilled.

The trouble perhaps was that he had won the musical directorship of the SNO too late in his career. Born in Ayrshire, he

was as Scottish as Sir Alexander Gibson yet had never held a major
post in his homeland, other than the token, though greatly useful,
assistant conductorship of the BBC Scottish Symphony Orchestra. In the days when the SNO had 'associate' conductors, he (like
Roderick Brydon) was one of the associates. When Scottish Opera
was founded, he played harpsichord continuo in *Don Giovanni* but
did not conduct that work for the company until many years later
at the MacRobert Centre, Stirling. Comic Rossini was considered
more his scene (he did a new Scottish Opera *Cenerentola* in 1969
and a revival of *The Barber of Seville*) but most of his operatic
work took place abroad, in Oslo, Gothenburg, Stockholm and
Hamburg. Northern Europe, it seemed, suited his cool conducting
style and no-nonsense manner, though his knowledge of Stravinsky's *The Rake's Progress* – for which he won admiration abroad
– was never by Scottish Opera exploited. Indeed his talents were
never really exploited by Scotland at all, no doubt because so
much of his career took place elsewhere. The same at present
could be said of Donald Runnicles, the Edinburgh-born conductor
who ran a local chamber group called the Caritas Orchestra but
failed to be talent-scouted by the SNO or its peers. Today, in his
thirties, he conducts at Glyndebourne, Bayreuth and the Vienna
State Opera, and is musical director of the San Francisco Opera.
With that sort of experience, his Edinburgh Festival debut – which
took place in 1992 – seemed overdue.

But Scotland's treatment of native talent is so perplexing –
Roderick Brydon, after a brief spell as the SCO's musical director,
now lives and freelances in Switzerland – that one wonders at times
how Sir Alexander Gibson ever managed to become conductor of
the SNO and to hold his position for so long. James Loughran,
apart from a spell in charge of the BBC SSO, has likewise worked
little in Scotland. Loughran, it would seem, bears no grudges. His
guest appearances with the SNO carry kudos – in 1993 he conducts
Mahler's Ninth Symphony – and he has enough work outside
Scotland to enable him to be selective in what he chooses to do.

Thomson, on the other hand, did bear grudges – and it showed.
His rudeness offended some people as much as it attracted others.
When, as a young conductor, he returned to Glasgow from Hamburg with a testimonial from Hans Schmidt-Isserstedt, under
whom he had been working, he made remarks so careless that he
provoked William Fell into declaring: 'That young man will never
work with the SNO as long as I am its general manager.'

So when he was finally offered the job he had always desired,
it was with no dewy-eyed romantic notions that he accepted it.
He took it because it was there. He may have been cynical about
the way the SNO had always been run, yet, as one player confirmed, 'He had the good of the orchestra at heart.' Or, as Williamson put it, though Thomson would not have thanked him for it,
'We got value for money. I don't think he let us down on the
podium. He put on a series of interesting concerts, He was a
professional to his fingertips. His only downside was his mouth.'

As a critic who had first heard him conducting a crisp,
thoroughly unsentimental account of Schubert's Fifth Symphony
with the Northern Sinfonia of Newcastle in the nineteen-sixties,
I thought he lacked poetry – he would in any case have denounced
the word – but I grew to admire the directness of his interpretations and, in person, his sheer brassneck. Yet at least once, when
as guest conductor he went against the judgment of the then
leader, Sam Bor, by cutting the SNO strings down to a handful
of players for a performance of Mozart's *Eine kleine Nachtmusik* in
the Usher Hall, he obtained a performance so graceful, so poetic,
so mysteriously nocturnal that one realised there was a side to
Thomson that he himself, for reasons of his own, kept ruthlessly
in check.

Had he not been a Scot, his outspokenness might have been
considered an enjoyable eccentricity. In his later years, with his
little beard, sardonic eyes and the white shoes he sometimes
sported in competition with his sober suits, he could look like a
slightly mad professor. But as a Scot among Scots, he was not
allowed to get away with it. As a Scot in conjunction with an
Englishman, however, he had an additional problem, brought
about four months after his appointment when he found that
henceforward he would be working with Christopher Bishop, the
orchestra's new chief executive.

Such a title, never previously employed by the SNO, immediately symbolised the high-class managerial style that the orchestra could expect of its latest administrator. Rather than wait for a
possible candidate to turn up, the board had this time taken the
initiative and sought Bishop's services. They knew him to have
been one of EMI's top producers, with a flair for choral music and
a long, productive relationship with a conductor of the calibre of
Sir Adrian Boult; they knew he had risen to become general manager of the company's International Classical Division; and they

knew he had been invited by Riccardo Muti to become managing director of the Philharmonia Orchestra, later presiding over the appointment of Giuseppe Sinopoli as Muti's successor. Here was a man, complete with Cambridge education, who had the most impeccable musical credentials in the orchestra's history. True, he and the Philharmonia had finally agreed to part, but he had lasted nine years – and that, as he said himself, is an almost unprecedentedly long time in the cut-throat world of London music.

During that period Bishop raised £3 million in sponsorship and gained the patronage of The Prince of Wales. He also launched the first orchestral subscription scheme in London and started the Friends of the Philharmonia – both new ideas on the South Bank, though already long established by the SNO, whose Friends are a particularly faithful supporters' group. They have their own range of activities in the four main cities, including pre-concert lectures and post-concert parties, coffee mornings, lunchtime recitals by members of the orchestra, the running of the gift and record stalls, and a massive amount of fund raising. In November 1992, Sir Alexander Gibson, in his capacity as the RSO Society's honorary president, celebrated the tenth anniversary of the Glasgow Friends by conducting a concert for them at the RSO Centre. His choice of music included Sibelius, Vaughan Williams, Brahms and Bizet – all composers, as he explained to his audience, who had played a special role in his career.

Christopher Bishop, hailed by Raymond Williamson as 'someone at the pinnacle of his profession', was expected, with Bryden Thomson, to form a team that 'in artistic, administrative and commercial terms is unrivalled on the British orchestral scene'. That the two men hardly knew each other was not, at the time, considered a problem. Bishop vaguely recalled that Thomson had conducted the Philharmonia on one occasion, but not until they were working together in Glasgow did it become apparent that the unrivalled team consisted of chalk and cheese.

It would have been instructive, or at any rate entertaining, to eavesdrop on some of their private conversations. But it soon became clear that neither of them ever penetrated the other's personality, or even wanted to. Since Thomson wasn't around too much, perhaps it did not greatly matter. The first of his three seasons was, in any case, largely improvised, because during what should have been a major period of concert planning, neither

Thomson nor Bishop was yet appointed, and Erik Knussen was trying to hold things together.

Nevertheless the season proved better than anyone could have hoped, even if Thomson was not yet free from other commitments to conduct very much of it. But his decision to do Vaughan Williams's Fourth Symphony and Rakhmaninov's First Symphony seemed like a happy portent, and his willingness to learn Andrew Vores's unmemorably titled *Twistification* – the latest work to win the Ian Whyte Award – suggested that he would not be averse to taking on chores. In London he was entrusted with a Royal concert at the Barbican, where he conducted Strauss's *Don Juan* in the presence of the Queen Mother, but for the moment it was Matthias Bamert (winning a deserved accolade for accompanying Pierre Amoyal in Schoenberg's Violin Concerto) and a handful of Russian guest conductors who kept things going.

Among these Russians, Valery Gergiev and Alexander Lazarev were little-known names which soon would gain much greater resonance; Yuri Temirkanov, first brought to Scotland by Fiona Grant, was already winning acclaim for his studied blend of brilliance and eccentricity; and Gennadi Rozhdestvensky, with a stockade-like podium to help combat his terror of falling into the audience, was an obvious coup, more welcome on this occasion for his keenly defined performances of Prokofiev's *Scythian Suite* and Shnitke's Piano Concerto (with his wife, Viktoria Postnikova, as soloist) than for his vandalising of Bruckner's Fourth Symphony – he chose, for unspecified reasons, to conduct the truncated Mahler version of the score.

Bishop quickly established a public image of high urbanity. At the Usher Hall, the pastel stripes of his Garrick Club tie blended with the ice-creams he could be seen licking in flamboyant criticism of that concert hall's wretched bar facilities. His press conferences were brisk, witty, with a vein of not unbitchy English repartee that was quite the best of its kind since John Drummond's time, making everyone else's announcements of their forthcoming seasons seem dull and maladroit. That (again like Drummond in his Edinburgh Festival days) what he was actually announcing was not always so very important made his performance seem all the more virtuosic. His unwavering self-confidence (which was soon to make him enemies both inside and outside the orchestra) carried all before it. In all the years I have known him, right back to his Philharmonia days, I have never seen him abashed.

Thomson's profile as musical director, on the other hand, remained fairly low, and failed to rise between this season and the next. He cared nothing about his public image (the same, perhaps, could be said for Bishop, but Bishop was better at it). An expected invitation for the orchestra to appear at the London proms, one of the regular summer dates, failed to materialise in 1989. Worse, for the first time since 1950, the SNO was blatantly dropped from the Edinburgh Festival, which was now in the hands of Frank Dunlop, Drummond's successor. Some delicate negotiating would surely have solved the problem, which concerned nothing more than the choice of conductor for the performance of Berlioz's Requiem with which the SNO had been invited to close the Festival. Frank Dunlop stipulated that he wanted someone other than Thomson to do it. Bishop, feigning outrage, told Dunlop that if he wanted the orchestra he would have to have Thomson, too.

Bishop, at that point, would have been prepared to resolve the problem by the age-old device of a spot of horse-trading. A different conductor would be acceptable so long as it was a distinguished Berliozian of the calibre of Giulini or Sir Colin Davis, and so long as the orchestra was given an extra programme with its own musical director in charge. For a while nothing happened. 'I felt', said Bishop, 'that we were being forced into a situation where we would have to appear without Bryden Thomson in some way. Then I met Frank Dunlop one night in Edinburgh, and asked him what was happening. He told me: "Oh, it's the BBC Scottish Symphony Orchestra who are performing."' And indeed, in the end, the Requiem was performed by the rival band with the by no means exceptional Rafael Frühbeck de Burgos as conductor. Thomson, characteristically unappreciative of Bishop's efforts on his behalf, remarked caustically that he 'had never been in with the Edinburgh Festival, so what did anyone expect?'

What the episode made clear was that Bishop knew how to be combative, and was prepared to sacrifice an important date if the terms were unsatisfactory. Dunlop, for his part, claimed that Bishop had simply been slow to make up his mind, so he had approached a different orchestra instead. Each appeared to think he had won. Bishop, declaring that the orchestra would probably be on tour when the Requiem was performed, said 'After all, the Festival is not quite what it was, is it?' But in fact both organisations had lost.

The incident, in fact, was not an isolated one, but typical of Dunlop's high-handed use of local forces, whose services he employed in a far less creative way than did most of his predecessors. The SCO, for example, tended to find itself seconded to foreign ballet companies or accompanying the Stockholm Folk Opera's economy versions of the classics. The SNO was likewise undervalued. Järvi on one occasion had found himself relegated to a programme dimly inspired by the Age of Enlightenment; and when, a year after the Berlioz incident, it was decided that he would be the most satisfactory solution to the problem of who should conduct the SNO at the Festival, he was allotted – some say by his own choice – a Sunday afternoon slot, usually regarded as a suitably offpeak time for events the Festival has little faith in. It said much for the public's belief in Järvi that they supported him, even at that time of day, in a potentially suicidal programme of Enescu, Bartók and Khachaturian.

For the second of his three seasons with the SNO, Thomson had more scope for personal planning and his decision to champion the nonconformist and in his view underrated music of Bohuslav Martinů was typical of him. Equally typically, perhaps, he did the composer a disservice by programming all six of his symphonies in conjunction with Rakhmaninov's four piano concertos, the *Rhapsody on a Theme of Paganini* and the *Symphonic Dances*, a straitjacket which, by the end of the season, one had come to dread. The two composers proved neither compatible nor incompatible. There simply seemed no reason to place them side by side six times running, with Dvořák's symphonic poems added as makeweight. Their combined sound world proved fatiguing and unilluminating, and the programmes obeyed the law of rapidly diminishing returns.

Though Thomson captured the anger that sometimes erupted in Martinů's symphonies – when rehearsing one of these works during a visit to Australia later in the year, he told the players to 'Sound angry, think of Mrs Thatcher,' only to remember that Mrs Thatcher was irrelevant to Australians – he failed to establish that all six of these works were worth doing in a single season.

What did strike sparks – or would have done in a happier context – was the combination of Howard Shelley as soloist and Thomson as conductor. Between them they stripped Rakhmaninov to the bone and, in sharp edged, finely detailed performances, revealed his greatness anew. Programmed more effectively, the Rakhmaninov cycle would have been a highlight of Thomson's short reign as conductor. As testimony, the recordings of these works made in Dundee show a truly musical partnership at work.

Combining Carl Nielsen's symphonies with works by Haydn and Beethoven the following season, Thomson ran into the same sort of programme problems that had occurred with Martinů, Rakhmaninov and Dvořák. The mixture, for all the excellence of individual performances, simply did not work. Nor did Nielsen possess the novelty value of Martinů. Previous conductors had dealt with these works just as effectively, as part of less rigidly compiled programmes. Considering the size of Thomson's repertoire, it seemed a wasted opportunity – though how wasted one did not realise until after his period with the SNO had ended and he returned, emaciated and dying, as guest conductor of a series of performances of Prokofiev's Third Symphony. The lacerating intensity of the music – the work is based on parts of Prokofiev's opera *The Angel of Fire* – seemed to sum up the conductor's sometimes self-lacerating career. The audiences who heard it would never forget it. A week later, Thomson died after collapsing during a rehearsal with the London Philharmonic. As Christopher Bishop quoted, 'Nothing in his life became him like the leaving it.' Thomson had been due back in Scotland at the end of the season to conduct three short works by the Scottish composer, John Maxwell Geddes, followed by Beethoven's Ninth Symphony. As a memorial to him, James Loughran took over the programme intact.

14

Welcoming Weller

So now, as I begin my final chapter, the orchestra is midway between the centenary of its founding in 1891 and that of its first concert under George Henschel in 1893. The Queen has endorsed its new, by no means yet fully accepted, Royal name by attending a gala concert in Glasgow's equally new Royal Concert Hall, where Walter Weller, the new conductor and music director, treated her to a programme, not of new music, but of Tchaikovsky, Respighi and Richard Strauss, with Margaret Marshall as soloist in the *Four Last Songs*. To *Till Eulenspiegel* he brought that rich Viennese glow which is his recognised hallmark and which, after just half a season, he has already imposed on his players. As in *Romeo and Juliet* and *The Pines of Rome*, the sound was ravishing, the textures scrupulously blended, the solos exquisitely articulated, particularly those for horn in Strauss's autumnal songs.

Weller's home in Vienna, it is said, contains rooms decorated in different Viennese styles, which means, I assume, that he can move as the mood takes him from Biedermeier to Jugendstil. But his performances so far have been less clearly differentiated. Starting with Beethoven's Seventh Symphony in January 1992, they have proved clean, weighty, well upholstered. The orchestra has played well, as it was bound to do, with violin and viola tone warmly layered upon a solid bedrock of cellos and basses. This is the sort of sound which, with Weller's help, the strings are particularly keen to cultivate, and which he, for his part, says he is stamping on them as his 'signature'. This, above all, is what he has been appointed for. Edwin Paling, the leader, has expressed the hope that he will thereby renovate the mainstream repertoire from Mozart to Richard Strauss – though beyond Strauss, one imagines, he will not tread far.

Weller was the players' choice, fully endorsed by the management. After Bryden Thomson said his official adieu with an aptly bitter-edged account of Mahler's First Symphony in the spring of 1991, there had been only two obvious contenders for the job. One, from the Bolshoy Opera, was Alexander Lazarev, who had recently made some striking appearances in Scotland, both with his own orchestra and with the RSO. The other was Weller, an old friend who had conducted an exemplary account of Prokofiev's emotionally complex Sixth Symphony in 1975, a performance still spoken of with awe by those who took part in it. Since then, he had been invited back eight times.

In matters of string tone, Weller knows what he is talking about. After years of experience as leader of the Vienna Philharmonic, in which his father also played, he formed the breakaway Weller String Quartet, excelling in the Viennese classics, until the lure of conducting grew irresistible. Both as player and conductor, he exudes solid Viennese know-how. Big, burly and – by the time he reached middle age – bearded, he looks like someone who could devour a fillet steak before a concert, and a Wiener schnitzel afterwards. He wears a massive wrist-watch, though whether to time his performances or the trains and model trains which are his passion one can only guess. More importantly, he has won wide admiration for what is regarded as his straightforwardness as a musician. He lets the strings play freely (in contrast with Thomson, who was prone to needle them) and – high accolade in orchestral circles – 'does not get in the way'.

Yet by the nineteen-nineties in Britain, where he has spent a surprising amount of his life, his career was unexpectedly hanging fire. What seemed a promising relationship with Scottish Opera two decades ago, when he conducted a fine *Fidelio* and a brilliantly detailed *Der Rosenkavalier*, had fizzled out. Periods with the Royal Liverpool Philharmonic (1977–79) and the Royal Philharmonic Orchestra in London (1980–85) began better than they ended. Abroad he tended to work with second-run orchestras, and in his native Vienna his reputation was nothing special. At the age of fifty-two, he possessed a repertoire which was not only alarmingly small but failing to develop.

Lazarev, on the other hand, offered the excitement – and the risk – of the almost unknown. As a Russian, he was undoubtedly different but, so soon after Järvi, was he different enough? His repertoire was similarly slanted towards the East, and in other music – such as, during visits to Scotland, the *Eroica* symphony and Debussy's *Three Nocturnes* – he was disturbingly idiosyncratic, grinding out the mysterious central section of *Fêtes* like a threatening procession of tanks. On the other hand, Prokofiev's *Alexander Nevsky* at the Edinburgh Festival was shattering enough to suggest that here, if properly nurtured, was a very special talent indeed. The question, however, was whether, or how, it could be nurtured. Clearly, like Järvi, Lazarev was eager to develop a career in the West, but would he be someone else who just wanted to make records? Moreover – this time unlike Järvi – he would continue to have numerous Russian responsibilities at the Bolshoy and elsewhere. Opera conducting, symphony concerts and programmes with his own progressive Moscow-based chamber ensemble – which he had once brought to Glasgow for an avant-garde concert under BBC auspices – would all demand his attention. How much time would he be able to spare for an orchestra in Scotland, albeit one he was keen to conduct? That was something that would have to be sorted out before contracts were signed.

What remained equally uncertain was his reputedly volatile temperament, and how it would manifest itself if he became music director. Orchestras – British ones especially – pride themselves on their ability to size up a conductor the moment he steps on to the podium, and there was an instinctive feeling about Lazarev that, for all his technical expertise, he was someone who, as more than one player put it, might 'turn nasty'.

Interviewing him during Glasgow 1990, when he had brought the Bolshoy Opera to the Exhibition Centre and was staying at the Moat House Hotel next door, I thought him remote and stiff. Though it was said that he understood English, he insisted on speaking to me formally through an interpreter, whereas his more amiable rival from St Petersburg, Valery Gergiev, talked English eagerly when I interviewed him at the Edinburgh Festival the following year. And though casually wearing a T-shirt, Lazarev did not relax until my last question, when he permitted a ghost of a smile to cross his lips. That was when I asked him about his future relationship with the SNO, and he replied that it 'created the possibility of cycles of concerts' which might include 'a great deal of Brahms'.

Well, I had expected him to be guarded about whether he was interested in the job, but Brahms – from a conductor with a real interest in contemporary music – was a surprise. It was a surprise, too, to Christopher Bishop who, when I quizzed him about it later, said the subject of a Brahms cycle had never been raised in any of his discussions with Lazarev. But then, perhaps the passionate commitment the Bolshoy's musical director brought to all those Russian works hid the possibility that his musical ambitions actually lay in the German mainstream. Or else, as Bishop later suggested to me, the mention of Brahms was merely a Russian joke.

But if Lazarev (even making jokes) was enigmatically Russian, and potentially nasty with it, what about the seemingly genial Weller? A player who has worked frequently with him, though not in Scotland, claims that he is no exception to the rule that relationships between conductors and players almost invariably grow tricky once the initial bonding is over. Weller, in his opinion, could turn nasty, too, but 'not perhaps so quickly'. At any rate, the orchestra voted overwhelmingly for him to be Bryden Thomson's successor. And because he was free, and claimed to have 'happy memories' of the SNO, he got the job.

Who the other contenders were, apart from Lazarev, remains unclear. Perhaps there was nobody else, though Yuri Temirkanov – another volatile Russian and an attractive showman whose regular guest appearances with the orchestra were continuing to prove good value, especially if they included works by Tchaikovsky or his own puppet-like impersonation of Stravinsky's *Petrushka* – must have been considered, along with, perhaps, Valery Gergiev, who had appeared one season as an impressively capable stand-in. Then there were Sian Edwards, Jane Glover, James Judd and Christopher Seaman as possible British candidates, none really apt enough to generate much enthusiasm. Lazarev, with no offer coming from Scotland, eventually accepted the principal guest conductorship of the BBC Symphony Orchestra in London. In Glasgow, it seemed, an opportunity had been missed, though according to Christopher Bishop they remain on friendly terms. Lazarev as principal guest conductor of the RSNO is not yet an impossibility.

But the orchestra was content with Weller. Allowed entry to his first Glasgow rehearsal after his appointment as music director, I detected nothing but mutual admiration and bonhomie. The honeymoon had begun. To an onlooker, it's true, he was not good value. There were no tantrums, no threats, no insults, no quips, no tears, nothing that would stick in the memory the way Paul Kletzki's advice to the SNO's cellos had stuck in mine after I heard him rehearse Brahms's Third Symphony at the Usher Hall in

1953. Demanding ever increasing expressiveness from them in the long soulful opening to the third movement, Kletzki (famous for the occasion he broke down and wept at a London rehearsal) beseeched: 'Please, is no good unless your fingers bleed.'

Weller, in contrast, was matter of fact. As he progressed through Beethoven's Seventh Symphony, nothing much seemed to be happening – which meant that there was probably more than met the eye. Wearing a navy-blue polo neck, he had walked into the Henry Wood Hall at one minute past ten, amid applause and merry laughter. Soon, perched on a stool and conducting without a score, he was deep into the first movement, pausing to discuss, in brisk if fractured English, the tempo change after the slow introduction, and to explain how he wanted the dotted rhythms of the *vivace* to be treated. The basses, on reaching the sepulchral passage which had prompted the young Weber to declare that Beethoven was ripe for the madhouse, were told to play more quietly – 'it's *misterioso*'.

By now Weller was on his feet, conducting with big circling gestures. Before launching the slow movement, he discussed its basic dactylic pulse, then set it in motion, drawing deep, resonant tone from the cellos and basses, upon whose efforts he kept concentrating. Unlike Sir Colin Davis – who once, rehearsing a London orchestra on television, told his players he would 'talk them through' the whole of this movement – he spoke little while the music was playing.

At eleven o'clock precisely, the scherzo started. Here there were more stops than in the previous movements, and much verbal emphasis on the whirling rhythm, which Weller kept articulating as 'pa-pree-a, pa-pree-a,' as if his mind were on the peppery Austro-Hungarian spice for which Viennese cuisine is famed.

At a quarter past eleven, before the finale, there was a coffee break. The mood remained affable. In orchestra-speak, Weller had made plain that he 'knew the score' and that his interruptions were to the point. The actual performance, later in the week, was broad in flow, weighty in tone, with much structural signposting – a perceptible *rallentando* to mark the start of the first movement's recapitulation, an unusually attentive, long-drawn-out underlining of the quiet, slow-moving harmonies that steer the D major trio section back to the F major of the scherzo.

This was, above all, comfortable Beethoven, muscular but unsparkling, in which the deep pile of the strings softened the rasp of the wind, even if that rasp was an essential ingredient of Beethoven's texture in the Seventh Symphony. It was the Weller sound, and it would be heard again later in the season when he returned to conduct Dvořák's Fifth Symphony (Weller's excursions outside German and Austrian music tend to be into Czechoslovakia and other areas of Middle Europe) and in Beethoven's *Pastoral* symphony, a work that could be described as ready and waiting to receive the Weller treatment. The effect here was serene, the slow shifts of harmony – a special feature of the music – perfectly judged, the timbres shining.

Yet the performance of the *Pastoral* was also an illustration of Désiré-Emile Inghelbrecht's acid essay on false conducting traditions, walking as it did straight into one of the most famous of his traps – the *sotto voce* passage on the strings near the end of the finale, a few peaceful bars that have been likened to a last soft hymn of thanksgiving, during which there is the most restrained and narrow of crescendos from *pianissimo* up to *piano*. If this crescendo is at all exaggerated – if it is raised to *mezzo-forte* then suddenly hushed – Beethoven's melodic line is disturbed and distorted. Weller exaggerated it. His control of his little superimposed 'swell' of string tone was masterly and beautiful. But it was also self-conscious – an example, in Inghelbrecht's book, of how not to conduct Beethoven, though Weller, as a Viennese, would doubtless reckon his interpretation more authentic than that of any effete, Debussy-soaked Parisian musician.

Performances as large-scale as these, employing a full complement of strings, may be against today's stylistic trends, but they are heard to advantage in the spacious acoustics of Glasgow Royal Concert Hall, which opened in the autumn of 1990 as the most expensive and enduring celebration of Glasgow as European City of Culture. As successor to St Andrew's Hall it had been a long time coming. Was it worth the wait? The answer must be yes, with reservations. Its splendid central site, dominating the slope of Buchanan Street the way Wagner's great Festspielhaus crowns the hill above Bayreuth, had demanded a building of distinction, but the stripped down classicism of Sir Leslie Martin's design – I quote Frank Arneil Walker's sharp new Phaidon Architectural Guide to Glasgow – was of a kind that would 'make even Bucharest look interesting'.

Happily, there are more ways than one of judging a concert hall. Exciting modern concepts can be expensive and difficult to realise – think of the Sydney Opera House – and can lead, all too easily, to acoustical disaster. Arguing that the inside matters more than the outside may seem dull and unadventurous, yet it is a priority that would absolve many a boring building from charges of architectural dreariness. Departing from the traditional shoebox shape invariably involves risk. When fan forms and curves began to enter the world of music making, when suspended reflectors replaced coffered ceilings, troubles arose.

Glasgow's new auditorium looked like a compromise between a traditional Gewandhaus and a hall dependent on modern acoustical devices. To increase audience capacity – it holds some 2,500 people – the conventional rectangle was broadened until it became more square than oblong. To compensate for this, and to keep listeners in all parts of the capacious auditorium inside the sound of the orchestra, a series of large white reflectors were hung at an angle – a striking visual effect – along both sides of the auditorium. 'Well, at least it's not a disaster,' declared a senior BBC producer on hearing one of the first live acoustical tests with an orchestra on the platform. Faint praise perhaps; but to be able to say as much for any modern hall can be considered an achievement.

In fact the £30 million Glasgow Royal Concert Hall is a success, even if its name is as unexciting as its architecture. One felt bound to wonder why the thoroughly appropriate and historically relevant idea of calling it the New St Andrew's Hall was rejected in favour firstly of something as dismal as Glasgow International Concert Hall (whose acronym, as Michael Tumelty jeered in *The Herald*, would have been the cheerlessly guttural GICH) and finally of something carrying all the Victorian appeal of Glasgow Royal Infirmary?

But if, whatever it is called, it can be hailed as a good hall, the question remains: how good? Here opinions differ. Certainly it is not the equal of the even newer Birmingham Symphony Hall, upon which rather more money was spent, with rather more vision, to rather better effect. Nor, acoustically, can it compare with Glasgow's own smaller City Hall (whose future, as I write, hangs in the balance), though it is certainly more pleasant to sit in, and to promenade around. Corporate sponsors – alas, an influential factor today – are said to like its facilities. As a result it is attracting more business clients, for what they are worth, than the City Hall was ever able to.

Acoustics being at best a quasi-science – some would call it a backward one – luck plays a larger part in the success or failure of a hall than most acousticians are prepared to admit. In the end our ears, rather than technical equipment, are what matter. Moreover, psychological factors come into play. In halls where you cannot see certain instruments – and in Glasgow's, if you are sitting in the balcony at the right-hand side, you cannot easily see the double basses – you may also get the impression that you cannot hear them.

What is unpleasantly 'cold' to some ears may be enjoyably 'clear' to others; what some praise as 'warm,' others may dismiss as 'bathroomy'. Modern acousticians, such as those who helped to plan London's Royal Festival Hall and many of its successors, are frequently said to favour clarity over resonance, and find themselves forced to 'add' warmth, perhaps by way of extra reflectors or resonators, at a later date. And sometimes they succeed: the Royal Festival Hall is better now than when it was built, and the Royal Albert Hall – an auditorium of earlier vintage – much improved by its 'flying saucers'.

In terms of clarity, Glasgow Royal Concert Hall has 'modern' acoustics. Orchestral textures can usually be heard in sharply etched detail, yet are not unresonant. Soft solo timbres, in spite of the size of the place, stand out. At the opposite extreme, the climaxes of a big Shostakovich symphony are properly shattering, and the grinding discords of Stravinsky's *Rite of Spring* are accommodated in a way they could never have been in the more cramped acoustics of the City Hall.

Yet when Ernest Fleischmann, the administrator of the Los Angeles Philharmonic, brought his orchestra to Glasgow in 1991, he complained that the building lacked 'bloom'. String tone was not parched, as in many other modern halls, but it was never radiant. The sound of the full orchestra smacked you, but did not engulf you. Walter Weller's considerable success in these surroundings, therefore, must count as a happy omen. Already he has learnt to play on the hall as if it were a musical instrument and, under his baton, the orchestra is sounding increasingly at ease there.

To start with, things had seemed less promising. The SNO's opening concert, in the presence of The Princess Royal in October 1990, was one of those batty, bitty gala events, with a sprinkling of innocuous new music, which tend to be assembled at such times

and manage to displease almost everybody. The short commissioned works by Thea Musgrave and Thomas Wilson, each
employing the colourful orchestration all too vividly suggested by
titles as unpromising as *Rainbow* and *Carillon*, seemed simply to
cancel each other out. Elgar's square old choral version of the
National Anthem was chosen in preference to Britten's more dra-
matic, modern and acoustically testing one. But the sound of
the SNO Chorus in Beethoven's *Choral Fantasia* and in Vaughan
Williams's *Serenade to Music*, composed for the Jubilee Concert of
Sir Henry Wood in 1938, in any case demonstrated that choral
music had not been regarded by the hall's designers as a high
priority.

There were, however, further causes for concern. The critic of
The Independent complained that, from where he was sitting, the
piano in Liszt's First Piano Concerto was inaudible, though that
could hardly have been the fault of Scotland's bright-fingered
wunderkind, David Horne. The acoustics, therefore, were to
some extent directional. Unusually in a concert hall, downstairs
seats seemed better than upstairs ones.

But inaugural programmes are notoriously hard to assess,
because so many factors come into play. It was certainly not the
sort of occasion to which the brusque Bryden Thomson could be
expected to rise. His conducting of it, as expected, seemed more
dutiful than inspired. The event was, at best, a semi-success, and
though the hall itself was deemed more or less a triumph – especially by Glasgow District Council, who had ample cause to feel
pleased with their investment – there were nevertheless urgent
questions to be answered.

One of them soon came from Arthur Oldham, director of the
Edinburgh Festival Chorus, who wanted to know why the choir
gallery was really just an audience gallery, complete with padded
seats, perched steeply and awkwardly high above the orchestra.
The unconvincing explanation was that wrapping the audience
round the platform had been a special feature of the design plan.
Choristers, in other words, were of secondary importance, as
Oldham was able to confirm when the 250 lustrous voices of his
distinguished chorus, in their performance of Mahler's *Resurrection*
symphony later that season, were sucked – as he had feared – into
the roof of the hall through a gap in the overhead reflectors.

Oldham's diagnosis of the problem was, of course, subjective,
and an acoustician would doubtless reject it. Yet as a leading

chorus director who has worked in some of Europe's best halls, his words should have been heeded. The RSO Chorus, moreover, was steadily encountering the same problem. In its performances of Britten's *War Requiem* and *Spring Symphony* during the 1991–92 season, meticulously though these had been prepared by Christopher Bell (the latest in its line of chorusmasters), a true fortissimo proved difficult to achieve. The singers, indeed, felt so distanced, not only from the orchestra but from each other, that low-powered backward-facing loudspeakers had to be installed to enable them to hear their own voices.

But almost all modern halls – even Berlin's sublime Philharmonie – have required acoustical adjustments, and to have expected instant perfection in Glasgow would have been over-optimistic (though it does seem to have been achieved in Birmingham, in a hall modelled on an already proven auditorium in the United States). To Glasgow District Council it was all irrelevant anyway. At a press conference not long before the opening, I had raised the subject of the acoustics, because none of the officials had remembered to mention them. What were they going to be like? The senior councillor who had been extolling the splendours of the building, and was answering questions, looked puzzled and said 'Eh?' and 'Ah?' and 'The what?' Someone whispered in his ear. Swelling with Glasgow pride, he announced: 'They will be superb.'

Still, Glasgow pride usually gets results more quickly than Edinburgh. Concerts in the new hall have continued to be monitored by the acousticians, who are aware that improvements are called for if choral music is to sound well, and that the rumble of Glasgow's underground railway remains audible from down below, even though the building was constructed on rubber pads in order to suppress this. Something, we have been assured, will be done. Of the orchestras that appear regularly there, the RSNO is the one that generally sounds the best. The strings have polish and, in soft passages, beauty and delicacy. Matthias Bamert speedily showed its possibilities in twentieth-century music with a witty, pungent performance of Kurt Weill's Second Symphony. Sir Alexander Gibson, conducting some of his beloved Sibelius for the first time in these surroundings, turned to the audience at the end and publicly praised the place – a nice and, at that point, much needed comment from someone who, for years, had really cared about music in Glasgow, and who was now the orchestra's president.

As for Christopher Bishop, chided though he is for not having Scotland's interests at heart, he has consistently championed Glasgow's new hall over Birmingham's.

But what remains needed at the intersection of Buchanan Street and Sauchiehall Street is a unified artistic policy. Far from being, as was originally hoped, the hall's 'orchestra-in-residence', the RSNO is simply one of numerous users. It has no priority, no supreme right of access. It rents the hall each week (for a fee high enough to enrage not only Bishop but the entire board of directors) just like any other orchestra. RSNO rehearsals continue to take place in the RSNO Centre. Things are different in England, where the Royal Liverpool Philharmonic owns the Liverpool Philharmonic Hall and is thus genuinely an orchestra-in-residence. The City of Birmingham Symphony Orchestra, at least as long as Simon Rattle remains in charge, is the acknowledged glory of Birmingham Symphony Hall – as even the hall's name implies. Manchester still has the scope to make its soon-to-be-built auditorium the Hallé's hall. In Glasgow, this status was never extended to the RSNO. But then, it could be argued, the RSNO is at least spared the responsibility of running the place, and having to make it pay, as Scottish Opera must do with the Theatre Royal.

A special advantage, or so it initially seemed, of a hall that was independently run and democratically open to all was the grand international orchestra series that brought Glasgow 1990 to its musical climax, and augured encouragingly for the future. Two concerts by the Berlin Philharmonic, even with the sour Kurt Sanderling rather than the smooth (but by then deceased) Herbert von Karajan as conductor, showed the possibilities that a large, ambitiously exploited new Glasgow auditorium could open up. A Brahms cycle from Kurt Masur and the Leipzig Gewandhaus Orchestra, Bruckner's Fifth Symphony from Riccardo Chailly and the Concertgebouw, Russian delights from various Russian orchestras and an uncompromisingly tragic performance of Shostakovich's Tenth Symphony from the Los Angeles Philharmonic under Sanderling whetted appetites for a diet of splendours.

Sadly, it was a diet that proved too rich to sustain. As time passed, the international orchestra series dwindled, along with the civic thrust that had established Glasgow as European City of Culture. Fears that the building would prove no more than a garage for whatever orchestras or groups happened to be passing through – Christopher Bishop's old orchestra, the Philharmonia, dropped in one night with a programme it was also giving in London and Eastbourne – rather than an integrated orchestral palace, with the RSNO at its heart, showed signs of being realised.

But better times may come again; and, in defence of his own policies, Cameron McNicol, the hall's Scottish-born manager who had progressed from the running of the Lochgelly Centre to that of the Royal Albert Hall in London, would claim that he was doing just what he had been hired to do. His brief was to fill the hall, on a hire basis, with as many suitable events as he could. If that meant quantities of rival *Messiahs* in December – an example he put to me – it was of no consequence to him, so long as the performers paid their fees. It was certainly one way of running a concert hall, even if in London the method had resulted in a preponderance of Viennese nights, *Battle* symphonies, *1812* overtures and Tchaikovsky B flat minors.

In Glasgow, these particular slots were promptly filled by a blatantly populist organisation called the Glasgow Philharmonic, which began to appear regularly and about whose easy success the RSO soon became resentful. So in the spring of 1992, at the orchestra's suggestion, an attempt was made to beat the Philharmonic at its own game with a series of similar programmes which merely proved that the Philharmonic did these things rather better. But it certainly suggested that Scotland's senior orchestra was overreacting to events which at one time would have seemed outside its own sphere of activities. The trouble was that, with a deficit as big as the RSO's, nothing could be considered outside that sphere any more.

Yet audiences, so it was claimed, were holding firm. Weller, in box-office terms, was good news. But backstage, as nobody could fail to perceive, things were in disarray. At one time, no doubt, the management would have managed to conceal that there was deep discontent inside the orchestra, along with the possibility of industrial action buttressed by the now predictable votes of no confidence. In a series of audacious leaks to the The Herald, however, the grievances of the players were not only aired but supported by a root-and-branch examination of their causes, written by *The Herald*'s music critic.

For Christopher Bishop, who in his Philharmonia days had had to fight many battles, it must have been embarrassing, though not yet a cause for alarm. 'I'm a fairly hardened old warrior,' he remarked at one point. But in the hitherto sheltered world of

Scottish music, it was all something new and, for newspaper readers, utterly enthralling. As disclosure followed disclosure, people could not get enough of it. If it was *The Herald*, rather than *The Scotsman*, which seemed to print all the best stories, this was doubtless because Michael Tumelty knew all the players and had a Glaswegian's sympathy for their problems. What began as a series of audacious exclusives soon developed into a relentless crusade whose aim, quite clearly, was to question, if not disparage, just about every policy decision that had been made since Bishop became chief executive.

There was certainly plenty to ventilate. The difficulty, in comparing the statements of the players with those of the management, was in deciding which were actually true. For example, on a fundamental level, had the players agreed, or had they not, to share hotel rooms on foreign tours? The ambiguities surrounding what, to non-musicians, might have seemed an absolutely straightforward question were complex and unending. There were dialogues with Walter Weller to be weighed up, and letters from Christopher Bishop.

'What's this I hear about you not wanting to share rooms?' Weller suddenly asked his players after a rehearsal, pointing out that the Vienna Philharmonic shared rooms, and that a possible RSO tour in 1993 might depend on it. The players replied that they never said they would not share rooms. Bishop, on hearing this, immediately demanded confirmation in writing, adding that he was fascinated to know that they were prepared to share rooms, because he had received a letter from the Musicians' Union saying that all members were entitled to single-room accommodation unless they specifically wished to share with someone else. And so the debate continued, with everybody denying that it was an issue but simultaneously demonstrating that it was.

Bishop, for his part, knew perfectly well that the Philharmonia, in common with other leading London orchestras, traditionally refuses to share rooms. In private, indeed, he was quite prepared to sympathise with those who wanted rooms to themselves, touring being nerve-racking enough without nocturnal or early morning personality clashes. The problem was simply one of costing. The Philharmonia, during the nine years he was in charge of it, had been abroad no fewer than twenty-five times and simply possessed better bargaining power with foreign agents.

That is an example of the fine detail of a contract orchestra's life outside London. What Bishop and the board of directors may regard as reasonable and hardly non-negotiable items of cost-cutting are seen by the players as insensitive interference with their lifestyle and with cherished work practices – such as how much, and in what way, they can charge travel expenses for their concerts inside Scotland, and whether they are defrauding the management if they demand a train fare although travelling by car. As for medium-haul trips, cheapness has increasingly begun to take precedence over comfort. A visit to Belfast by bus and boat, rather than by air, caused immense displeasure – perhaps because Scottish Opera had recently flown there and agitated members of the RSO by proclaiming 'Welcome to the RSO boat people' – though when orchestras perform in Orkney they usually go, without demur, by the Pentland Firth.

But then, players everywhere battle with their bosses over what, to an onlooker, must seem petty details. Weller, as an ex-player, knows this very well, and is conscious that he must strike a prudent balance in his relationship with his new orchestra and its management. As a citizen of Vienna, where zephyrs traditionally blow rumours and rancours hither and thither, he has doubtless learnt the art of diplomacy, if not wiliness, and of how to show himself, if necessary, to be on everybody's side.

In Glasgow, in any case, bigger issues than travel expenses soon proved to be at stake. These were merely the tip of a very substantial iceberg. A private, and possibly damaging, letter about the threatened non-renewal of the orchestra's important contract with Chandos Records found its way into the hands of *The Herald*, where its implications were assessed beneath a six-column heading, 'Symptoms of malaise in RSO'.

Now here was something that could really cut deep, though like much else it was open to misunderstanding. Not all leaks are quite what they seem, and in order to appraise the problem one needed to know more than what *The Herald* was able to divulge. But when Lord Goold, the new chairman, soon afterwards publicly put the blame for the orchestra's unrest on a small group of troublemakers, that was a very different matter. Seventy-eight of the orchestra's eighty-three members promptly signed a letter to *The Herald* stating 'unequivocally that the concerns and fears expressed by our elected representatives are not those of "a small minority", as Lord Goold claims, but are shared by all the undersigned players of the orchestra.' *Touché, sans doute*, and a photocopy of the letter, complete with signatures, was front-paged by *The Herald* to immense effect.

It was like the Fiona Grant and Stephen Carpenter periods all over again, only considerably worse and publicly exposed each morning like a running sore. The lack of foreign touring was diagnosed as just another serious malaise. Yet to do anything other than what he was doing, Bishop might have argued, would have made each of these activities a potential loss-maker, and the RSO could no longer afford to make a loss.

The trouble, it became clear, was that with a deficit of more than £200,000, and with now regular cash top-ups from the orchestra's life-saving Endowment Fund, Bishop could afford to do very little. A trip to Greece and Turkey, with the immature and not exactly coruscating James Judd as guest conductor, carried little prestige.

The orchestra's substantial centenary tour of Scotland, at any rate, was appropriate and successful. With heavy sponsorship from British Telecom, it proved enjoyable – worth doing and, indeed, worth repeating (as happened, in more concentrated form, in the autumn of 1992). It took the players to many places in the High-lands, Islands and Borders which they had not visited for years.

Yet of a true centenary celebration, something that would go down in history, there remained little sign. In America, the New York Philharmonic had commemorated its 150th anniversary by commissioning more than thirty new pieces, many of them from major composers. How many composers – and in particular how many Scottish composers – were approached by the RSO for something new? The answer requires little guesswork.

Nor was it merely a matter of commissions. In Birmingham, Simon Rattle had conceived a visionary ten-year programme entitled 'Towards the Millennium', to provide his orchestra with a progressive repertoire for the nineteen-nineties. Its basis was nothing less than the entire history of twentieth-century music. But where, with a centenary to commemorate in the last decade of the century, was the RSO's vision? Where was Walter Weller's? Was anyone even thinking in those terms, or in terms in any way beyond, say, the next Beethoven or Brahms cycle?

No doubt everything came down to cash. Everything, indeed, seemed to possess that improvised air – so familiar in Britain – of an orchestra, or at any rate a management and board of directors, not quite in command of a situation, and with insufficient money or inclination to do anything much about it. Having been at the top of what, in financial terms, is known as the 'regional' league – a word much disliked in Scotland – the orchestra's salary scale was now, with Bournemouth's, at the bottom. Yet the offer of a fourteen per cent rise, in exchange for the sacrifice of a number of long-established work practices, failed to pour oil on troubled waters and was refused. As Gerald Larner speculated in *The Guardian*, the fact that Christopher Bishop was 'having so much trouble in getting the RSO to accept a rise like that while other orchestras have settled for far less, indicates either an extraordinary lack of negotiating skills or a more deep-seated dissatisfaction with management of the orchestra's affairs'. In Bishop's words, however, 'it might equally have indicated how deeply entrenched and financially rewarding to themselves the orchestra's work practices were'.

Meanwhile, an artistic toe-hold had been regained in the London proms in 1991, when Sir Alexander Gibson conducted *The Mary Bean*, a new concert overture by Martin Dalby commissioned by the BBC in celebration of the RSO's centenary, alongside his evergreen interpretation of Rakhmaninov's Second Symphony. Further performances of *The Mary Bean*, again with Gibson as conductor, were given in October 1992 in Glasgow, Edinburgh, Dundee and Aberdeen (Dalby's home town).

The Edinburgh Festival – which in Frank Dunlop's farewell year had given the RSO its most prominent role for ages with a performance of Britten's *War Requiem*, again conducted by Gibson – continued to be genuinely encouraging, now that it had Brian McMaster in command. In 1992 the orchestra was allotted three important dates as part of a massive Tchaikovsky retrospective which anticipated by a year the centenary of the composer's death.

Tchaikovsky, in normal circumstances, might seem no more than business as usual to a symphony orchestra, but this was different. The players came under the guest conductorship of three notable exponents of Russian music, among them two old friends, Neeme Järvi (since 1989 Conductor Laureate of the orchestra thanks to the efforts of Christopher Bishop) and Gennady Rozhdestvensky, the latter with a typically probing programme devoted to the Russian view of *Hamlet* – not only Tchaikovsky's overture, but also the world premiere of music by Shostakovich, along with some Prokofiev new the the RSO's repertoire.

This was encouraging; but if managerial problems continued, at least it could be claimed that they were not confined to the RSO during the financial recession which Britain was still undergoing. Most of Scotland's musical scene had been in disarray for at least a year. Richard Mantle, the latest in Scottish Opera's line of managing directors, had departed suddenly, leaving a vast deficit and much speculation about the circumstances of his going. His mounting problems were inherited by the more likeable Richard Jarman, formerly John Drummond's assistant at the Edinburgh Festival, who soon won everybody's sympathy, even when he was forced to cancel the second half of a new *Ring* cycle.

The Edinburgh Festival itself had parted company with Frank Dunlop, again in not the friendliest of fashions. There were also, as one member put it, 'trials and tribulations' inside the Scottish Chamber Orchestra, though at least, with regular foreign tours and a plan to become Scotland's first truly European orchestra with a residency in Paris, this did remain an organisation with an outward semblance of imagination, financial prosperity and recognisable ambition. Over the BBC Scottish Symphony Orchestra, on the other hand, there again lay the old fear of disbandment that invariably occurs when its masters in London are feeling the financial pinch.

So Christopher Bishop was not the only beleaguered man in Scotland in 1992. But if he has a special administrative attribute, it lies in his ability – in public at least – to keep his *sang froid* when the going gets rough. While *The Herald* continued to rail against him, he elegantly sustained a Harold MacMillanesque façade that it was all no more than a little local difficulty. In this, he had what appeared to be the full support of Lord Goold and his outsize board of directors, whose membership, it was now generally agreed, needed to be cut by half. Goold, a former chairman of the Scottish Tories and a zealous Unionist, was unquestionably – from one point of view – the right man to keep the unruly orchestra in order. But in combination with Christopher Bishop, and with editorial support from *The Scotsman* and the *Sunday Times*, he represented what the players all too palpably considered to be the unacceptable face of the Thatcher and post-Thatcher era. Clearly, they thought, the intention was simply to bully them into submission.

But in a centre-page article in the *Independent on Sunday*, Neal Ascherson, a staunch Edinburgh-born, London-based crusader for

Scottish independence, characteristically entered the fray over the question of the orchestra's new name and the loss of its 'national' identity tag. In a diatribe against the disease-like spread of the word 'Royal' in cultural circles, he pointed out how in 1988 the National Theatre had become the Royal National Theatre. Until then, he said, the theatre had seemed to belong to the public. To be 'Royal' suddenly diminished it. Would it become 'just another scroll of gilded plaster in the Ancient British Pageant?' The question could soon have been asked equally of the SNO.

The excuse for the transmogrification of the orchestra was put down largely to cash: 'When Thatcherite cultural policy began to tip subsidised music into the shark pool of commercialism, the SNO did badly in the scrabble for tour bookings. But in 1987, Japanese impresarios arrived demanding an orchestra with a "Royal" handle. None was available. They fell back on "royal sponsorship," and the SNO – whose patron is The Queen – won the Japanese award.'

That, of course, was in Stephen Carpenter's time. But the success, Ascherson surmised, must have made the board think. Since the SNO already had The Queen as its patron, why not have the word 'Royal' added to the orchestra's name? Most organisations which receive Royal status let it be assumed that the initiative comes from The Queen herself. Not so; you have to apply informally to the Home Secretary (or, if it is Scotland, via the Scottish Office to the Palace) asking for a favourable recommendation to be made to the Crown. Once this has been done, the rest is automatic. So the SNO chairman made his confidential plea, and in the spring of 1991 the SNO became the RSO.

More than a year later, however, the name was still refusing to stick in the minds of the Scottish public, who went on happily talking about the SNO, even though the management thought that the word 'national' was nowadays narrow and provincial and did the orchestra a disservice abroad.

Local supporters, however, did not care in that sort of way about the orchestra's foreign image. They cared about its Scottish one. In any case, the orchestra was already quite widely known abroad as the SNO. Why change? 'National' was a reminder of what the orchestra actually was. True, nobody had ever attempted to call Scottish Opera the Scottish National Opera, but there was a sound reason for that. The name would inevitably have been initialised as SNO, thus causing confusion in Scottish musical circles. Perhaps, now that the initials have been freed, Scottish Opera could respond to the RSO by renaming itself Scottish National Opera; indeed it has been proposed that its orchestra, if the merger with the BBC SSO goes through, should be known as the National Orchestra of Scotland – which, in December 1992, quickly prompted the RSO to revert to calling itself the RSNO.

What's in a name? The question with which this book began clearly continues to matter. But the players themselves might at present consider it a side-issue. The quality of the orchestra, they would say, is what really counts. And indeed the Oslo Philharmonic, which nobody could describe as one of the world's more thrilling names, was nothing exciting until Mariss Yansons got hold of it and brought it fame. The Orchestre de la Suisse Romande, on the other hand, lapsed into Swiss anonymity after Ernest Ansermet's death. The European Community may be big in Brussels but who can name a Belgian orchestra of world class?

Conductors, in other words, matter. Orchestras, like politicians, rise and slide, and British critics take particular pleasure in naming bests and worsts. In London, the LPO, LSO and Philharmonia rotate in excellence, with the BBC Symphony Orchestra offering the most interesting programmes and the Royal Philharmonic, as always, heading nowhere. The City of Birmingham Symphony will flourish as long as Rattle is around, but even he will move one day or, if he remains, the players will eventually say they want a change. In Manchester, there are high hopes for Kent Nagano, who will be as different from Barbirolli as he is from James Loughran and the unspellable, unmemorable, though musically thoroughly sound Stanislaw Skrowaczewski. In Liverpool, Libor Pešek seemed good news, though whether he has the staying power is now in doubt. Bournemouth, having advanced from the grimness of Rudolph Barshai to the blandness of Andrew Litton, seems as far as it has ever been, at least since Constantin Silvestri's day, from any major rating in the British league table.

But how the RSNO rates is, or should be, perfectly clear. With a really meaningful concert policy, it would be – as it has been, off and on, for many years – the best British orchestra outside London. If it does not at present score as high as Birmingham, it is for reasons of programming, and for the lack of – let us say – genuinely interesting interpretations of the works it performs, rather than for any shortcomings in the quality of its playing. Whether it will achieve its potential with Weller remains to be seen. If one's criterion is what Michael Tilson Thomas is doing, or what someone like Istvan Kertesz used to do, with the LSO, then fine. There are probably good times ahead. If something more than that is wanted, much will depend on choice of guest conductors. Christopher Bishop, no doubt, would put it somewhat differently, and so, I expect, would the players, who wanted Weller, after all, and have a high respect for him.

And Weller himself, it must be said, is bursting with enthusiasm, describing the orchestra as 'something special' and 'fantastic people' and confirming that he and they are 'a family, a mafia in a positive way' (how this makes Christopher Bishop feel would be interesting to know). Speaking to him at the Moat House Hotel, which has replaced the defunct Moore's as the place which the orchestra's more resident conductors regard as home, I found him just the jolly Viennese he is said to be, his face clouding only momentarily when he touches on 'the problem', saying that 'there is no need, it is not necessary, it is absolute nonsense. I am unhappy about, the orchestra is unhappy about, all are unhappy about, but I can't say who is guilty.'

Pressed to continue, he bubbles on about how things will change: 'We have many tours in the next years, to Germany, Spain, Austria, Prague, Budapest, maybe Switzerland and Japan. In recording we may have lost the Chandos connection, but now we have Collins.' He leans forward confidentially, saying he has other ideas. In Copenhagen he has just conducted a concert performance of Wagner's *Tristan*, uncut, three times, all five hours of it. 'And the audience went wild. Thirty-two minutes of applause! In Copenhagen! Around the world this is what people now want, concert performances of opera, of Wagner, just to listen to the music. I have identified the trend. I am one of the men of it. Here we could do *Elektra*, *Salome*, *Tannhäuser*, with the best singers we can get, from Bayreuth, Munich. A new idea. We don't disturb Scottish Opera.'

Well, maybe not. What he will definitely not disturb is Musica Nova, not personally anyway, since it is no more his scene than it was Neeme Järvi's or Bryden Thomson's. Indeed, of the orchestra's four musical directors since Musica Nova was founded, only one – Sir Alexander Gibson – has shown any interest in it, and in recent years only Matthias Bamert's fortitude has kept it going, though even he lost heart last time when he had the chance to bring Boulez and Stockhausen to Glasgow and ended up with

John Cage and Wolfgang Rihm instead. It happened, admittedly, at a time when there was nobody in the orchestra's office to act on Bamert's advice. Carpenter had just left. Bishop had not yet arrived. Knussen, holding the fort, could not say yes. The opportunity passed. But it didn't in England, where the Huddersfield Contemporary Music Festival, combining Cage with Boulez, and throwing in Messiaen as well, all of them in person, was steadily stealing Musica Nova's thunder, and providing, as *The Guardian* put it, 'the ultimate festival achievement'.

Whether, and in what form, Musica Nova survives the RSNO's financial and artistic troubles remains to be seen. Christopher Bishop is known to disapprove of the 'ghetto-ising' of contemporary music, and to believe that it should take its chance out in the open, as part of the general repertoire, in front of an ordinary audience. Thus a piano concerto enticingly entitled *The Berserking*, by one of the most talented of the new generation of Scottish composers, James MacMillan, found its way into the winter season (conducted, predictably, by the tireless Matthias Bamert) after its Musica Nova premiere. By propping it up with Tchaikovsky's *Pathétique* symphony, Bishop ensured it a sizeable audience not only in Glasgow and Edinburgh but also in Aberdeen and Dundee.

What Bishop does have, and he knows it, is a good orchestra, and one which, whatever working practices it wants to hang on to, is ready for other sorts of change. 'It would be tactless but true', he says, 'to point out that the quality of players in London is higher individually, but the degree of unanimity you get from having an orchestra that plays together all the time offsets that. I am immensely impressed by the playing of the RSNO as it now is.'

So although London has a larger pool of talent to draw from, the RSO has distinct advantages of its own. Because it is a contract orchestra, it can rely on its members to be there when needed, whereas in London's self-governing orchestras, where the players operate on a freelance basis, a section leader can vanish for periods in order to pursue a private career.

At one time, praising the unanimity of the SNO would have meant little. In Rankl's day, it was not a good enough orchestra for unanimity, if that was the word, to matter very much. But most British orchestras have steadily improved, and the RSNO is no exception. 'Even in small ways,' says Christopher Bishop, 'I would take credit for a certain tightening up of discipline. The players come on stage as an orchestra now, instead of in straggly ones and twos like chamber groups. And I insist on an extra half-hour rehearsal immediately before every concert, which is particularly useful if a conductor doesn't know a hall. It helps to concentrate everybody's mind. The players argued at first, but they soon saw the wisdom of it.'

No doubt it is statements like this which make the players say Bishop is intransigent. As one of them put it to me: 'If he had not reacted to us the way he did, we wouldn't have reacted to him.' Though this sounds suspiciously like what used to be said about Robert Ponsonby and Fiona Grant, there may be some truth in it. 'What we were told, at least by implication,' says another player, 'was that we had tried to get rid of our two most recent administrators, and that in the end we made life so unpleasant for them that they went. So this time the board of directors wanted a tough nut, with brass neck and a thick skin, who could stand up to pressure and was impervious to criticism.'

Against the background of British politics today, it certainly sounds plausible. As a way of getting the best out of a maverick body of people like an orchestra, however, it was courting trouble. 'What they should really have been doing', says yet another player, 'was looking for reasons for the problems and making sure they were solved, rather than trying to call us to heel. It's a question of attitude. All we want is someone fired with enthusiasm, who is imaginative and inventive, promoting the orchestra the way it should be promoted, and capable of using its resources in new and different ways.'

So would the orchestra's interests perhaps be better served by an administrator elected from among the players themselves? Bishop reports that, in exasperation, he once put the idea to them. 'If you want to be self-governing', he told them, 'then just say so.' But the players did not rise to the challenge, and perhaps they never will. 'We don't actually see that as a solution. We don't want to be self-governing, not at the moment anyway. People seem to think that we're dissatisfied with the system, but we're not. It works elsewhere, after all. People also say we're looking for power, but that just isn't the case, it's not even a topic. It's just a red herring to say we're after self-government. A self-governing orchestra still has to employ a chief executive.'

What this player did not add was that a self-governing orchestra can get rid of an unpopular administrator or conductor more easily, though without necessarily finding a superior replacement. The Philharmonia had about fifteen managers between the time it became self-governing in the nineteen-sixties and the start of Bishop's nine-year tenure in the nineteen-seventies. To suggest that orchestras get the managers they deserve would obviously be too simplistic, but there are moments when it is tempting to say so all the same.

So where, at the age of a hundred, is the RSNO heading? All one can take is the long view. Bishop, as reported in the introduction to this book, has stated that he will return to London in the autumn of 1993, thus providing ample time for a replacement to be found. In response to his decision, Jeremy Fletcher, chairman of the players' committee, expressed feelings of joy and sadness on behalf of the orchestra – joy that Bishop was leaving, but 'sadness that it was not for another year'. To this, Bishop replied 'How very witty'.

Whoever replaces Bishop and, ultimately, Weller – a conductor whose restricted Central European repertoire will be increasingly a liability, unless he is counterbalanced by a principal guest conductor more progressive in outlook, and with Sir Alexander Gibson's belief in Scottish music – may turn out to be superior or inferior. Finances may improve or they may not. The halcyon days, if ever there were any, may be over but they may return. All I can say is that things are very different now from when I first heard Scotland's senior orchestra, and very different from when, as a young music critic in Edinburgh, I first wrote about it.

In spite of the recent unrest, no harm has been done to the playing, which by common consent is better than ever. In spite of uncertainty among the players about the idea of self-government, self-government may come in the end – and perhaps sooner than is thought. Indeed, as Christopher Bishop (who has experience of both sorts of set-up) is prepared to admit, self-governing orchestras can be easier to manage, because a more equable *modus vivendi* thereby tends to establish itself between players and administrators. As this book goes to press, discussions have been quietly proceeding about radical changes in the running of the orchestra, and Lord Goold, after only twenty months as chairman, has announced his intention to resign – thus, by implication, leaving the way clear for a player rather than an outsider to be the orchestra's next chairman.

Meanwhile, in an independent review of the state of the orchestra, the Scottish Arts Council in October 1992 identified a variety of 'strengths and weaknesses' within the RSNO's current strategies, and recommended 'options for change to achieve greater realisation of objectives'. Though sternly worded, and containing more rebukes than compliments, the report stated that there were few external threats to impede the orchestra's progress to a brighter future.

Tantalisingly, my final page leaves the Royal Scottish National Orchestra in a state of flux. But its achievements are already part of history. What Barbirolli did, what Gibson did, what Järvi did – all these contributions have helped to make the orchestra what it is, and given it its place in the development and progress of symphonic music. The present recriminations will doubtless lead to others. Orchestras are like that. But they are also people who can perform Mahler's Eighth Symphony. And that is what matters most of all.

BIBLIOGRAPHY

A select list of books consulted

Beranek, Leo L.: *Music, Acoustics and Architecture* (Wiley, 1962)
Bing, Rudolf: *5000 Nights at the Opera* (Hamish Hamilton, 1972)
Bookspan, Martin and Yockey, Ross: *Zubin Mehta* (Robert Hale, 1978)
Cardus, Neville: *Cardus on Music* (Hamish Hamilton, 1988)
Culshaw, John: *Putting the Record Straight* (Secker & Warburg, 1981)
Haltrecht, Montague: *The Quiet Showman* (Collins, 1975)
Holst, Imogen: *Gustav Holst, a biography* (OUP, 1959)
Hughes, Spike: *Glyndebourne* (David & Charles, 1981)
Inghelbrecht, D-E.: *The Conductor's World* (Peter Nevill, 1953)
Kennedy, Michael: *Barbirolli, Conductor Laureate* (MacGibbon & Kee, 1971)
Lebrecht, Norman: *The Maestro Myth* (Simon & Schuster, 1991)
Porter, Andrew: *Music of Three Seasons, 1974–77* (Chatto & Windus, 1979)
Prieberg, Fred K.: *Trial of Strength* (Quartet, 1992)
Rosenthal, Harold: *Opera at Covent Garden* (Gollancz, 1967)
Rubinstein, Arthur: *My Young Years* (Jonathan Cape, 1980)
Shaw, George Bernard: *Shaw's Music* (Max Reinhardt, 1981)

APPENDIX I

Conductors, Associate Conductors, Principal Guest Conductors and Leaders of the orchestra from 1891 to 1993

CONDUCTORS

George Henschel	1893–95	Robert Heger	1929
Willem Kes	1895–98	Robert Heger	1930
Wilhelm Bruch	1898–1900	Albert van Raalte	1930
Frederic Cowen	1900–1910	Landon Ronald	1930
Emil Mlynarski	1910–1916	John Barbirolli	1930
		Nikolai Malko	1930
Concerts abandoned	1916–1919	Albert van Raalte	1931
Landon Ronald	1919–1923	John Barbirolli	1931
Serge Koussevitzky	1923	Landon Ronald	1931
Adrian C. Boult	1923	Basil Cameron	1931
Landon Ronald	1923	Constant Lambert	1931
Maurice Besly	1923	Issay Dobrowen	1931
Emil Mlynarski	1923	Albert van Raalte	1932
Felix Weingartner	1924	John Barbirolli	1932
Václav Talich	1924	John Barbirolli	1933–36
Emil Mlynarski	1924	Robert Heger	1933
Landon Ronald	1924	Landon Ronald	1933
Felix Weingartner	1925	Adrian C. Boult	1934
Václav Talich	1925	George Schnéevoight	1934
Emil Mlynarski	1925	Georg Szell	1936–39
Hermann Abendroth	1925	Aylmer Buesst	1939–40
Václav Talich	1926	Warwick Braithwaite	1940–45
Vladimir Golschmann	1927	Walter Susskind	1946–52
Hermann Abendroth	1927	Karl Rankl	1952–56
Albert Coates	1927	Hans Swarowsky	1957–59
Vladimir Golschmann	1928	Alexander Gibson	1959–84
Albert Coates	1928	Neeme Järvi	1984–88
Albert van Raalte	1928	(Conductor Laureate 1989–)	
Albert van Raalte	1929	Bryden Thomson	1988–91
Vladimir Golschmann	1929	Walter Weller	1992–

ASSOCIATE CONDUCTORS

Julius Harrison	1920–21	Roderick Brydon	1966–68
Thomas Matthews	1953–59	Alan Suttie	1966–71
Leon Lovett	1963–68	Julian Dawson	1971–74
Bryden Thomson	1966–68		

PRINCIPAL GUEST CONDUCTORS

Gary Bertini	1971–81	Matthias Bamert	1988–90
Paavo Berglund	1981–84		

LEADERS

Maurice Sons	1891–1903	Thomas Carter	1936–37
Henri Verbrugghen	1903–14	Henri Temianka	1937–39
Horace Fellowes	1914–20	David McCallum	1939–40
Barry Squires	1920–23	Reginald Whitehouse	1940–47
Horace Fellowes	1923–26	Jean Rennie	1947–53
Loris Blofield	1926–29	Thomas Matthews	1953–59
Sidney Bowman	1929–31	Sam Bor	1959–74
Max Jaffa	1931–32	Michael D. Davis	1974–76
David McCallum	1932–36	Edwin Paling	1976–

APPENDIX II

Premieres performed since 1950

SNO or RSNO Commission★

1950	Cedric Thorpe Davie	Festival Overture★
1951	Iain Hamilton	Variations for Strings
1952	Iain Hamilton	Symphony No 1
1953	Bruce Montgomery	*The Century's Crown*★
1959	Iain Hamilton	Ecossaise★
1961	*Musica Viva*	Sinfonia for two orchestras
	Iain Hamilton	Piano Concerto★
	Thea Musgrave	*Obliques*★
	Gordon Jacob	Fantasia on Scottish Tunes★
1963	Anthony Hedges	Comedy Overture
	Thea Musgrave	Festival Overture
1964	John Purser	Opus 7 for Orchestra★
1966	Martin Dalby	Waltz Overture
	David Dorward	Choral Settings of George Mackay Brown
	Thomas Wilson	Carmina Sacra
1967	Thomas Wilson	Symphony No 2
1968	David Dorward	Concerto for wind and percussion
1969	Thomas Wilson	Concerto for Orchestra
	Wilfrid Mellers	*Yeibichai*
	Robin Orr	*From the Book of Philip Sparrow*
	Arthur Oldham	Scots Songs
1970	Martin Dalby	Symphony
	Ronald Stevenson	Scots Dance Toccata
1971	*Musica Nova*	
	Iain Hamilton	*Alastor*★
	Thomas Wilson	Sequentia Passionis★
	Luciano Berio	*Bewegung*★
	Douglas Young	*Departure* (Rankl Prize)★
	Thea Musgrave	Horn Concerto★

	Thomas Wilson	Te Deum
	John Purser	Comedy Overture★
	Kenneth Leighton	Dance Overture★
1972	Graham Williams	Symphony (Ian Whyte Award)★
	Sebastian Forbes	Symphony★
	John Currie	Christmas Scene No 1
1973	Musica Nova	
	Luciano Berio	Still★
	Martin Dalby	The Tower of Victory★
	Peter Maxwell Davies	Stone Litany★
	John Purser	The Undertaker
		(Scottish Opera)
	John Currie	Christmas Scene No 2
1974	John Currie	A String of Scots Songs★
		Christmas Scene No 3
	Iain Hamilton	The Catiline Conspiracy
		(Scottish Opera)
1975	Iain Hamilton	Aurora★
	Colin Matthews	Fourth Sonata (Ian Whyte
		Award)★
	Robin Orr	Weir of Hermiston
		(Scottish Opera)
	John Currie	Christmas Scene No 4
1976	Musica Nova	
	Morton Feldman	Orchestra★
	David Dorward	Piano Concerto★
	Harrison Birtwistle	Melencolia I★
	George Newsom	To the Edge of Doom★
	Wilfred Josephs	Clarinet Concerto★
	William Wordsworth	Confluence
	John Currie	Christmas Scene No 5
		'The Christmas Animals'
1977	Kenneth Leighton	Symphony No 2 (Sinfonia
		Mistica)
	Alan Hoddinott	Passagio
	Arthur Oldham	Psalms in Time of War
	John Currie	Christmas Scene No 6
		'The Weather'
	Wilma Paterson	Et in Arcadia Ego
1978	Bruce Cole	The Foundry of Minstrels★
	John McLeod	Lieder der Jugend
	John Currie	Christmas Scene No 7
		'The Christmas Dance'
	Tomasz Sikorski	Music in Twilight

1979	Edward Harper	Symphony*
	Lyell Cresswell	*Salm* (Ian Whyte Award)*
	Musica Nova	
	Brian Ferneyhough	*La Terre est un Homme**
	Robin Holloway	Concerto for Orchestra No 2*
	Thomas Wilson	Symphony No 3*
1981	Anthony Burgess	A Glasgow Overture
	William Wordsworth	*Cosmos*
	Simon Thorne	*3D for orchestra* (Ian Whyte Award)*
	Musica Nova	
	Jonathan Harvey	*Whom Ye Adore**
	Judith Weir	*Ballad**
	Alexander Goehr	*Deux Etudes**
1982	John McLeod	*The Seasons of Dr Zhivago**
1983	Iain Hamilton	Symphony No 4 in B*
1984	*Musica Nova*	
	Lyell Cresswell	Cello Concerto*
	Per Nørgaard	*Illumination**
	John Casken	*Orion over Farne**
	Robert Parris	Chamber Music*
1985	John Marlow Rhys	*Aquileia* (Ian Whyte Award)*
	Garrett O'Brien	A Lowland Rhapsody
	William Sweeney	*Sunset Song*
1987	*Musica Nova*	
	Toru Takemitsu	Two Fanfares*
	James Dillon	*Helle Nacht**
	Mark Anthony Turnage	*Gross Intrusion**
	Thomas Wilson	Piano Concerto
	Douglas Young	*Rain, Steam and Speed**
1988	Andrew Vores	*Twistification* (Ian Whyte Award)*
	Thomas Wilson	*Passeleth Tapestry*
1990	William Sweeney	Air, Strathspey and Reel
	Musica Nova	
	James MacMillan	*The Beserking* (Piano Concerto)*
	Wolfgang Rihm	*In's Offene**
	Thomas Wilson	*Carillon*
	Thea Musgrave	*Rainbow*
	Gordon Crosse	Sea Psalms (SNO Chorus Commission)
1991	Martin Dalby	*The Mary Bean*
1992	Edward McGuire	Symphonies of Scots Song*

APPENDIX III

Discography

Compact Discs and Cassettes

CHAN 8947 / (1991)
Bartok/Enescu Concerto for orchestra etc.   Neeme Järvi
ABTD 1067 / CHAN 8316 / (1982)
Berlioz Five Overtures   Alexander Gibson
ABTD 1343 / CHAN 8657 / (1989)
Britten *Les Illuminations/4 Chansons Francs./Serenade*
                    Lott/Rolfe Johnson/Thompson/Bryden Thomson
ABTD 1257 / CHAN 8556 / (1988)
Tchaikovsky *Nutcracker* Act 2 Complete/*Swan Lake* (Excerpts)
                                                              Neeme Järvi
ABTD 1307 / CHAN 8618 / (1988)
Copland/Nielsen Clarinet Concertos/**Lutoslawski** *Dance Preludes*
                                              Hilton/Matthias Bamert
CBT 1003 / (1972)
Dukas *Sorcerer's Apprentice*/**Saint-Saëns** *Danse Macabre*/**Rossini-
Respighi** *La Boutique Fantasque*   Alexander Gibson
DBTD 2019 / CHAN 8798/9 / (1989)
Dvořák Complete Symphonic Poems/Overture *My Home*
                                                              Neeme Järvi
ABTD 1143 / CHAN 8406 / (1985)
Dvořák *Slavonic Dances* Op. 46 & 72   Neeme Järvi
ABTD 1291 / CHAN 8597 / (1988)
Dvořák Symphony No 1/*Hero's Song*   Neeme Järvi
ABTD 1283 / CHAN 8589 / (1988)
Dvořák Symphony No 2/Slavonic Rhapsody No 3   Neeme Järvi
ABTD 1270 / CHAN 8575 / (1988)
Dvořák Symphony No 3/*Carnival* Overture/Symphonic Variations
                                                              Neeme Järvi
ABTD 1251 / CHAN 8608 / (1988)
Dvořák Symphony No 4/*Biblical Songs*   Neeme Järvi

ABTD 1258 / CHAN 8552 / (1987)
Dvořák Symphony No 5/*Water Goblin*   Neeme Järvi
ABTD 1240 / CHAN 8530 / (1987)
Dvořák Symphony No 6/*Noon Witch*   Neeme Järvi
ABTD 1211 / CHAN 8501 / (1987)
Dvořák Symphony No 7/*Golden Spinning Wheel*   Neeme Järvi
ABTD 1352 / CHAN 8666 / (1989)
Dvořák Symphony No 8/*Wood Dove*   Neeme Järvi
ABTD 1220 / CHAN 8510 / (1987)
Dvořák Symphony No 9/*My Home*, overture Op. 62   Neeme Järvi
CHAN 9008–13
Dvořák The Complete Symphonies   Neeme Järvi
ABTD 1007 / CHAN 8384 / (1979)
Elgar Cello Concerto/**Walton** Cello Concerto
                        Kirshbaum/Alexander Gibson
CBT 1013 / CHAN 8430 / (1977)
Elgar *Coronation Ode/Spirit of England*
            Cahill/Collins/Rolfe Johnson/Howell/Alexander Gibson
CBT 1029 / CHAN 8431 / (1979)
Elgar *Falstaff*, Symphonic Study/*Enigma Variations*   Alexander Gibson
ABTD 1077 / CHAN 8309 / (1983)
Elgar *Froissart/Cockaigne/In the South*/Overture in D minor
                            Alexander Gibson
CBT 1012 / CHAN 8429 / (1978)
Elgar *Pomp and Circumstance Marches* Op. 29/Other Items
                            Alexander Gibson
CBR 1011 / CBT 1011 / (1977)
Elgar Symphony No 2   Alexander Gibson
CRD 40267 / CRD 33267 / (1976)
Elgar *The Dream of Gerontius*
            Hodgson/Tear/Luxon/SNO Chorus/Alexander Gibson
ABTD 1235 / CHAN 8525 / (1987)
Eller *Elegia/5* String Pieces/*Dawn*/RAID Symphony No 1 in C
                            Neeme Järvi
ABTD 1159 / CHAN 8447 / (1986)
Glazunov *Raymonda*, Ballet Music Op. 57   Neeme Järvi
ABTD 1432 / CHAN 8804 / (1990)
Glazunov Suites – *From the Middle Ages – Scenes de Ballet*/**Lyadov** *A Musical Snuffbox*   Neeme Järvi
ABTD 1285 / CHAN 8596 / (1988)
Glazunov *The Seasons*/Violin Concerto Op. 82 Shumsky/Neeme Järvi
ABTD 1010 / CHAN 8302 / (1979)
Holst *The Planets*   SNO Ladies' Chorus/Alexander Gibson
ABTD 1299 / CHAN 8611 / (1988)
Kalinnikov Symphony No 1/**Glazunov** *The Sea/Spring*   Neeme Järvi

ABTD 1433 / CHAN 8805 / (1990)
Kalinnikov Symphony No 2/Overture *Tsar Boris/The Cedar and the Palm*
Neeme Järvi
ABTD 1250 / CHAN 8542 / (1987)
Khachaturian Piano Concerto/*Gayaneh* and *Masquerade* Suites
Orbelian/Neeme Järvi
ABTD 1519 / CHAN 8918 / (1990)
Khachaturian and **Kabalevsky** Violin Concertos
Lydia Mordkovich/Neeme Järvi
ABTD 1529 / CHAN 8927 / (1991)
Khachaturian Ballet Suites 1–3
Neeme Järvi
ABTD 1541 / CHAN 8945 / (1991)
Khachaturian Symphony No 2
Neeme Järvi
ABTD 1380 / CHAN 8741 / (1989)
Leighton Cello Concerto/Symphony No 3 *Laudes Musicae*
Mackie/Wallfisch/Bryden Thomson
ABTD 1025 / (1981) – CHAN 8951 / (1991)
Mahler Symphony No 4
Marshall/Alexander Gibson
ABTD 1454 / CHAN 8829 / (1990)
Mahler Symphony No 5
Neeme Järvi
ABTD 1525 / CHAN 8917 / (1991)
Martinu Symphonies 3 & 4
Bryden Thomson
ABTD 1524 / CHAN 8916 / (1991)
Martinu Symphonies 2 & 6
Bryden Thomson
ABTD 1523 / CHAN 8915 / (1991)
Martinu Symphonies 1 & 5
Bryden Thomson
ABTD 1144 / CHAN 8407 (1985)
Mozart Wind Serenades in C minor and E flat major
Paavo Järvi
ABTD 1259 / CHAN 8552 / (1987)
Mozart Serenade for Thirteen Wind Instruments
Paavo Järvi
ABTD 1342 / CHAN 8656 (1989)
Music from Estonia Lemba – Tobias – Eller – Tormis – Part
Neeme Järvi
CHAN 8880 / (1991)
Nielsen Symphonies No 1 in G Minor/No 2, *The Four Temperaments*
Bryden Thomson
CHAN 9047 / (1992)
Nielsen Symphonies 4 & 5
Bryden Thomson
ABTD 1275 / CHAN 8584 / (1988)
Prokofiev *Alexander Nevsky/Scythian Suite*
Finnie/SNO Chorus/Neeme Järvi
ABTD 1369 / CHAN 8729 / (1989)
Prokofiev Suites *Chout, Le Pas D'Acier, Love for Three Oranges*
Neeme Järvi

ABTD 1221 / CHAN 8511 / (1987)
Prokofiev *Peter and the Wolf/Cinderella* Suite
                                    Narr. Lina Prokofiev/Neeme Järvi
ABTD 1368 / CHAN 8728 / (1989)
Prokofiev *Prodigal Son/Divertimento/Andante/Symphonic Song*
                                                      Neeme Järvi
ABTD 1431 / CHAN 8803 / (1990)
Prokofiev *Semyon Kotko* Symphonic Suite Op. 81/*The Gambler* (Four
Portraits) Op. 49   Neeme Järvi
ABTD 1354 / CHAN 8709 / (1989)
Prokofiev Violin Concerto No 1/Violin Concerto No 2
                                    Mordkovitch/Neeme Järvi
ABTD 1183 / CHAN 8472 / (1986)
Prokofiev *Romeo & Juliet* Suite No 2/*Dreams/Pushkiniana* Neeme Järvi
ABTD 1218 / CHAN 8508 / (1987)
Prokofiev Sinfonia Concertante for Cello and Orchestra
                                    Wallfisch/Neeme Järvi
ABTD 1137 / CHAN 8400 / (1985)
Prokofiev Symphony No 1/Symphony No 4 (original version)
                                                      Neeme Järvi
ABTD 1134 / CHAN 8368 / (1985)
Prokofiev Symphony No 2/*Romeo & Juliet* Suite No 1   Neeme Järvi
ABTD 1138 / CHAN 8401 / (1985)
Prokofiev Symphony No 3/Symphony No 4 (revised)   Neeme Järvi
ABTD 1160 / CHAN 8450 / (1986)
Prokofiev Symphony No 5/Three Waltzes Op. 110   Neeme Järvi
ABTD 1122 / CHAN 8359 / (1985)
Prokofiev Symphony No 6/Waltz Suite Nos. 1, 5, 6   Neeme Järvi
ABTD 1154 / CHAN 8442 / (1986)
Prokofiev Symphony No 7/Sinfonietta Op. 5/48   Neeme Järvi
ABTD 1434 / CHAN 8806 (1990)
Prokofiev *Lieutenant Kije* Suite etc.   Neeme Järvi
ABTD 1535 / CHAN 8939 (1991)
Prokofiev *Cinderella* Suites Nos. 1 & 3   Neeme Järvi
ABTD 1536 / CHAN 8940 (1991)
Prokofiev *Romeo & Juliet* Suites Nos. 1, 2 & 3   Neeme Järvi
CHAN 8931–34 (4 disc set) (1991)
Prokofiev The Complete Symphonies   Neeme Järvi
ABTD 1021 / CHAN 8423 / (1981)
Rakhmaninov Symphony No 2   Alexander Gibson
ABTD 1187 / CHAN 8476 / (1986)
Rakhmaninov *The Bells/Vocalise/***Tchaikovsky** 3 Items
                    Murphy/Lewis/W. Johnson/SNO Chorus/Neeme Järvi

DBTD 2025 / CHAN 8882/3 / (1990)
Rakhmaninov The Four Piano Concertos
Howard Shelley/Bryden Thomson
DBTD 3004 / CHAN 8327–9 / (1984)
Rimsky-Korsakov Overture & Suites from Six Operas   Neeme Järvi
ABTD 1191 / CHAN 8479 / (1986)
Rimsky-Korsakov *Sheherazade*/**Glazunov** *Stenka Razin*   Neeme Järvi
CFP 40086 / TC CFP 40086 / (1975)
Saint-Saëns/Bizet/Ravel Children's Pieces   Alexander Gibson
CD CFP 4086 / TC CFP 40086 / (1991)
Saint-Saëns *Carnival of the Animals*   Alexander Gibson
ABTD 1308 / CHAN 8619 / (1988)
Schoenberg *Pelleas und Melisande*/**Webern** PassacagliaMatthias Bamert
ABTD 1032 / CHAN 8379 / (1981)
Scottish Overtures/*Hebrides*/*Land of the Mountain and Flood* etc.
Alexander Gibson
ABTD 1176 / CHAN 8462 / (1986)
Skryabin Symphony No 2 Op. 29/Reveries Op. 24   Neeme Järvi
ABTD 1148 / CHAN 8411 / (1985)
Shostakovich Symphony No 1/Symphony No 6   Neeme Järvi
ABTD 1328 / CHAN 8640 / (1989)
Shostakovich Symphony No 4   Neeme Järvi
ABTD 1336 / CHAN 8650 / (1989)
Shostakovich Symphony No 5   Neeme Järvi
ABTD 1312 / CHAN 8623 / (1988)
Shostakovich Symphony No 7   Neeme Järvi
ABTD 1396 / CHAN 8757 / (1990)
Shostakovich Symphony No 8   Neeme Järvi
ABTD 1279 / CHAN 8587 / (1988)
Shostakovich Symphony No 9/Festival Overture/*Katerina Ismailova*
Suite/*Tea for Two*   Neeme Järvi
ABTD 1319 / CHAN 8630 / (1988)
Shostakovich Symphony No 10/Ballet Suite No 4   Neeme Järvi
ABTD 1370 / CHAN 8730 / (1989)
Shostakovich Ballet Suites Nos. 1, 2 & 3   Neeme Järvi
ABTD 1445 / CHAN 8820 / (1990)
Shostakovich Violin Concerto No 1 Op. 99/Violin Concerto No 2
Op. 129   Mordkovitch/Neeme Järvi
CBT 1027/8 / CHAN 8395/6 / (1978)
Sibelius Complete Tone Poems   Bryn-Julson/Alexander Gibson
ABTD 1086 / CHAN 8344 / (1983)
Sibelius Symphonies Nos. 1 & 7   Alexander Gibson
ABTD 1062 / (1982)
Sibelius Symphony No 2   Alexander Gibson

ABTD 1097 / (1984)
Sibelius Symphonies Nos. 3 & 6   Alexander Gibson
ABTD 1074 / CHAN 8388 / (1983)
Sibelius Symphonies Nos. 4 & 5   Alexander Gibson
CBT 1026 / CHAN 8394 / (1978)
Sibelius *Lemminkainen Legends* incl. *Swan of Tuonela*
                                                     Alexander Gibson
CBT 1025 / CHAN 8393 / (1977)
Sibelius *Scènes Historiques* Suites Nos 1 & 2/*Rakastava* Suite/*Valse Lyrique*
                                                     Alexander Gibson
ABTD 1246 / CHAN 8538 / (1987)
Strauss, Richard *Also Sprach Zarathustra*/Two Songs Lott/Neeme Järvi
ABTD 1263 / CHAN 8557 / (1987)
Strauss, Richard *Alpine Symphony*/Four Songs   Lott/Neeme Järvi
ABTD 1383 / CHAN 8744 / (1989)
Strauss, Richard *Aus Italien*/Four Songs   Lott/Neeme Järvi
ABTD 1397 / CHAN 8758 / (1989)
Strauss, Richard *Der Rosenkavalier* Suite/*Salome's Dance*/Suite from *Cap-riccio*   Lott/Neeme Järvi
ABTD 1320 / CHAN 8631 / (1988)
Strauss, Richard *Don Quixote*/Two Songs/Romanze in F
                                    Lott/Wallfisch/Neeme Järvi
ABTD 1228 / CHAN 8518 / (1987)
Strauss, Richard *Ein Heldenleben*/Four Last Songs   Lott/Neeme Järvi
ABTD 1457 / CHAN 8834 / (1990)
Strauss, Richard *Macbeth*/*Der Rosenkavalier* 1st & 2nd Waltz Sequence
                                          Finnie/Neeme Järvi
ABTD 1267 / CHAN 8572 / (1987)
Strauss, Richard Sinfonia Domestica/*Till Eulenspiegel*/Two Songs
                                          Lott/Neeme Järvi
ABTD 1374 / CHAN 8734 / (1989)
Strauss, Richard *Tod und Verklärung*/*Metamorphosen*/*Drei Hymnen*
                                          Lott/Neeme Järvi
CHAN 9054 / (1992)
Strauss, Richard Orchestral Songs   Lott/Neeme Järvi
DBTD 2004 / CHAN 8345/6 / (1981)
Stravinsky Symphony in E flat major/Symphony in C/Symphony in 3 movements   Alexander Gibson
ABTD 1123 / CHAN 8360 / (1985)
Stravinsky *Fairy's Kiss*/**Tchaikovsky** *Bluebird*/*Pas de Deux*
                                                Neeme Järvi
ABTD 1095 / CHAN 8313 / (1983)
Walton Symphony No 1   Alexander Gibson

ABTD 1315 / CHAN 8626 / (1988)
Wilson Piano Concerto/*Introit – Towards the Light*
Wilde/Bryden Thomson

Collect Series

MBTD 6503 / CHAN 6503 (1990)
Dukas *The Sorcerer's Apprentice*/**Saint-Saëns** *Danse Macabre*/**Rossini-Respighi** *La Boutique Fantasque*   Alexander Gibson
MBTD 6504 / CHAN 6504 (1990)
Elgar *Enigma Variations*/*Pomp and Circumstance* Marches 1–5
Alexander Gibson
MBTD 6523 / CHAN 6523 (1991)
Elgar Symphony No 2 in E flat major/*Crown of India* Suite
Alexander Gibson
MBTD 6523 / CHAN 6523 (1991)
Mahler Symphony No 4   Margaret Marshall/Alexander Gibson
MBTD 6538 / CHAN 6538 (1991)
Mendelssohn *The Hebrides* Overture/**Berlioz** *Le Corsaire*/**Bridge** *Seascape*/**Bax** *Tintagel*/**Sibelius** *The Oceanides*
Alexander Gibson/Vernon Handley/George Hurst/Bryden Thomson
MBTD 6524 / CHAN 6524 (1991)
Nielsen Symphony No 4 *The Inextinguishable*/*Pan and Syrinx*/*Rhapsodic Overture*/*An Imaginary Journey to the Faroe Islands*/**Sibelius** *The Dryad/ En Saga*   Alexander Gibson
MBTD 6533 / CHAN 6533 (1991)
Nielsen Symphony No 5/*Helios* overture/**Sibelius** *Night Ride and Sunrise/Spring Song*   Alexander Gibson
MBTD 6511 / CHAN 6511 (1990)
Russian music: Tchaikovsky/Rimsky-Korsakov/Prokofiev/Shostakovich/Glazunov/Stravinsky/Khachaturian   Neeme Järvi
MBTD 6555 / CHAN 6555 (1991)
Sibelius Symphonies 1 & 4   Alexander Gibson
MBTD 6556 / CHAN 6556 (1991)
Sibelius Symphonies 2 & 3   Alexander Gibson
MBTD 6557 / CHAN 6557 (1991)
Sibelius Symphonies 3, 6 & 7   Alexander Gibson
CHAN 6559
Sibelius The Complete Symphonies (No 1–No 7)
Alexander Gibson

Long-Playing Records

WAVERLEY YLP 060 / SYLP 061 (1963)
Arnold Four Scottish Dances   Alexander Gibson
EMI CFP 40232 (1974)
Beethoven Piano Concerto No 1/Choral Fantasy
                              John Lill/Alexander Gibson
EMI CFP 40271 (1975)
Beethoven Piano Concerto Nos 2 & 4   John Lill/Alexander Gibson
EMI CFP 40259 (1975)
Beethoven Piano Concerto No 3   John Lill/Alexander Gibson
EMI CFP 40087 (1974)
Beethoven Piano Concerto No 5 *Emperor*
                              John Lill/Alexander Gibson
DECCA PFS 4367 (1975)
Beethoven Symphony No 3 *Eroica*   Carlos Paita
EMI CFP 40248 (1975)
Bruch Violin Concerto No 1/*Scottish Fantasy*
                              Maurice Hasson/Alexander Gibson
RCA RL 25158 (1978)
Elgar Overture *Cockaigne/Crown of India/Pomp and Circumstance* Marches
                              Alexander Gibson
RCA RL 25206 (1979)
Elgar *Enigma Variations/Falstaff*
                              Alexander Gibson
RCA LRL 15130 / VICS 2010 (1976)
Elgar Symphony No 1 in A flat   Alexander Gibson
WAVERLEY LLP 1021 / SSLP 1022 / EMI CFP 172 (1963)
Elgar Symphony No 2 in E flat   Adrian Boult
RCA RL 25104 (1977)
Elgar Symphony No 2 in E flat   Alexander Gibson
EMI ASD 2810 (1973)
Hamilton Violin Concerto/**Goehr** Violin Concerto
                              Manoug Parikian/Alexander Gibson
EMI CFP 40226 (1974)
Mahler *Das Lied von der Erde*
                  Alfreda Hodgson/John Mitchinson/Alexander Gibson
EMI CFP 40270 (1975)
Mendelssohn Symphony No 3/*Hebrides* Overture   Alexander Gibson
WAVERLEY YLP 158 / SYLP 059 (1962)
Mozart Four German Dances   Alexander Gibson
WAVERLEY YLP 057 (1962)
Mozart/Handel Four Arias   William McCue/Alexander Gibson

DECCA HEAD 8 (1975)
Musgrave Horn Concerto/Concerto for Orchestra
                    Barry Tuckwell/Alexander Gibson/Thea Musgrave
RCA RL 25226 (1979)
Nielsen Symphony No 4/*Pan and Syrynx*/*Imaginary Journey to the Faroes*
                                        Alexander Gibson
RCA RL 25148 (1977)
Nielsen Symphony No 5/*Helios* Overture   Alexander Gibson
WAVERLEY LLP 1011 / SLLP 1012 (1962)
Oldham *Laudes Creaturarum*/*Hymns for the Amusement of Children*/
Mozart Ave Verum/Laudate Dominum
        Eileen McLoughlan/St Mary's Cathedral Choir/Arthur Oldham
WAVERLEY LLP 1025 / 1026 (1963)
Prokofiev Symphony No 5   Alexander Gibson
EMI SXLP 20099
Prokofiev Symphony No 5/**Shostakovich** *Festival* Overture/**Kabalev-**
sky *Colas Breugnon* Overture   Alexander Gibson
EMI CFP 40086 / TC CFP 40086 (1974)
Saint-Saëns *Carnival of the Animals*/**Bizet** *Jeux d'enfants*/**Ravel** *Mother*
Goose   Alexander Gibson
WAVERLEY YLP 055 SYLP 056 (1962)
Shostakovich *Festival* Overture/**Kabalevsky** *Colas Breugnon* Overture
                                                   Alexander Gibson
EMI CFP 4054 / CFP 40055 (1973)
Sibelius Symphony No 1   Alexander Gibson
EMI CFP 40047 (1972)
Sibelius Symphony No 1   Alexander Gibson
ALPHA PHA 3011 / SPHA 3012 / SAGA 5284 (1964)
Sibelius Symphonies Nos. 3 & 4   Alexander Gibson
EMI CFP 40218 (1974)
Sibelius Symphony No 5/*En Saga*   Alexander Gibson
RCA FL 25172 (1978)
Sibelius *Legends*   Alexander Gibson
EMI HQM 1070 / HQS 1070 / CFP 40173 (1967)
Sibelius *King Christian II* Suite/*Karelia* Overture/*The Bard*/*Festivo*
                                                   Alexander Gibson
RCA RL 25136 (1977)
Sibelius *Luonnatar*/*En Saga*/*Finlandia*/*Varsang*/*The Bard*/*The Dryad*/
Pohjola's Daughter/*Night Ride and Sunrise*/*Oceanides*/*Tapiola*
                    Phyllis Bryn-Julson/Alexander Gibson
RCA RO 25051 (1976)
Sibelius *Scènes Historiques*/*Rakastava*/*Valse Lyrique*   Alexander Gibson
EMI TWO 299 / MFP 57016 (1969)
Strauss, Johann *Wine, Woman and Song*/Waltzes and Polkas
                                                   Alexander Gibson

EMI CFP 40217 (1974)
Strauss, Richard *Der Rosenkavalier* (excerpts)
Helge Dernesch/Anne Howells/Teresa Cahill/Michael
Langdon/Alexander Gibson
EMI CFP 40228 (1974)
Tchaikovsky Symphony No 4 Alexander Gibson
EMI CFP 40054 (1973)
Tchaikovsky Symphony No 5 Alexander Gibson
EMI CFP 40252 (1975)
Verdi *Un Ballo in Maschera* (excerpts)
Cristina Deutekom/Patricia Hay/Charles Craig/William
McCue/Alexander Gibson
RCA RL 25105 (1977)
Walton *Belshazzar's Feast*/Te Deum
Sherrill Milnes/Alexander Gibson

Collections

EMI ALP 2279 / ASD 2279 (1965)
Orr Symphony in one movement/**Musgrave** Triptych/**Hamilton** Sinfonia for two orchestras   Duncan Robertson/Alexander Gibson
EMI ASK 2400 / ED 29028 (1968)
Music of Four Countries: **MacCunn** *Land of the Mountain and the Flood*/**Smyth** Overture: *The Wreckers*/**Harty** *With the Wild Geese*/**German** *Welsh Rhapsody*   Alexander Gibson
WAVERLEY ZLP 2040 / SZLP 2041 (1962)
Prom Encores: **Rossini** Overture *Il Signor Bruschino*/**Handel** *Arrival of the Queen of Sheba*/**Mozart** *Figaro* aria/**Prokofiev** March and Scherzo (*Love for Three Oranges*)/**Lehar** *Gold and Silver* Waltz/**Handel** *Messiah* aria/**Mozart** German Dance No 3/**Hamilton** Scottish Dance No 5
Alexander Gibson
POLYDOR 2383 3522
Russian music: **Tchaikovsky** 1812 Overture/*Eugene Onegin* (excerpts)/**Borodin** Polovtsian Dances/**Glinka** Overture *Ruslan and Ludmilla*
Vivian Dunn
WAVERLEY LLP 1009 / SLLP 1010 (1962–3)
Scottish Dances: **Arnold** Scottish Dances/**Hamilton** Scottish Dances/**Shostakovich** Festival Overture/**Prokofiev** March and Scherzo (*Love for Three Oranges*)/**Kabalevsky** Overture *Colas Breugnon*
Alexander Gibson
WAVERLEY YLP 005 (1961)
Musorgsky Gopak (*Sorochinsky Fair*)/**Lehar** *Gold and Silver* Waltz/**Rossini** Overture *Il Signor Bruschino*   Alexander Gibson

EMI CFP 40056 (1973)
New and Traditional Carols   SNO Chorus/Alexander Gibson
ENIGMA K 23541 (1981)
Christmas Carols   SNO Chorus/John Currie
POLYDOR 2383.396 (1976)
Great Scottish Songs   SNO Chorus/Alexander Gibson
CHANDOS GAC 101
A Question of Music: Study project devised by John McLeod – extracts
from **J. S. Bach, Beethoven, Berlioz, Britten, Mahler**
          John McLeod/Alexander Gibson
(Sponsored by General Accident. Limited circulation)

INDEX